MIKHAIL ZOSHCHENKO

BEFORE SUNRISE

A Novella

The First Complete
Text, Translated, with
an Afterword, by

Gary Kern

Ardis
Ann Arbor

BEFORE SUNRISE

A NOTE ON THE TEXT

The first six chapters of *Before Sunrise (Pered voskhodom solntsa)* were published in 1943 in the journal *Oktyabr'* (Nos. 6-7 & 8-9). These chapters were reprinted in 1967 as a separate volume by the Inter-Language Associates (Munich-New York). The intensely personal nature of these chapters outraged contemporary Soviet critics, who considered any psychological probing unnecessary in time of war. A campaign of vilification was launched against the author. "This is a filthy spit in the face of our reader," wrote one critic. "The novella is full of the persona of Zoshchenko himself." The self-analysis in the spirit of Freud (anathema in the USSR), even though combined with the theory of Pavlov (approved), particularly incensed the critics. Zoshchenko was called anti-socialist, cynical, depraved. Publication of *Before Sunrise* was naturally suspended.

With the end of the war, critics resumed their attack on Zoshchenko. Party spokesman on the arts, Andrei Zhdanov, took the occasion of Zoshchenko's publication of a story in the journal *Zvezda* to make an example of the author. Recalling *Before Sunrise,* Zhdanov declared: "In this novella Zoshchenko turns his vile and vulgar little soul inside out, and he does it with pleasure, with relish, with the desire to show everyone—look, what a hooligan I am! It's hard to find anything more repulsive in our literature than the moral which Zoshchenko preaches in the novella *Before Sunrise,* depicting people and himself as abominable, wanton beasts, who have neither shame nore conscience..." *(On the Journals "Zvezda" and "Leningrad."* Central Committee Directives, 1946). The editorial board of *Zvezda* was replaced. Zoshchenko was expelled from the Union of Soviet Writers and not permitted to publish his own works. For the next seven years he worked as a translator.

With the death of Stalin and the waning of Zhdanovism, Zoshchenko's fate improved. In June 1953 he was restored to the Union of Soviet Writers and allowed to publish. He died in 1958. In the sixties literary historians took the first tentative steps in re-evaluating his career. Anthologies of his works began to appear. The best of these, a two-volume collection of stories and novellas, came out in 1968. Finally, without fanfare, the remaining nine chapters of *Before Sunrise* were published in 1972. Appropriately enough, they appeared in the journal *Zvezda* (No. 3). According to reliable sources, the text was not altered; the title of these nine chapters, however was given as "A Novella on Reason" *(Povest' o razume)*.

The present translation is the first to combine the two halves of this ill-fated work, Zoshchenko's masterpiece.

August 1973

ACKNOWLEDGEMENTS

I wish to thank Janice Hyde for typing the final manuscript. After making the first rough draft, I consulted the translations by Sidney Monas and by Maria Gordon and Hugh McLean (see Short Bibliography). They helped me in many instances. Mrs. Margaret Feldman (a native Russian) cleared up a good dozen dilemmas for me. Professor Cyrus Hoy identified the quotations of Shakespeare from my literal version of the Russian. My wife Jean prevented Lara and Kira from interrupting me more than 38 times a day. The project was supported by a summer fellowship from the University of Rochester.

Contents

List of Illustrations

Unless otherwise specified, all illustrations are by Edvard Munch.

FOREWORD

I conceived this book a very long time ago. Immediately after I brought out my *Youth Restored.*[1]

For almost ten years I collected materials for this new book and waited for a calm year to sit down and work in the quiet of my study.

But this did not happen.

On the contrary. German bombs fell twice near my materials. The portfolio containing my manuscripts was littered with lime and bricks. The burning flames licked them. And I am surprised that they escaped without damage.

The collected material flew with me in an airplane across the German front, out of besieged Leningrad.

I took twenty heavy notebooks with me. To lessen their weight I tore off their calico bindings. And still they weighed close to eight kilograms of the twelve kilograms of baggage allowed on the airplane. And there was a moment when I sorely grieved for having taken this rubbish with me instead of warm underpants and an extra pair of boots.

But the love of literature triumphed. I resigned

myself to my unhappy fate.

In a torn black portfolio I carried my manuscripts into central Asia, into the city—blessed forever after—of Alma-Ata.

Here I was busy for a whole year writing various scenarios on themes needed in the days of the Great Fatherland War.[2]

I kept the material I had carried with me in a wooden couch on which I slept.

From time to time I raised the top of my couch. There, on the plywood bottom, rested twenty of my notebooks along with a bag of biscuits I had gotten ready in the Leningrad fashion.

I leafed through these notebooks, bitterly regretting that the time had not come to take up this work, which now seemed so unnecessary, so far removed from the war, from the rumble of artillery and the whistling of bullets.

"Never mind," I said to myself, "as soon as the war ends, I'll take up this work."

I again packed my notebooks away in the bottom of my couch. And, lying on top of them, I tossed over in my mind when, in my opinion, the war might end. It turned out, not very soon. But when exactly—this I could not determine.

"But then why hasn't the time come to take up this work of mine?" I now thought. "After all, my materials deal with the triumph of human reason, with science, with the advance of consciousness. My work refutes the 'philosophy' of fascism, which says that consciousness causes people innumerable miseries, that human happiness lies in a return to barbarism, to savagery, in a denial of civilization."

So it may be more interesting to read about this now than at some time in the future.

In August 1942 I put my manuscripts on the table and, without waiting for the war to end, set to work.

I. PROLOGUE

For good intent toward the game
The actor is forgiven his performance.

Ten years ago I wrote my novella entitled *Youth Restored.*

It was an ordinary novella, one of those which writers write by the score, but to it were added commentaries—etudes of a physiological nature.

These etudes explained the behavior of the novella's heroes and gave the reader some information on the physiology and psychology of man.

I did not write *Youth Restored* for men of science, but it was precisely they who turned to my work with special interest. There were many disputes. Arguments took place. I heard many caustic remarks. But kind words were also said.

I was disconcerted by the fact that the scientists argued so seriously and so heatedly with me. This meant not that I knew a lot (I thought), but rather that science had evidently not dealt sufficiently with those problems which I, by virtue of my inexperience, had the audacity to touch upon.

Whatever the case, the scientists conversed with me almost as with an equal. And I even began to receive announcements to conferences at the "Brain Institute." And Ivan Petrovich Pavlov invited me to his Wednesdays.[3]

But, I repeat, I had not composed my work for science. It was a literary work, and the scientific material was only a component part.

It always did amaze me: an artist, before he draws the human body, is obliged in his training to study anatomy. Only a knowledge of this science spares him from making mistakes in representation. But a writer, who must know more than the human body—his psyche, his consciousness, often does not strive for the same sort of knowledge. I considered it my duty to study something in this regard. And afterwards I shared my study with the reader.

This is the way *Youth Restored* was created.

Now that ten years have passed, I can see the defects of that book quite clearly: it was incomplete and one-sided. And probably I deserved to be scolded even more than I was scolded.

In the fall of 1934 I became acquainted with a certain remarkable physiologist.

When the subject of my work came up, this physiologist said:

"I prefer your usual stories. But I admit that what you write about is worth writing about. The study of consciousness is not the concern of the scientist alone. I suspect that as yet it is even more the concern of the writer than of the scientist. I'm a physiologist, and so I'm not afraid to say this."

4

I answered him:

"I think so too. The province of consciousness, the province of higher psychological activity, belongs more to us than to you. The behavior of man can and must be studied with the aid of the dog and the lancet. But a man (and also a dog) sometimes has fantasies which in some extraordinary way change the force of a sensation, even when the stimulus remains one and the same. And here it is sometimes necessary to talk to the dog in order to decipher its fantasies in all their complexity. And as for talking to the dog—that's our province completely."

Smiling, the scientist said:

"You're partly right. The correspondence between the force of a stimulus and the response is often inexact, especially in the area of sensations. But if you have pretensions to this province, it is precisely here that you must get together with us."

Some years passed after this conversation. Upon learning that I was doing a new book, the physiologist asked me to tell him about this work.

I said:

"In brief, it's a book about how I got rid of many unnecessary sorrows and became happy."

"Will it be a treatise or a novel?"

"It will be a literary work. Science will enter into it, just as in other cases history enters into a novel."

"Will there again be commentaries?"

"No. This will be something complete. Like a gun and a shell can be a complete unit."

"Therefore, this work will be about yourself?"

"Half of the book will be taken up with my person. I will not conceal from you—this greatly disturbs me."

"You will tell things about your life?"

"No, worse. I will speak of things which one does not usually speak of in novels. But I am comforted by the fact that the book will deal with my youthful years. This is the same thing as speaking of the dead."

"Up to what age do you take yourself in your

book?"

"Up to about thirty years."

"Perhaps there's good reason to toss in another fifteen years. Then the book would be fuller—about your whole life."

"No," I said. "After thirty, I became an entirely different man—no longer an appropriate subject for my composition."

"Did such a change really take place?"

"You can't even call it a change. An entirely different life began, completely unlike what had been before."

"But in what way? Was this psychoanalysis? Freud?"

"Definitely not. It was Pavlov. I made use of his principle. It was his idea."

"But what did you yourself do?"

"I did something essentially quite simple: I swept away the thing that was bothering me—the incorrect conditioned connections which were mistakenly established in my consciousness. I destroyed the false connection between them. I severed the 'temporary connection,' as Pavlov called them."

"In what way?"

At that time I had not fully thought through my materials and therefore had difficulty in answering this question. But I was able to speak of the principle. True, very vaguely.

After pondering a moment, the scientist answered:

"Write it. Only don't promise people anything."

I said:

"I'll be careful. I'll promise only what I myself have already obtained. And only to those people who have qualities close to my own."

Laughing, the scientist said:

"That's not too much. And that's right. Tolstoi's philosophy, for example, was useful only to him and to no one else."

I answered:

6

"Tolstoi's philosophy was a religion, and not a science. It was faith which helped him. But I am far from religion. I speak neither of faith nor of a philosophical system. I speak of ironclad formulas verified by a great scientist. My role in this matter is modest: I verified these formulas through the experience of a human life and I united something which it seemed could not be united."

I parted with the scientist and have not seen him since. Probably he decided that I had been unable to cope with my book and had given it up.

But—as you have already been informed—I was only waiting for a calm year.

This did not happen. It's a pity. I write considerably worse to the rumble of artillery. Beauty, no doubt, will be diminished. My emotional agitation will make the style shaky. Anxiety will stifle knowledge. Nervousness will be taken for hastiness. In this there will be seen a careless attitude toward science, a lack of respect for the scientific world...

Scientist!
Where my speech strikes you as impolite—
Rub it out, I assure you it's all right.

May the informed reader forgive me my transgressions.

II. I AM WRETCHED—AND KNOW NOT WHY

> *O woe! To flee from the sunshine*
> *And to seek delights in a cell*
> *By the light of a lamp...*

When I recall my early years, I am amazed at how much woe, unnecessary anxiety and despair I experienced.

The most wonderful years of youth were painted in black.

As a child I had not experienced anything like this.

But my very first steps as a young man were overshadowed by this remarkable despair, for which I know no comparison.

I was attracted to people, I delighted in life, I sought friends, love, happy meetings... But in none of these things could I find solace. Everything grew dim in my hands. Gloom pursued me at every step.

I was wretched without knowing why.

But I was eighteen years old, and I found an explanation.

"The world is horrible," I thought. "People are vulgar. Their actions are comical. I'm not one of the herd."

Over my desk I hung these lines from Sophocles:

Incomparably best is not to be.
And next to this, once a man sees the day,
Is with all speed to hasten whence he came.[4]

Of course, I knew that there were other views—joyful, even ecstatic ones. But I did not respect people who were able to dance to the coarse and vulgar music of life. Such people seemed to me on a level with savages and animals.

Everything I saw around me strengthened this viewpoint.

Poets wrote sad verses and took pride in their despair.

"Despair has come—my sovereign lady, my grayhaired one." I used to mutter some such lines, I don't remember the author.

My favorite philosophers spoke of melancholy with respect. "Melancholics possess a sense of the sublime," wrote Kant. And Aristotle held that "a melancholic cast of mind aids profound thought and accompanies genius."

But not only poets and philosophers added fuel to my dim fire. Strange to say, in my time sadness was considered the mark of a thinking man. In my class, people were respected who were pensive, melancholic and even somehow removed from life.[5]

In short, I began to believe that a pessimistic view of life was the only view for a thinking and refined man, born into the gentry class, from which I myself hailed.

10

This means, I thought, that melancholy is my normal state, and despair and a certain repugnance for life are qualities of my mind. And, evidently, not of my mind alone. Evidently—of every mind, every consciousness which strives to be higher than the consciousness of an animal.

It's very sad if this is so. But probably it is so. In nature the coarse fibers conquer. Coarse feelings, primitive thoughts triumph. Everything that becomes refined—perishes.

This is the way I thought at my eighteen years of age. And I will not conceal from you that I also thought this way considerably later.

But I was mistaken. And now I am happy to inform you of this horrible mistake of mine.

This mistake almost cost me my life then.

I wanted to die, since I could see no other way out.

In the autumn of 1914 the world war began and after quitting the university, I joined the army to die valiantly at the front for my country, for my native land.

Yet in the war I almost ceased to experience despair. It came from time to time. But it quickly passed. And in the war I felt almost happy for the first time.

I thought: how come? And I arrived at the thought that I had found excellent comrades here and that this was why I had ceased to be gloomy. It was logical.

I served in the Mingrelsky Regiment of the Caucasian Grenadiers Division. We lived together as friends. But perhaps it just seemed that way to me.

At the age of nineteen I was already a lieutenant.

At the age of twenty I had five decorations and had been recommended to the rank of captain.

But this did not mean that I had been a hero. It meant that I had been in the lines for two years straight.

I participated in many battles, was wounded, poisoned by gas. Damaged my heart. Nevertheless, my joyful mood hardly ever vanished.

11

With the beginning of the Revolution, I returned to Petrograd.

I experienced no nostalgia for the past. On the contrary, I wanted to see a new Russia, not the miserable one I had known. I wanted to be surrounded by healthy, flourishing people, not those like myself—inclined to gloominess, melancholy and sadness.

I did not experience any so-called "social disorientation." Nevertheless, I began to experience despair as before.

I tried changing cities and professions. I wanted to flee from this horrible despair of mine. I felt it would ruin me.

I traveled to Archangel. Then to Mezen on the Arctic Ocean. Then I returned to Petrograd. I traveled to Novgorod, to Pskov. After this, to the Smolensky province, to the city of Krasny. Again I returned to Petrograd...

Gloom followed close on my heels.

In three years I changed twelve cities and ten professions.

I was a policeman, an accountant, a cobbler, an instructor in poultry farming, a telephone operator on the border patrol, a detective, a court secretary, a business manager...

This was not a firm course through life, this was bewilderment.

I spent a half-year at the front again with the Red Army—outside Narva and Yamburg.

But my heart had been damaged by gas, and I had to think about a new profession.

In 1921 I began to write stories.

My life greatly changed by my becoming a writer. But the gloom remained as before. In fact, it began to visit me more and more frequently.

Then I turned to physicians. Besides gloominess, there was something wrong with my heart, with my digestion and with my liver.

The physicians went at me energetically.

They began to treat me for these three illnesses with pills and water. Mainly with water—inside and outside.

It was decided to chase away my gloom with a massive blow—from all four sides at once, on the flanks, in the rear, at the front—with traveling, bathing in the sea, Charcot sprays and the amusements so necessary at my youthful age.

I began to travel twice a year to resorts—to Yalta, Kislovodsk, Sochi and other blessed places.

In Sochi I became acquainted with a man whose despair was considerably greater than my own. A minimum of twice a year they removed his head from the noose he had slipped into because he was tormented by an unfounded despair.

With a feeling of the greatest respect I began to converse with this man. I assumed I would see wisdom, a mind overflowing with knowledge and the pained smile of a genius who must manage to dwell on our transitory earth.

I saw nothing of the sort.

He was a short-sighted man, uneducated and without even a trace of enlightenment. He had not read more than two books in his whole life. And besides money, food and women, he wasn't interested in anything.

Before me stood the most ordinary man, with vulgar thoughts and obtuse desires.

I did not even understand at once that such was the case. At first it seemed to me that someone had been smoking in the room, or that the barometer had fallen, a storm was in the offing. Somehow I was not myself when talking with him. Then I look—it's simply a fool. Simply a blockhead whom you couldn't talk to for more than three minutes.

My philosophical system cracked open. I understood that it was not only a matter of higher consciousness. But what was it then? I didn't know.

With the greatest humility I placed myself in the

13

hands of the physicians.

In the course of two years I consumed a half-ton of powders and pills.

Without a murmur I drank every kind of nasty stuff, which made me nauseous.

I allowed myself to be pricked, shone through and set into baths.

Yet the treatment had no success. And soon it even got to the point that my acquaintances ceased to recognize me on the street. I grew ridiculously thin. I was like a skeleton with skin stretched over it. All the time I had horrible chills. My hands shook. And the yellowness of my skin astonished even the physicians. They began to suspect that I was a hypochondriac to such an extent that medical procedures had become superfluous. Hypnosis and the clinic were necessary.

One of the physicians succeeded in putting me to sleep. Once I was asleep, he began to suggest to me that my gloom and despair were in vain, that everything in the world was beautiful, and there was no reason to be distressed.

For two days I felt hardier, then I got considerably worse than before.

I almost stopped going out of the house. Each new day was a burden to me:

> It might be months, or years, or days—
> I kept no count, I took no note,
> I had no hope my eyes to raise,
> And clear them of their dreary mote.[6]

I barely moved myself down the street, gasping from heart seizures and from pains in my liver.

I stopped traveling to resorts. More accurately, I went, languished through two or three days, returned home again in even more terrible despair than when I had gone.

Then I turned to books. I was a young writer. I was

14

all of twenty-seven years old. It was natural that I should turn to my great comrades—the writers, the musicians... I wanted to find out if they had ever had something similar. If they had ever had a despair like mine. And if they had, then what had caused it, in their opinion. And what had they done to get rid of it.

And so I began to note down everything relating to gloominess. I began to note down things without any particular scheme or rationale. However, I did try to pick what was characteristic of the man, what was repeated in his life, what did not seem to be an accident, a flight of imagination, an outburst.

These notes struck my imagination for several years.

...I leave the house, walk down the street, feel despair and again return home. What for? To suffer depression...
(Chopin, *Letters,* 1830)

I did not know what to do with myself in my despair...I myself did not know where this despair came from...
(Gogol to his mother, 1837)

I have attacks of such depression that I'm afraid I'll throw myself into the sea. Dear one! It's very sickening...
(Nekrasov to Turgenev, 1857)

I am so *ill*—so terribly, hopelessly *ill* in body and mind that I CANNOT live...
(Edgar Allan Poe to Annie, 1848)[7]

I am suffering under a depression of spirits such as I have never felt before. I have struggled in vain against the influence of this melancholy... I am

wretched, and know not why.
(Edgar Allan Poe to Kennedy,
1835)[8]

Twenty times a day the thought of a pistol comes into my mind. And with this thought things become better...
(Nekrasov to Turgenev, 1857)

Everything has repulsed me. It seems to me I could hang myself with pleasure now—only pride prevents me...
(Flaubert, 1853)

I live miserably, feel horrible. Every morning I get up with the thought: isn't it better to shoot myself...
(Saltykov-Shchedrin to Pantele-
yev, 1886)

To this was added a despair for which there is no description. I positively did not know what to do with myself, what to lean against...
(Gogol to Pogodin, 1840)

Everything in the world is so repellent, so unbearable... It's boring to live, to speak, to write...
(Leonid Andreyev, *Diary,* 1919)

I feel tired, so enervated that I come close to crying from morning till night... The faces of friends irritate me... Everyday conversations, sleeping in one and the same bed, my own voice, my face, its reflection in the mirror...
(Maupassant, *Under the Sun,* 1881)

Hanging or drowning seemed to me like some sort

of medicine or relief.
(Gogol to Pletnev, 1846)

I am tired, tired of all relationships, all people have exhausted me and all desires. To go away somewhere into the wilderness or to fall asleep with the "last sleep."
(Valery Bryusov, *Diary*, 1898)

I hide the rope so as not to hang myself from the crossbeam in my room, in the evening, when I am left alone. I do not go hunting any more with a gun so as not to fall to the temptation of shooting myself. It seems to me that my life has been a stupid farce.
(Lev Tolstoi, 1878. *The Truth About My Father* by L.L. Tolstoi[9]

I filled a whole notebook with similar entries. They amazed and even shook me. For I had not picked people who had just then experienced grief, misfortune, death. I had picked a condition which was repeated. I had picked people many of whom had said themselves that they could not understand where this condition came from.

I was shaken, disconcerted. What suffering is this to which people are subject? Where does it come from? And how can one struggle with it, by what means?

Perhaps this suffering arises from the disorder of life, from social disorientation, from world problems? Perhaps this provides the soil for such despair?

Yes, this is the case. But here I recalled the words of Chernyshevsky: "It's not world problems that make people drown themselves, shoot themselves and go mad."

These words perplexed me even more.

I could find no solution. I did not understand.

Perhaps, after all (I once again thought), this is that worldly pain to which people are subject by virtue of

17

their higher consciousness?

No! Alongside the great men I have listed, I saw no fewer great men who had experienced no despair at all, although their consciousness was just as elevated. And there were even considerably more of these men.

At an evening devoted to Chopin, his "Second Concerto for Piano and Orchestra" was performed.

I sat in the back rows, exhausted, enervated.

But the "Second Concerto" chased away my melancholy. Powerful, masculine sounds filled the hall.

Joy, struggle, extraordinary strength and even exultation sounded in the third part of the concerto.

Where did this weak man discover in himself such tremendous strength, this musician of genius whose sad life I now knew so well?—I thought. Where did he discover such joy, such rapture? Did it mean that he had all this inside him? And it was only fettered? By what?

Here I thought of my stories which made people laugh. I thought of the laughter which was in my books, but which was not in my heart.

I will not conceal from you: I was frightened when I suddenly thought that I must find the cause: why was my strength fettered and why was I so unhappy in life; and why are there people like me, inclined to melancholy and unfounded despair.

In the autumn of 1926 I forced myself to travel to Yalta. And forced myself to stay there four weeks.

For ten days I lay in my hotel room. Then I began to take strolls. I walked into the mountains. And sometimes I sat by the seashore for hours, rejoicing that I was better, that I was well.

I improved a lot within a month. My soul grew calm, even gay.

To strengthen my health even more, I decided to prolong my rest. I got a ticket on a motorboat to Batum. From Batum I intended to travel to Moscow by direct train.

I got a private cabin. And in a wonderful mood, I

left Yalta.

The sea was calm, untroubled. And I sat on deck all day, admiring the Crimean shore and the sea which I so loved and for the sake of which I usually came to Yalta.

In the morning, at the first glimmer of light, I was again on deck.

A marvelous morning was arising.

I sat on a chaise lounge, enjoying my excellent condition. My thoughts were most pleasant, even gay. I thought of my trip, of Moscow, of the friends I would meet there. Of the fact that my despair was now behind me. And let it remain a riddle, so long as it never returns.

It was early morning. I gazed pensively at the light rippling of the water, the spots of sunlight, the gulls which sat down on the water with a disgusting cry.

And suddenly, in one instant, I felt bad. This was not only despair. It was anxiety, trembling, almost terror. I could barely get up from the chaise lounge. I barely made it back to my cabin. For two hours I lay without moving on my bunk. And once again despair rose, to a degree I had not yet experienced.

I tried to struggle against it. I went out on deck. Began to listen to people's conversations. I wanted to distract myself. But I did not succeed.

It seemed I should not and could not continue the journey.

I was barely able to wait for Tuapse[10] I went ashore with the idea of continuing my trip a few days later.

A nervous fever shook me.

I rode a streetcar to the hotel. And there I took to my bed.

By an effort of will, only after a week, I forced myself to prepare for the road.

The road distracted and diverted me. I began to feel better. The horrible despair vanished.

The trip was long, and I began to think over my unfortunate illness which could vanish as quickly as it arose. Why? And what were the causes?

Or were there no causes?

. It was as if there were no causes. It must be simply a "weakness of the nerves," excessive "sensitivity." It must be that this could swing me like the pendulum of a clock.

I began to think: Was I born so weak and sensitive, or had something happened in my life that had ruined my nerves, damaged them and made me a wretched speck of dust to be driven and buffeted by any wind?

And suddenly it seemed to me that I could not have been born so wretched, so defenseless. I could have been born weak, scrofulous, I could have been born with one arm, with one eye, without an ear. But to be born to feel gloomy, let alone to feel gloomy without any cause—because the world seems vulgar! But I am no Martian. I am a child of my own earth. And, like any animal, I should feel rapture in my existence. Feel happiness if all is well. And struggle—if bad. But to feel gloomy?! When even an insect which is given but four hours of life exults in the sun! No, I could not have been born such a monster.

And suddenly I saw clearly that the cause of my misfortunes lay hidden in my life. Without a doubt, something had happened, something had occurred that had acted on me in an oppressive manner.

But what? And when had it happened? And how could I search for this unfortunate experience? How could I find the cause of my despair?

Then I thought: I must recall my life. And I began to recall feverishly. But I immediately understood that nothing would come of this unless I introduced some sort of system into my recollections.

It's not necessary to recall everything, I thought. It suffices to recall only the strongest, the brightest things. It suffices to recall only those things that were connected with some emotional agitation. In this alone lay the solution to the riddle.

And so I began to recall the brightest pictures left

in my memory. I saw that my memory had retained them with unusual precision. Trifles, details, colors, even smells were retained.

My emotional agitation, like a magnesium flash, illuminated everything that had occurred. These were snapshots left in my brain as memories.

With unusual agitation I began to study these snapshots. And I saw that they agitated me even more than had the desire to find the cause of my misfortunes.

III. FALLEN LEAVES[11]

The life of each repeats the same event
Which was accomplished well before his time.
And if a man should dip into the past,
He may be able truly to foretell
The course of things to come...

And so I decided to recall my life in order to find
the cause of my misfortunes.

I decided to find the event, or series of events,
which had had an oppressive effect on me and had turned
me into a wretched speck of dust, tossed about by any
gust of wind.

For this purpose I decided to recall only the brightest scenes from my life, only those scenes connected
with great emotional agitation, rightly calculating that
here alone could lie the solution to the riddle.

Yet there is no need to recall my childhood years, I thought. What kind of emotional agitation can a kid have? Just think of his great deeds! He lost three kopecks. The other boys beat him up. He tore his pants. They stole his stilts. The teacher gave him a one...[12] Here you have the tribulations from the time of childhood. Much better for me, I thought, to recall scenes from my conscious life. Especially since I fell ill not in my childhood years, but when I had already grown up. I will start at about sixteen years old, I thought.

And so I began to recall the brightest scenes, starting at the age of sixteen.

1912-1915

O, the legend revived by a retold tale!
O, the wings of a butterfly battered and pale!

I'm Busy

The yard. I'm playing soccer. The playing has already bored me, but I go on playing, stealing glances at the window of the second floor. My heart contracts in despair.

Tata T. lives there. She's grown up. She's twenty three. She has an old husband. He's forty. And we gimnaziya[13] students always mock him when he, bent-over slightly, returns from work.

And now the window opens. Tata T. adjusts her hairdo, stretching and yawning.

Seeing me, she smiles.

Oh, she's very pretty. She's like a young tigress from the zoo—the same bright, shining, blinding colors. I almost have to stop looking at her.

Smiling, Tata T. says to me:

"Mishenka, come up to my place for a second."

My heart pounds with happiness, but without raising

24

my eyes I answer:

"Don't you see—I'm busy. Playing soccer."

"Then hold out your hat. I'll throw you something."

I hold out my gimnaziya hat. And Tata T. throws down a little package with a ribbon tied around it. A piece of chocolate.

I stick the chocolate in my pocket and go on playing.

At home I gobble up the chocolate. And the ribbon, after touching it for a moment to my cheek, I stick in my desk.

A Letter

The dining room. Cinnamon wallpaper. A crystal saltshaker in the shape of an inverted pyramid.

At the table sit my sisters and mother.

I was delayed at the gimnaziya, came home late, and they have begun dinner without me.

Glancing at each other, my sisters titter softly.

I sit down at my place. By my setting is a letter.

A long lilac-colored envelope. Unusually fragrant.

With trembling hands I rip open the envelope. And take out an even more fragrant sheet of paper. The smell of the paper is so strong that my sisters, unable to contain themselves, burst out laughing.

Frowning, I begin reading. The letters leap in front of my eyes.

"Oh, how happy I am that I met you..." I memorize this one phrase and mentally repeat it.

I encounter my mother's laughing eyes.

"Who from?" she asks.

"From Nadya," I answer drily, almost angrily.

The sisters become even more hilarious.

"I don't understand," says the elder sister. "They live in the same house, see each other every day and still they write letters. It's funny. It's stupid."

I give my sister a threatening look. Silently I swallow my soup and munch my bread, suffused with the fragrant smell.

Rendezvous

Petersburg. Kamenoostrovsky Prospect. The monument to the Steregushchy.[14] Two sailors by an open Kingston valve. Bronze water flows into the hold of the ship.

Unable to tear myself away, I look at the bronze sailors and at the bronze stream of water. I like this monument.

I love to look at this tragic scene of a ship's sinking.

Next to me on the bench sits the gimnaziya student Nadya V. We are both sixteen years old.

Nadya says:

"I really shouldn't have fallen in love with you. Positively all the girls advised me not to do it..."

"But why is that?" I ask, tearing myself away from the monument.

"Because I have always liked gay, witty men... You, though, are able to sit without talking for a half-hour or more."

I answer:

"I do not consider it a merit to say words which were uttered by tens of thousands before me."

"In that case," says Nadya, "you should kiss me."

Glancing around, I say:

"We can be seen here."

"Then let's go to the movie."

We go to the "Molniya"[15] Theater and sit there kissing for two hours.

True to the Original

I come out of the gimnaziya and meet Seryozha K., who goes to trade school. He's a tall, fair-haired, dejected youth.

Biting his lips nervously, he says to me:

"Yesterday I broke with Valka P. I. for good, and can you imagine—she asked me to return all her letters."

"You'll have to return them," I say.

"Of course, I'll return the letters to her," says Seryozha, "but I want to keep copies... As a matter of fact, I want to ask a favor of you. I need you to confirm these copies..."

"What for?" I ask.

"Well, for whatever," says Seryozha. "Later she will say that she didn't love me at all... But if there are confirmed copies..."

We come up to Seryozha's house. Seryozha is the son of a fire chief. And so it's interesting for me to drop in on him.

Seryozha lays three letters on the table and three copies already written out.

I don't feel like signing the copies, but Seryozha insists. He says:

"We're grown up already. Our childhood years have passed... I really want you to sign."

Without reading them, I write on each sheet of the copies: "True to the original." And I sign my name.

As a token of his appreciation, Seryozha leads me out into the yard and shows me a fire ladder and some fire hoses drying there in the sun.

Easter Eve

I'm hurrying for matins. I stand before the mirror drawn up in my gimnaziya uniform. In my left hand I hold white kid gloves. With my right hand I adjust my

27

stunning part.

I'm not especially pleased with my appearance. Very young.

At sixteen years of age one could look a bit older.

Carelessly tossing my overcoat over my shoulders, I go out onto the stairway.

Up the stairs comes Tata. T.

Today she is remarkably pretty, in her short fur jacket, with a muff in her hands.

"Aren't you going to church?" I ask.

"No, we're meeting at home," she says with a smile. And, coming up closer to me, she adds: "Christ is risen!.. Mishenka..."[16]

"It's not yet twelve," I mumble.

Wrapping her arms around my neck, Tata T. kisses me.

This is not the three Easter kisses. This is one kiss which lasts a minute. I begin to realize that this is not a Christian kiss.

At first I feel joy, then surprise, then—I laugh.

"What are you laughing about?" she asks.

'I didn't know people kiss like that."

"Not people," she says, "but men and women, you ninny!"

She caresses my face with her hand and kisses my eyes. Then, hearing a door slam on her landing, she goes more quickly up the stairs—beautiful and mysterious, precisely the type I would always want to love.

I'm Not Coming Home

We're walking to Novaya Derevnya.[17] There are a-bout ten of us. We're very excited. Our comrade Vaska T. has quit the gimnaziya, left home and now lives on his own, somewhere on Chornaya Reka.[18]

He left the eighth grade of the gimnaziya.[19] Without even waiting for final exams. In short, he spits on the

28

whole deal.

We are secretly thrilled by Vaska's act.

A wooden house. A shaky rotten staircase.

We go up almost to the roof, enter Vaska's room.

Vaska sits on an iron cot. The neck of his shirt is unbuttoned. On the table are a bottle of vodka, bread and sausage. Next to Vaska sits a skinny girl, about nineteen years old.

"She's the one he left for," someone whispers to me.

I look at this slender girl. Her eyes are red from crying. Not without fear she peers at us.

Vaska deftly pours out the glasses of vodka.

I go down to the garden. In the garden stands an old lady. It's Vaska's mama.

Holding up her fist threateningly, Mamasha screams shrilly, and some aunts or other listen in silence to her outcries.

"It's all her doing, that hussy!" screams Mamasha. "If it weren't for her, Vaska would never have left home."

Vaska appears in the window.

"Go on away, Mamasha," he says. "You hang around here for days on end. You bring nothing but trouble... Go on, go on. I'm not coming home, I told you."

Pressing her lips grievously, Mamasha sits down on the slats of the staircase.

Torture

I lie on the operating table. Beneath me, a cold white oilcloth. Ahead, a huge window. Beyond the window, a bright blue sky.

I swallowed a crystal of mercuric chloride. I kept these crystals for photographic purposes. Now they're going to pump my stomach.

A physician in a white gown stands motionlessly

29

by the table.

The nurse hands him a long rubber tube. Then, taking a glass pitcher, she fills it with water. I follow this procedure with revulsion. Well, so they are going to torment me. If only I could have died. At least all my sorrows and vexations would have ended.

I got a one in Russian composition. Beside the one, there was a remark written in red ink, at the bottom of the composition: "Drivel." True, the composition was on a Turgenev subject—"Liza Kalitina"[20]—and what do I care about her?... But all the same it's impossible to endure this...

The physician shoves the rubber hose down my gullet. Deeper and deeper goes this repulsive brown tube.

The nurse raises the pitcher of water. The water pours into me. I gasp. Squirm in the hands of the physician. Wave my hand with a groan, begging them to stop the torture.

"Calm down, calm down, young man," says the physician. "Now, aren't you ashamed of yourself... Such faint spirits...over trifles."

The water pours out of me like a fountain.

At the University

At the gates stands a police officer. Besides my entry pass, he demands that I show my student registration. I produce the documents.

"Pass," he says.

In the yard stand armed soldiers and policemen.

Today is the anniversary of Tolstoi's death.

I walk down the university corridor. There is noise, bustling about, excitement.

Down the corridor, stepping slowly, comes the warden of the educational district—Prutchenko. He's tall, solid, red-faced. On the white breast under his uniform shine little diamond buttons.

30

Around the warden is a living wall of students: these are students of the academic corporation "the "White Linings." Holding hands, they have formed a chain around the warden and guard him against any possible excesses. Some sort of long-jawed, pimply student in a uniform with a sabre at his side directs them and bustles about more than the others.

Noise and hell all around. Someone shouts: "They led the elephant through the streets." Jokes. Laughter.

The warden steps forward slowly. The warden's living wall respectfully moves along with him.

A student appears. He's short. Not handsome. But his face is surprisingly intelligent, energetic.

Coming up to the "wall," he stops. Involuntarily, the wall with the warden also stops.

Raising his hand, the student calls for silence.

When it becomes quieter, the student, enunciating each word, shouts: "We have two calamities here in Russia: at the bottom—the power of darkness,[21] at the top—the darkness of power."

A burst of applause. Guffaws.

The lanky student grabs the handle of his sabre theatrically. The warden mumbles wearily: "Hold it, there's no need..."

The student with the sabre says to someone: "Get the name of that wiseacre."

Was It Worth the Hanging

The student Mishka F. hanged himself. He left a note: "Don't blame anyone. The cause was unsuccessful love."

I knew Mishka a bit. Ungainly. Disheveled. Unshaven. Not very intelligent.

The students, though, had good relations with him—he was an easy, companionable fellow.

Out of respect for his tragedy, we decided to drink

to his repose.

We gathered in the beerhouse on Maly Prospect.

First we sang "Quick as the Waves are All the Days of our Life." Then we began to reminisce about our comrade. However, no one could recall anything in particular.

Then someone recalled how Mishka F. had eaten up several dinners at one time in the student dining room. Everyone started to laugh. They began to recall all sorts of trivia and nonsense from Mishka's life. The guffawing became incredible.

Choking with laughter, one of the students said:

"Once we were getting ready to go to a dance. I dropped by for Mishka. He didn't feel like washing his hands. He was in a hurry. He stuck his fingers in a box of face powder and whitened the dirt under his nails."

A burst of laughter rang out.

Someone said:

"Now you know why his love was unsuccessful."

Laughing, we began to sing "Quick as the Waves" again. This time one of the students stood up and conducted with an exaggerated motion of his hand every time the song came to the words: "You'll die and get buried, as if you hadn't lived on the earth."

After this, we sang "Gaudeamus," "Evening Bells" and "Dir-lim-bom-bom."

The Name-Day Party

Evening. I'm walking home. I feel very sad.

"Oh, student!" I hear someone's voice.

Before me, a woman. She's painted and powdered. Beneath her feathered hat I see a plain face with high cheekbones and fat lips.

Frowning, I want to leave, but the woman says with an embarrassed smile:

"It's my name day today... Come and visit me—to

drink some tea."

I mutter:

"Excuse me... I don't have time..."

"I go with all who invite me," says the woman. "But today I decided to celebrate my name day. I decided to invite someone myself. Please don't refuse..."

We climb the dark staircase, amid cats. Enter a little room.

On the table, a samovar, nuts, jam and rolls.

We drink the tea in silence. I don't know what I am to say. And she is embarrassed by my silence.

"Do you really have no one—no friends, no relations?"

"No," she says, "I'm a newcomer, from Rostov."

Having drunk some tea, I put on my coat to leave.

"Do I actually displease you so much that you don't even want to stay with me?" she says.

I feel gay and amused. I don't feel any disgust toward her. I kiss her fat lips in farewell. And she asks me:

"Will you drop by another time?"

I go out on the staircase. Maybe I should remember her apartment? In the dark I count the number of steps to her door. But I lose count. Maybe I should light a match—just glance at the number of her apartment? No, it's not worth it. I won't come to her place again.

A Proposition

I'm walking through the cars of a train. In my hands I have clippers for punching holes in tickets.

My clippers cut out a half-moon.

The chic branch line of Koslovodsk-Mineralnye Vody[22] is served by university students in the summer. And that's why I'm here, in the Caucasus. I came here to make some money.

Kislovodsk. I go out onto the platform. At the gates

of the station stands a huge gendarme with medals on his chest. He stands frozen, like a monument.

Politely bowing and smiling, the cashier comes up to me.

"Colleague," he says to me (though he's not a student), "a couple of words with you... Next time don't punch the tickets with your clippers, but return them to me..."

He utters these words calmly, smiling, as if he were speaking of the weather.

Disconcerted, I mutter:

"What for?.. So that you will...sell them again?..."

"Well, yes... I have an agreement with almost all of you... Split fifty-fifty..."

"Bastard!... You're lying!" I mutter. "With all of us?"

The cashier shrugs his shoulders.

"Well, not with all," he says, "but... with many... And what do you find so surprising about that? They all do it... After all, do you think I can live on thirty-six rubles... I don't even consider it a crime. They push us into it..."

Turning sharply, I walk away. The cashier catches up to me.

"Colleague," he says, "if you don't want to, you don't have to, I won't insist... only don't take it into your head to tell anybody about this. In the first place, no one will believe it. In the second place, you can't prove it. In the third place, you'll get the reputation of a liar, a troublemaker."

I wander home slowly... It's raining...

I am more surprised than at any time in my life.

Elvira

The train stop "Minutka." I have a quiet room with windows looking out on a garden.

My quiet and my happiness do not last long. The

next room is taken by a circus performer arriving from Penza, Elvira. According to her passport, she's Nastya Gorokhova.

She's a hefty soul, almost illiterate.

In Penza she had a brief romance with a general. The general presently arrived with his spouse in "Kislye vody."[23] Elvira arrived right after him, counting on no one knows what.

From morning to night, all of Elvira's thoughts are turned in the direction of the unfortunate general.

Showing her arms, which have held three men under the big top, Elvira tells me:

"I'm telling you, I could kill him quite calmly. And they wouldn't give me more than eight years for it... What do you think?"

"But what exactly do you want from him?" I ask her.

"What do you mean, what!" says Elvira. "I came here expressly for his sake. I've been living here almost a month and, like a fool, paying for everything myself. I want him, at least for the sake of decency, to pay my fare both ways. I want to write him a letter about this."

Because of Elvira's illiteracy, the letter is written by me. I write with inspiration. My hand is guided by the hope that once Elvira gets the money, she'll leave for Penza.

I don't remember what I wrote. I only remember that when I read this letter to Elvira, she said: "Yes, this is the cry of a woman's soul... And I'll definitely kill him if he doesn't send my anything after this."

My letter churned up the general's insides. And he sent Elvira five hundred rubles by messenger. This was a huge and even grand sum in those times.

Elvira was dumbfounded.

"With this much money," said she, "it would be plain stupid to leave Kislovodsk."

She stayed. And stayed with the thought that I alone was the cause of her wealth.

Now she almost never left my room.

It's a good thing the world war began soon after.
I left.

1915-1917

Fate treated me more kindly
Than a multitude of others...

Twelve Days

I'm riding from Vyatka to Kazan to get reinforcements for my regiment. Riding with post-horses. There's no other connection. I'm riding in a kibitka,[24] wrapped in a blanket and fur coats.

Three horses race over the snow. Desolate all around. A fierce frost.

Beside me sits Ensign S. We're riding together for reinforcements.

It's the second day we've been riding. All the words have been said. All the recollections repeated. We're bored like mad.

Taking the revolver from his holster, Ensign S. shoots at the white insulators on the telegraph poles.

These shots irritate me. I get mad at Ensign S. I say to him gruffly: "Cut it out... you bonehead!"

I expect an uproar, a shout. But instead of this I hear a plaintive voice in reply. He says:

"Ensign Zoshchenko... no need to stop me. Let me do what I want. I'll arrive at the front and get killed."

I gaze at his upturned nose, I look into his pitiful bluish eyes. I recall his face after almost thirty years. He actually was killed on the second day after he took his position.

In that war ensigns lived on the average no more than twelve days.

Feeling Sleepy[25]

We enter a ballroom. At the windows, raspberry velvet curtains. In between, mirrors in golden frames.

A waltz is booming. It's played on the piano by a man in tuxedo. An aster in his buttonhole. But the mug on him—it's that of a murderer.

On the sofas and armchairs sit officers and ladies. Several couples dance.

A drunken cornet enters. Sings: "The Austrians are stupid men, if war with Russia they begin..."

Everyone takes up the song. They laugh.

I sit down on the sofa. Beside me, a woman. She's about thirty years old. A bit plump. Dark. Merry.

Glancing into my eyes, she says:

"Shall we dance?"

I sit somber, morose. Shake my head no.

"Feeling sleepy?" she asks. "Then come to my place."

We go to her room. In the room, a Chinese lantern. Chinese screens. Chinese robes. It's amusing. Funny.

We go to bed.

It's already twelve. My eyelids grow heavy. But I can't fall asleep. Feel bad. Miserable. Uneasy. I'm weary.

She's bored with me. She tosses, sighs. Reaches over to my shoulder. Says:

"Don't get angry if I go to the ballroom for a short while. They're playing lotto there now. They're dancing."

"As you wish," I say.

She kisses me gratefully and leaves. I fall asleep immediately.

Toward morning she's not there, and I again shut my eyes.

A bit later she is sleeping peacefully, and I, dressing quietly, leave.

The First Night

I enter the hut. On the table, a kerosene lamp. The officers are playing cards. On an army cot, puffing on a pipe, sits the lieutenant-colonel.

I salute.

"At ease," says the lieutenant-colonel. And turning to the players, he nearly yells: "Lieutenant K. Eight o'clock. Time for you to go to work."

The crafty-looking lieutenant, handsome, with thin moustaches, dealing the cards, answers:

"Yes, sir, Pavel Nikolaevich... At once... As soon as I finish this hand."

I gaze rapturously at the lieutenant. In a moment he has to go to work—into the night, into the darkness, on a scouting party, to the rear. Maybe he'll be killed, wounded. But he answers so easily, so gaily and jokingly.

Looking over some papers, the lieutenant-colonel says to me:

"Take a rest for now, but tomorrow we'll send you 'to work' too."

"Yes, sir," I answer.

The lieutenant goes out. The officers go to bed. Quiet. I listen to the distant gunshots. This is my first night near the front. No sleeping for me.

Toward morning Lieutenant K. returns. He's dirty, tired.

I ask him sympathetically:

"Not wounded?"

The lieutenant shrugs his shoulders.

I say:

"I also have a spot of 'work' ahead of me today."

Smiling, the lieutenant says:

"What do you think, that I went out on a military operation? I went to work with the battalion. Three kilometers from here, to the rear. We're fortifying the second line there."

I'm horribly uncomfortable, ashamed. I come close

to crying in my vexation.

But the lieutenant is already snoring.

Nerves

Two soldiers are cutting up a pig. The pig squeals so badly you can't stand it. I go closer.

One soldier is sitting on the pig. The hand of the other, armed with a knife, skilfully slits open the belly. White lard of immeasurable thickness spreads out on both sides.

The squeal is so bad it's time to stop up your ears.

"Hey, fellows," I say, "you could have stunned it, shut it up with something. What's the point of slicing it up that way?"

"Can't be helped, your honor," says the soldier sitting on the pig. "You won't get the same taste."

Catching sight of my silver sabre and the emblem on my epaulets, the soldier leaps up. The pig shoots out.

"Sit, sit," I say. "Finish it up already."

"Quick isn't good either," says the solider with the knife. "Too much quickness spoils the fat."

Looking at me with sympathy, the first soldier says:

"It's war, your honor! People are moaning. And you feel sorry for a pig."

Making the final gesture with the knife, the second soldier says:

"His honor has a case of nerves."

The conversation is taking on a familiar tone. This isn't proper. I want to leave, but I don't leave.

The first soldier says:

"In the Augustowo forest the bone was shattered on this hand here. Went right to the table. A half-glass of spirits. They start cutting. And I have a bite of sausage."

"And it didn't hurt?"

"How could it not hurt? It hurt most excessively...

I ate the sausage. Give me, I say, some cheese. I had just eaten up the cheese when the surgeon says: Finished, let's sew it up. My pleasure, I say... Now you, your honor, you wouldn't have been able to stand it."

"His honor has weak nerves," the second soldier says again.

I leave.

An Attack

Exactly at midnight we leave the entrenchments. It's very dark. I hold a revolver.

"Softly, softly," I whisper, "don't bang your canteens."

But it's impossible to get rid of the rattling.

The Germans open fire. How vexing. That means they've noticed our maneuver.

Amid the whistling and screeching of bullets, we rush forward to drive the Germans out of their trenches.

A hurricane of fire swells up. Machine guns, rifles are firing. And the artillery enters the affair.

Men are falling around me. I feel a bullet has singed my leg. But I rush forward.

Now we're right at the German obstructions. My grenadiers cut the wire.

Furious machine-gun fire cuts short our work. It's impossible to raise your hand. We lie still.

We lie an hour, maybe two.

Finally the telephone man extends the telephone receiver to me. It's the battalion commander speaking:

"Retreat to your former positions."

I pass the order down the line.

We crawl back.

Next morning they bandage me up in the regimental infirmary. A minor wound. And not made by a bullet, but by a shell fragment.

The regimental commander, Prince Makayev, tells

me:

"I'm very pleased with your company."

"We didn't do anything, your excellency," I answer in some confusion.

"You did what was demanded of you. You see, it was a diversion and not an assault."

"Ah, it was a diversion?"

"It was simply a diversion. We had to draw the foe from the left flank. That's the place where the assault was."

In my heart I feel unbelievable vexation, but I don't let on.

In the Garden

In front of the balcony of a dacha there is a beautiful flower-bed with a yellow glass ball on a stand.

They bring the dead in carts and lay them out in the grass alongside this flower-bed.

They lay them out like logs, one next to the other.

They lie there yellow and motionless, like wax dolls.

Removing the glass ball from the stand, the grenadiers dig a grave for their brothers.

By the porch stand the regimental commander and the staff officers. The regimental priest walks up.

Quiet. Somewhere far off, the artillery is bellowing.

The dead are lowered into the pit on towels.

The priest walks around and pronounces the words of the last rites. We hold our hands up in salute.

They batter down the grave with their feet. Erect a cross.

Unexpectedly, another cartload of dead rolls up.

The regimental commander says:

"Well, how can this be, men. It should all be done together."

A Feldwebel,[26] arriving on a cart, reports:

"We didn't find them all at first, your excellency.

41

These were on the left side, in a hollow."

"What can we do?" says the commander.

"Permit me to append, your excellency," says the Feldwebel, "why not just let 'em lie a bit. Maybe tomorrow ther'll be some more. And then we can bury 'em all together."

The commander agrees. The dead are carried off to the barn.

We go to dinner.

The Regiment in a Pocket

The regiment spreads out over the highway. The soldiers are exhausted, tired. For the second day, almost without resting, we have been marching across the fields of Galicia.

We are retreating. We have no shells.

The regimental commander orders us to sing songs.

The machine gunners, prancing on their horses, strike up "Over the Blue Waves of the Ocean."   .

From all sides we hear shots, explosions. The impression is, we are in a pocket.

We march through a village. The soldiers run up to the cottages. We have an order to destroy everything along the highway.

It's a dead village. No pity for it. There's not a soul here. There's not even any dogs. Not even a single chicken, which usually are found in abandoned villages.

The grenadiers run up to the little cottages and set fire to the straw roofs. Smoke rises up to the sky.

And suddenly, in an instant, the dead village comes alive. Women, children go running. Men appear. Cows moo. Horses neigh. We hear shouts, crying and screeching.

I see how one soldier, having just lit a roof, beats it out in his confusion with his cap.

I turn away. We march on.

We march until evening. And then we march at night. All around, the red glow of fires. Shots. Explosions.

Toward morning the regimental commander says:

"Now I can say it. For two days our regiment has been in a pocket. Tonight we came out of it."

We drop on the grass and immediately fall asleep.

Breakthrough

I memorized the name of this village: Tuchla.

We hastily dug out some trenches here. But we hadn't time to string up the obstructions. The barbed wire lay behind us in big rolls.

In the evening I receive an order—report to headquarters. Amid the whistling of bullets I go there with my orderly sergeant.

I enter the dugout of regiment headquarters.

The regimental commander, smiling, says to me:

"Lad, stay here with the staff. The adjutant will be getting a battalion. You'll take this place."

I lie down to sleep in a low hut. Take off my boots for the first time in a week.

In the early morning I am awakened by a burst of shells. I run out of the hut.

The regimental commander and the staff officers are standing beside saddled horses. I see they are all agitated and even shaken. Shells fall around us, fragments hiss and trees crash down. Nevertheless, the officers stand motionless, stonelike.

The chief signal officer, biting out his words, says to me:

"The regiment is surrounded and taken captive. In about twenty minutes the Germans will be here... There's no link with division headquarters... The front is broken up for six kilometers."

Nervously tugging on his gray sidewhiskers, the regi-

43

mental commander shouts at me:

"Quick, ride to division headquarters. Ask what are the directives. Tell them we headed for supplies, where our reserve battalion is waiting..."

Jumping on a horse, I dash down a forest road along with an orderly.

Early morning. The sun gilds a meadow, visible to my right.

I ride out into the meadow. I want to see what is happening and where the Germans are. I want to get a complete picture of the breakthrough.

I jump off the horse and walk up to the top of a knoll.

I am all aglitter in the sun—with my sabre, epaulets and binoculars, which I put to my eyes. I see some distant columns and the German artillery on horseback. I shrug my shoulders. It's very far away.

Suddenly, a shot. One, two, three. Three-inch shells land beside me. I hardly have time to lie down.

And, lying there, I see a German battery below the knoll. No more than a thousand paces away.

Again shots. And now the shrapnel explodes above me.

The orderly waves his hand at me. With his other hand he points to the road below where a battalion of Germans is moving.

I jump on my horse. And we dash away.

I Came for Nothing

I ride up to the high gates at a gallop. This is division headquarters.

I'm excited and agitated. The collar of my field jacket hangs open. The cap sits on the back of my head.

Jumping off my horse, I go through a wicket gate.

A staff officer, Lieutenant Zradlovsky, comes directly up to me. He hisses through his teeth:

44

"Looking like that... Button up your collar."

I button my collar and adjust my cap.

The staff officers are standing beside saddled horses.

Among them I see the division commander, General Gabayev, and the chief of staff, Lieutenant Shaposhnikov.

I make my report.

"I know," the general says irritably.

"What should I relay to my commander, your eminence?"

"Relay that..."

I sense some sort of curse on the general's tongue, but he holds it back.

The officers glance at each other. The chief of staff almost laughs out loud.

"Relay that... Well, what can I relay to a man who has lost his regiment... You came for nothing..."

I walk away in confusion.

I gallop off on my horse again. And suddenly I see my regimental commander. He's tall, lean. His cap's in his hand. The wind ruffles his gray sidewhiskers. He stands in the field and halts the departing soldiers. These are not soldiers from our regiment. The commander runs up to each one shouting and entreating.

The soldiers obediently go to the edge of the forest. There I see our reserve battalion and some two-wheeled supply wagons.

I go up to the officers. The commander also comes up to them. He mutters:

"My glorious Mingrelsy Regiment is lost."

Throwing his cap on the ground, he stomps on it in a rage.

We console him. We say that five hundred of us have remained. That's no small number. We'll have a regiment again.

We're sitting in some sort of kiln. It's seven hundred paces to the trenches. Bullets are whistling. And shells blow up nearby. But regimental commander Balo Makayev is joyful, almost gay. We have a regiment again—a hastily reinforced battalion.

For three days and nights we have sustained the assault of the Germans without retreating.

"Write," the commander dictates to me.

On my field stachel lies a notebook. I write a communique to division headquarters.

A heavy shell explodes ten paces from the kiln. We are sprayed with trash, filth, straw.

Through the smoke and dust I see the commander's smiling face.

"It's nothing," he says, "keep writing."

I take up my writing again. My pencil literally jumps up and down from the nearby explosions. Across the yard from us the house is burning. Again a heavy shell explodes with a horrible rumble. This one was right beside us. The fragments go flying—squealing and moaning. For some reason I stick a little burning fragment in my pocket.

There's no need to sit in this kiln, which doesn't even have a roof on it.

"Your excellency," I say, "it would be more reasonable to transfer to the forward line."

"We stay here," the commander says stubbornly.

A hurricane of artillery fire descends on the village. The air is filled with moaning, howling, squealing and screeching. It seems to me I have fallen into hell.

It seemed to me I was in hell! Twenty-five years later, I was in hell when a German bomb weighing a ton and a half exploded next door.

I Go On Leave

I have a suitcase in hand. I'm standing in the station "Zalesye." In a moment the train will pull up and I'll return to Petrograd via "Minsk" and "Dno."

The coaches pull up. They are all heated freight cars, with one passenger car. Everyone rushes to the train.

Suddenly, shots. By their sound: ack-acks. German planes appear in the sky. Three of them. They begin to circle around the station. The soldiers shoot at them haphazardly with their rifles.

Two bombs fall from the planes with an oppressive howl and explode near the station.

We all run into the field. In the field there are vegetable gardens, a hospital unit with a red cross on its roof and, farther off, fences of some kind.

I lie down on the ground by a fence.

Having circled the station and dropped another bomb, the planes set their sights on the hospital. Three bombs fall almost simultaneously by the fences, throwing up the earth. This is really swinish. There's a huge cross on the roof. You can't fail to notice it.

Three more bombs. I see how they break away from the planes. I see the beginning of their fall. And then, only the howling and whistling of air.

Our ack-acks fire again. Now the fragments and jackets of our shrapnel spray the field. I press against the fence. And through a chink I see an artillery dump.

Hundreds of cases of artillery shells stand under the open sky.

A watchman sits on the cases, eyeing the planes.

I rise up slowly and peel my eyes for a place to hide. But there's no place. One bomb in the cases, and everything will be turned upside down for several kilometers.

After dropping a few more bombs, the planes leave.

I walk slowly back to the train and give my heart-

47

felt blessing to inaccurate shooting. War will become absurd, I think, when technology achieves perfect aim. This year I would have been killed at least forty times.

I Love

I ring. Nadya V. opens the door. She cries out in surprise. And throws her arms around my neck.

On the threshold stand her sisters and mama.

We go out on the street to talk without disturbance. We sit down on a bench at the "Steregushchy" monument.

Squeezing my hands, Nadya weeps. Through tears she says:

"How stupid. Why didn't you write me anything. Why did you leave so unexpectedly. Now a year has passed. I'm getting married."

"Do you love him?" I ask, without yet knowing who he is.

"No, I don't love him. I love you. And I'll never love anyone else. I'll turn him down."

She weeps again. And I kiss her face, wet with the tears.

"But how can I turn him down," says Nadya, interrupting herself in reflection. "We've already exchanged rings. And we've announced our engagement. On that day he gave me an estate in the province of Smolensk."

"Then don't," I say. "After all, I'm going back to the front. And so why should you wait for me? I may be killed or wounded."

Nadya says:

"I'll think everything over. I'll decide myself. You don't have to say anything to me... I'll give you an answer day after tomorrow."

The next day I meet Nadya on the street. She is walking arm in arm with her fiance.

There's nothing special about this. It's natural.

48

But I'm infuriated.

In the evening I send Nadya a note saying that I've been called immediately back to the front. And a day later I leave.

This was the most stupid and senseless act of my life.

I loved her very much. And this love has not left me to the present day.

Come Tomorrow

At the entrance I meet Tata T. She's so beautiful and so dazzling, that I turn my eyes away from her as from the sun.

She laughs on seeing me. She looks over my uniform with curiosity and touches my silver sabre. Then she says I've really grown up and it's even improper for people to see us together. There would surely be gossip.

We go up the stairs.

Clicking my spurs, I enter her apartment.

At the mirror Tata adjusts her hairdo. I go over to her and embrace her. She laughs. She's surprised that I've become so bold. She embraces me the way she once did on the stairway.

We kiss. And in comparison to this the whole world strikes me as negligible. And she also doesn't care what's going on around us.

Then she looks at the clock and cries out in terror. Says:

"My husband will be home in a moment."

At that very minute the door opens, and her husband comes in.

Tata barely has time to adjust her hairdo.

The husband sits down in an armchair and looks at us silently.

Tata, not losing her composure, says:

"Nikolai, just take a look at him, how he's changed.

Why, just this minute he arrived from the front."

With a sour smile, the husband looks at me.

The conversation doesn't catch on. And I leave with a ceremonious bow. Tata sees me out.

Opening the door to the stairway, she whispers to me:

"Come tomorrow afternoon. He leaves at eleven."

I nod my head silently.

The husband's face and his sour smile stick in my head all day. It strikes me as horrible—and even criminal—to go to her tomorrow afternoon.

In the morning I send Tata a note saying that I must leave immediately for the front.

That evening I go to Moscow and, after spending a few days there, return to my regiment.

The Thief

I'm the battalion commander. I'm upset that discipline is becoming lax among my men.

My grenadiers salute me with a smile. They almost wink at me. Probably I myself am to blame. I converse with them too much. People hang about my dugout all day. For some I have to write letters. Others come for advice.

What advice can I give when I hear them calling me "kiddie" behind my back.

It's come to the point where things have begun to disappear from my dugout. A pipe is missing. A shaving mirror. Candy, paper disappears.

I'll have to shake them up and be hard on them.

We're off duty. I'm sleeping in a cottage, on a bed.

In my sleep I suddenly feel someone's hand stretching across me to the table. I shudder in horror and wake up.

Some damn soldier springs headlong out of the cottage.

I run after him with a revolver in my hand. I am infuriated as never before in my life. I shout: "Halt." And had he not stopped I would have shot him. But he stopped.

I walk up to him. And he suddenly falls to his knees. In his hands he holds my safety razor in a nickel-plated box.

"What did you take it for?" I ask him.

"For *makhorka*,27 your honor," he mumbles.

I understand that he should be punished, turned over for court-martial. But I lack the strength to do it. I see his dejected face, pitiful smile, trembling hands. It disgusts me that I chased him.

Removing the razor, I hand the box over to him. And walk away, irritated with myself.

July the Twentieth

I stand in the trenches and look with curiosity at the ruins of the little town. This is Smorgon. The right wing of our regiment has dug in beside the vegetable gardens of Smorgon.

This is a famous town, the place from which Napoleon fled, leaving Murat in command.

It's growing dark. I return to my dugout.

A sultry July night. Taking off my field jacket, I write letters.

It's nearly one o'clock already. Ought to lie down. I want to call the orderly. But suddenly I hear some sort of sound. The sound grows louder. I hear the tramping of feet. And the rattling of canteens. But no shouts. And no shots.

I run out of the dugout. And suddenly a sweet, suffocating wave engulfs me. I shout: "Gas attack!.. Masks!.." And rush into the dugout. My gas mask is hanging there on a nail.

The candle went out when I ran headlong into the

51

dugout. I've found the gas mask with my fingers and begun to put it on. Forgot to open the lower valve. Choke. Opening the valve, I run out into the trenches.

Soldiers are running all around me, wrapping their faces with gauze masks.

After fumbling for matches in my pocket, I light the brushwood lying in front of the trenches. This brushwood was prepared in advance. In case of a gas attack.

Now the flames illuminate our positions. I see that all the grenadiers have come out of the trenches and are lying beside the fires. I also lie down by a fire. I feel bad. My head is spinning. I swallowed a lot of gas when I shouted, "Masks!"

It becomes easier by the fire. Even all right. The flames lift the gas, and it passes over without touching us. I take off my mask.

We lie there for four hours.

It begins to get light. Now you can see the gas moving. It's not a solid wall. It's a cloud of gas ten sazhens[28] wide. It slowly advances on us, pushed forward by a soft wind.

We can go to the right or the left—and then the gas will pass by without touching us.

Now it's not frightening. Already I hear laughter and joking somewhere. It's the grenadiers pushing each other into clouds of gas. Guffaws. Horseplay.

I look through the binoculars toward the Germans. Now I see how they release the gas from big bags. It's a repulsive sight. I'm overcome with fury when I see how methodically and coldbloodedly they do it.

I give the order to open fire on these bastards. I give the order to shoot with all the machine guns and rifles, although I realize we'll do little harm—at a distance of fiteen hundred paces.

The grenadiers shoot listlessly. And there aren't many riflemen. Suddenly I see that many of the soldiers are lying dead. They're—the majority. The others are moaning and can't raise themselves from behind the flames.

I hear the sounds of a bugle in the German trenches. It's the poisoners sounding retreat. The gas attack is over.

Leaning on a stick, I blunder to the infirmary. My handkerchief is bloodied from the horrifying vomiting.

I walk down the highway. I see the grass turned yellow and a hundred dead sparrows fallen on the road.

Finale

Our regiment is again off duty.

We're riding on *rozvalni*[29] to the second-class supplies unit: supper will be served there.

The chief of supplies meets his dear guests.

On the table are goatskins of wine, shashlik and all sorts of victuals.

I sit at the table with the nurse Klava. I'm already drunk. But I must drink some more. Every glass is accompanied by a toast.

I feel that I shouldn't drink any more. After the gas attack I have disorders of the heart.

In order not to drink, I go out on the street. And sit down on the porch.

Klava comes up and is surprised to find me sitting in the frost without a coat. She takes me by the hand to her room. It's warm there. We sit down on her bed.

But our absence has already been noticed. Laughing and joking, the officers knock on the window of our room.

We go back to the table.

In the morning we return to the regimental station. And I go to sleep like a log on my army cot.

I wake up from the howling and bursting of bombs. A German plane is bombing the village. This is not the bombardment which we know from the present war. This is four bombs—and the plane leaves.

I go out on the street. And suddenly I feel that I can't breathe. My heart stops. I try to take my pulse—there is no pulse.

With unbelievable difficulty, holding onto the fences, I make it to our location.

The physician, shaking his head, shouts:

"Camphor!"

They inject me with camphor.

I lie there, nearly dying. The left side of my chest grows numb. My pulse is forty.

"You shouldn't drink," says the physician. "Heart defect."

And I make a vow to myself not to drink anymore.

They transport me to the field hospital through the thawed February snow.

1917-1920

Back to his troops he dashed on his steed
And new was the wind blew over the land...

I Don't Understand Anything

The first days of March. I'm riding home from the train station in a buggy.

I ride past the Winter Palace. See a red flag on the palace.

This means a new life. The New Russia. And I am new, not the same as before. Let all that stay behind—my sorrows, nerves, my gloominess, my sick heart.

Ecstatic, I enter my own home. And that very day I make the rounds of all my friends. I see Nadya and her husband. Meet Tata T. Drop in on my university friends.

I see joy and exultation all around. Everyone is glad that the revolution has taken place. Except Nadya, who told me: "It's horrible. It's dangerous for Russia. I don't

54

expect any good to come of it."

For two days I feel splendid. On the third day I have depression again, I have palpitations, gloom and melancholy.

I don't understand anything. I get lost guessing where this despair came from. It simply shouldn't be!

Probably I need to work. Probably I need to give all my strength to the people, the country, the new life.

I go to staff headquarters, to a representative of the Provisional Government. I request that he reassign me to the army.

But I am unfit for the ranks, and they assign me as postmaster to the main post office and telegraph.

A most unpleasant thing for me—is done. I sit in an office and sign some papers or other. This work is repellent to me in the extreme.

I go back to headquarters and request a transfer to somewhere in the provinces.

They offer me Arkhangelsk—adjutant in the local militia. I accept.

In a week I must leave.

Five O'Clock Tea   .

The jurist L. stops by for me. We're getting ready to go to a very aristocratic house—to visit Princess B.

L. asks me to put on my medals.

"She'll like it," he says. "Her husband is still at the front. He commands a division of the guards."

I show him my medals. One medal is on my Caucasian sabre. Two medals are fastened to my cigar box. A fourth medal is worn around the neck. It's awkward somehow for me to put it on. A fifth medal never came into my hands—it's only on paper.

L. insists. He adjusts the medal under the collar of my field jacket.

Feeling awful, I go with the jurist out onto Offi-tserskaya Street.

I have never before had occasion to be among the aristocracy. The February revolution has broken up class divisions. And so now I go to this house.

In a small drawing room stand two officers of the guards, several jurists and a *lycée*[30] student.

The princess isn't pretty—short in stature, with small facial features. But she has a very simple manner. And I don't feel any awkwardness.

The servants noiselessly roll a little glass table on wheels into the room. The princess pours out the tea.

The conversation constantly centers around the name of the czar. They are constantly talking about Nikolai, about his abdication, about the health of this or that member of the czar's family. About his spouse's condition. And about all sorts of affairs and activities at court.

I sit like a lump in an armchair, with my medal around my neck. I have absolutely nothing to say on the subject. I look despairingly at my friend the jurist. He turns his eyes away from me.

After tea, we move into the large drawing room. However, the subject of conversation does not change.

Finally someone from among the jurists begins to sing a song popular at the time: "A great big crocodile walked through the streets in style." Everyone takes up the tune.

They sing it five or six times, laughing all the while. One of the jurists sticks some sort of scarf in his teeth when the tune comes to the words: "In its teeth it gripped—a piece of a blanket..."

Everyone laughs madly. And the princess giggles indulgently.

At seven o'clock we go out on the street. L. asks me how I liked it. I shrug my shoulders.

Vava the Fiancée

I arrived in Arkhangelsk morose, in a horrible despair. Nevertheless, or perhaps therefore, people there began to make a match for me.

They found me a fiancée: Vava M., the daughter of a very wealthy fish merchant.

I had never seen this girl, and she had never seen me. But matchmaking of this kind was customary there. It occupied the ladies who had nothing else to do.

My meeting with my fiancée was solemnly arranged —in the conservatory of some wealthy home.

Before me stood a very young, very quiet girl.

They left us alone so we could have a little talk.

I had always been taciturn. But on that evening a near catastrophe occurred. I literally did not know what to say. I had to wrench the words out of myself to fill in the horrifying pauses.

The girl looked at me frightfully and also remained silent.

From nowhere could I expect salvation. Everyone had gone off to distant rooms, and they had tightly closed the door to the conservatory.

So I began to recite verses.

I began to recite the verses of a popular book by Vera Inber, *Sad Wine.* Then I began to recite Blok and Mayakovsky.

Vava listened to me attentively, without releasing a word.

When people came into the drawing room, I was almost gay. I asked Vava if she liked what I had recited. She said quietly:

"I do not like verses."

"Then whyever did you listen to them for a whole hour!" I exclaimed, mumbling under my breath: "You ninny."

"It would have been impolite on my part not to listen to what you said."

Almost like a soldier, I turned about-face on my heels and, infuriated, walked away from the girl.

Kid Gloves

On Tuesdays and Saturdays we visit D. This is a young woman, the widow of a naval officer.

It's always very merry at her place. She's witty and coquettish.

I have no success with her. She likes the midshipman T., a big-hearted, broad-shouldered officer.

Evening. We're playing poker at her place. D. plays the coquette with the midshipman. She touches her hand to his hand as if by accident and stares into his eyes for a long time. It looks like she'll invite him to visit her not merely on Tuesdays and Saturdays.

To be sure, she is also receptive to me. But not so much. She says I'm too inert, not masculine, sad. Melancholy is not her ideal.

We leave her at night. And on the street we rib the midshipman, who smiles enigmatically.

In the morning I can't find my gloves. I hate to lose them. They're English kid gloves. It must be I left them at D.'s place.

I telephone D. In reply I hear prolonged laughter. Through the laughter she tells me:

"Ah, so they're your gloves? For some reason I was certain they were the midshipman's gloves..."

I stop by her place at the appointed time. She does not let me go, and we drink tea in her boudoir.

After tea, she leans her head on my chest. And I leave her three hours later.

In the vestibule she hands me my kid gloves.

"Here's your gloves, you little rascal," she says with a smile. "You must admit that this was a somewhat naive ruse—leaving your gloves so you could come back to a lady."

I mumble my apologies. Laughing, she shakes her finger at me. Says with a sigh:

"As you see, I appreciated your clever trick. You're enterprising. I didn't expect it of you..."

"Madame," I say, "I assure you... I left my gloves by accident... I had no intention at all..."

I regretted saying this. Her face became unlovely, yellow, almost old.

"Ah, so that's how it is," she said through clenched teeth. "In that case I'm very sorry... O, let that be a lesson to me!"

She never invited me to visit her again.

I would have done the same thing in her place.

The Roads Lead to Paris

In the armchair across from me sits a French lieutenant. With a little snigger, he says:

"Tomorrow at twelve o'clock noon you can get a passport. Within ten days you'll be in Paris... You should thank Mademoiselle R. She's the one who sponsored you."

"I didn't request it of Mademoiselle R.," I tell the lieutenant.

Squinching, he looks at me:

"Ah, so that's how it is," he says. "In that case forgive me, I didn't know this ran counter to your desires."

I say:

"I'm not planning to travel anywhere, Lieutenant. It's a misunderstanding."

Shrugging his shoulders, he says:

"My friend, do you have any conception of what's going on in the country?... Above all, it's no small danger to your life—the proletarian revolution... Here in Arkhangelsk we don't feel this to such an extent... You should think about it. I'll expect you tomorrow at twelve."

59

"All right, I'll think about it," I say. Although there's nothing for me to think about. I have no doubts. I cannot, and do not want to leave Russia. I do not seek anything in Paris.

In the evening Mademoiselle R. comes to my place. She's a French woman. She's not very pretty. But she's very gay and amusing. There's something about her I don't understand. She keeps taking the stubs of my cigarettes from the ashtray and putting them in her bag. "As a momento," she says. I'm unable to talk her out of this bad practice. Probably she's from the provinces. But she claims she was born in Paris.

She asks me if I saw the lieutenant. I relate to her everything that happened. She's a bit irritated. Angrily she says:

"That's foolish. All of your lot are leaving. You won't stay here in any event. The roads lead to Paris."

She speaks rapturously about Paris and about how we shall live there fabulously.

I bring her down to earth. I tell her:

"In that case, why did you leave Paris? Here you can be a governess, a teacher. But there you'll be a seamstress."

She says:

"I came here to a millionaire's home. It's interesting... And there I will be not a seamstress, but a courtesan."

We laugh.

By the Gateway

I race up to the third floor in one breath. My heart is pounding.

I ring at Nadya's door. No one opens. I knock at the door softly at first, then start kicking it.

The neighbor's door opens.

"Do you want V." asks an old woman. "They've

60

all gone away. "

"Where to?"

"Don't know. Ask the janitor."

I stand by the gateway. Before me is the janitor. He recognizes me. Smiles.

"The V.'s have all gone away," he says almost joyfully.

"When?"

"A month ago. In February."

"And you don't know where they went?"

"Where could they go? To the Whites... After all, the papa's a general... And they gave your lot such a drubbing here—quite a sight!.. Of course they went away..."

Evidently noticing the dismay on my face, the janitor gives a sympathetic sigh.

"And who were you worried over?" he asks. "I don't quite get it—over Nadenka or Katenka?"

"Over Nadenka."

"A very sweet missus," he says. "The papa's a general, the husband's a landowner... A clear case... She took the little one and went away."

"You mean she had a baby?"

"Like I said—she took the newborn baby and went away."

I walk home. The whole world seems dim to me.

In the Basement

I'm sitting on a low stool. In my lap lies someone's worn-out shoe. With a rasp I level off a piece of leather just added to the sole.

I'm a cobbler. This is work I like. I despise intellectual work—it's just mental nitpicking, from which, it must be, melancholy and gloominess arise.

I'll never return to the past. I'm content with what I have.

61

Across from me, at a low, dirty table sits the master, Aleksei Alekseyevich—a fat cobbler in nickel-plated glasses. Next to him sits his nephew—the teenage Andryushka. They are both working with concentration.

The teenager hammers the sole quite deftly.

Behind, on a wooden settee, sits the master's fair-haired boy. A booby of twenty years. He's entering the conservatory to study violin. For this reason he does not work. He sits with a newspaper in his hands.

Breaking into laughter, the teenager Andryushka begins to relate a story about how one summer a certain tenant fell out of the second-story window. After drinking some denatured alcohol, he fell asleep on the windowsill, stretched out in his sleep and fell into the garden. He did himself harm, but didn't do himself in.

For three weeks now I have heard this story every day. Nevertheless everyone laughs. And I laugh too—it's funny somehow.

On occasion our laughter brings the master's wife out of the kitchen, and she stands in the doorway and laughs, rubbing her mouth and eyes with her apron.

The master, by the way, does not permit this story to be told. He gets angry and curses when the tale is begun. But he gets caught up in the details and laughs harder than anyone, clutching at his belly. He has a stomach ulcer and is forbidden to laugh. Therefore he prohibits this tale.

However, the teenager or the master's boy purposely turns the conversation toward it. They begin remotely, as if speaking of irrelevant matters—getting drunk, denatured alcohol, sleeping people. But every time they bring the conversation around to the actual event.

This time the teenager begins with a janitor who got scared. The master's boy tosses in a few remarks to the janitor's discredit. And then the teenager, squealing with laughter, fills in the details—how this janitor set off at a run when the falling tenant's hand struck him on the crown and shoulder.

The master squirms about on his stool, groaning and clutching his belly from time to time.

Finally, he scampers out into the kitchen.

I say:

"You shouldn't make him laugh. You see—he feels bad again."

The master's boy says:

"Rubbish. Papa has nausea. Everyone knows, it relieves people."

The master returns, rubbing his mouth on his sleeve.

We silently go back to work.

The Cast-Iron Shadow

"Mankovo," a former country estate in Smolensk province. Now there's a *sovkhoz*[31] there.

At the executive committee I got good marks on the examinations for the position of poultry breeder. And now I'm the manager of a poultry farm.

I wander among the birds with books in my hands. Some kinds of birds I've seen only in their roasted form. And so now the textbooks come to my aid.

For two weeks I don't leave the birds, almost spend the night with them, trying to learn their character and their ways.

On the third week I allow myself little strolls through the countryside.

I walk down the byroads. From time to time I encounter peasants.

These encounters confound me every time. Some fifteen paces away, the peasant doffs his hat and gives me a low bow.

I tip my cap politely and walk by in confusion.

At first I think these bows are accidental, but then I

see them repeated every time.

Perhaps they're taking me for some kind of bigwig.

I ask an old woman who has just given me a bow almost down to the earth:

"Granny," I say, "why do you bow that way to me? What's up?"

Kissing my hand and saying nothing, the old woman walks away.

Then I walk up to a peasant. He's elderly. Wearing *lapti*.[32] And a torn sackcloth. I ask him why he whipped off his hat ten paces away and gave me a bow from the waist.

Bowing again, the peasant tries to kiss my hand. I yank it back.

"What did I do to anger you, *barin?*"[33] he asks.

And suddenly in these words and in this bow of his I saw and heard all. I saw the shadow of a past manner of life. I heard the bellow of the landowner and the soft slavish response. I saw a life of which I had had no previous conception. I was startled as never before in my life.

"Father," I said to the peasant, "the workers and peasants have held the power for a year already. And here you are about to lick my hand."

"It hasn't reached us," says the peasant. "True, the lords have left their manors, live in huts... But who knows what will come tomorrow..."

I walk with the peasant to his village. I stop in his cottage.

Every step of the way I see the cast-iron shadow of the past.

An Old Man Dies

I'm standing in a peasant's cottage. On the table an old man lies dying.

He's been lying here three days already and hasn't died yet.

Today there's a wax candle in his hand. It falls and goes out, but they light it again.

At the head of the table stand the relatives. They stare at the old man unremittingly. There is unbelievable poverty all around, filth, rags, indigence...

The old man lies with his feet to the window. His face is dark, strained. The breathing uneven. Sometimes it seems he's already dead.

Leaning toward the old woman—his wife, I say to her softly:

"I'll go to town for the doctor. It's not right that he should lie on the table for three days."

The old woman shakes her head no.

"No need to bother him," she says.

The old man opens his eyes and looks over those present with a cloudy gaze. His lips whisper something.

One of the women, young and swarthy of face, leans over the old man and listens silently to his mumbling.

"What's with him?" asks the old woman.

"He wants the tit," answers the woman. And quickly unbuttoning her blouse, she takes the hand of the old man and places it on her bared breast.

I see how the old man's face beams. Something like a smile passes over his lips. He breathes more evenly, more calmly.

All stand in silence, without stirring.

Suddenly the old man's body shudders. The hand falls down helplessly. The face becomes stern and completely calm. He stops breathing. He's dead.

At once the old woman begins wailing. And immediately after her everyone wails.

I walk out of the cottage.

On the table sits a kerosene lamp with a coquettish pink shade. We're playing preference.[34]

My partners are a fat lady—Olga Pavlovna, an old man with rotten teeth, and his daughter—a beautiful young woman, Veronika.

These are former landowners from the neighboring districts. They did not want to move far away from their homesteads. Having rented this cottage from peasants, they lived here with the rights of private citizens.

We've been sitting at the table for four hours already. The game has bored me stiff. I'd give it up with pleasure. But it's uncomfortable for me—I've been losing, I have a big fine to pay.

My luck stinks. It's Olga Pavlovna who's lucky, and with every win she gets noisier and happier.

Taking a round, she slaps her palm on the table in delight.

"Lucky me!" she screams. "I've always been lucky at everything... Let two or three months go by, and I'm sure I'll get my estate back..."

The old man with rotten teeth begins to laugh.

"Cards are one thing, most respected Olga Pavlovna," he says, "but Russia, politics, revolution—that's another thing."

"No difference!" screams Olga Pavlovna. "We play cards in life as well. One is lucky, another is not lucky. But I've always been lucky at everything—both at life and at cards... You'll see, soon I'll get my 'Zatishe'[35] back..."

Dealing the cards, she says:

"Get my 'Zatishe,' whip my muzhiks a bit, and everything will be as before."

"After such a revolution you'll only whip them a bit?" asks the rotten-toothed old man, breaking off his laughter.

Olga Pavlovna, ceasing to deal, says:

"I'm not so brainless as to send my muzhiks to jail. I don't intend to remain without any labor. Keep that in mind..."

"My, no, most respected Olga Pavlovna," says the old man. "I categorically disagree with you... And I'll object to your policies... Two of them I'll hang—I know the ones. Five I'll send into hard labor. The rest—I'll whip and fine. They can work a full year for me alone."

I throw my cards down so hard that they bounce off the table and scatter over the floor.

"Oh!" Olga Pavlovna exlaims haughtily.

"Scoundrels, criminals!" I say softly. "It's because of you that there's such misery, such darkness in the village, such obscurity..."

I dig the money out of my pockets and hurl it onto the table.

A fever comes over me.

I dash out into the entryway and, fumbling with my coat, stick my arms into it with difficulty.

It's quiet in the room. No one even whispers. I wait for Veronika to come out into the entryway, but she doesn't come out.

I go out in the yard. Lead my horse through the gateway. Lie down in the rozvalnya.

The horse runs off friskily—it knows the way by itself.

Above my head, a dark sky, stars. All around, snow, fields. And a horrible silence.

Why did I come here? What am I here for, among the birds and the jackals? Tomorrow I'm leaving.

At Regimental Headquarters

I'm sitting at a desk. Copying an order for the regiment. I drafted the order today with the commander and commissar of the regiment.

I'm an adjutant of the first model regiment of the

village poor.

Before me is a map of northwestern Russia. The line of the front is marked off in red pencil—it proceeds from the shores of the Gulf of Finland through Narva to Yamburg.

Our regimental headquarters is in Yamburg.

I copy the order in a beautiful, precise hand.

The commander and commissar have ridden off to our positions. I have a heart defect. I'm forbidden to ride a horse. And so they rarely take me with them.

Someone raps at the window. I see some civilian figure in a dirty worn coat. Rapping at the window, the man bows.

I order the guard to admit the man. The guard reluctantly admits him.

"What can I do for you?" I ask.

Taking off his hat, the man hesitates in the doorway.

I see before me a very pitiful man, somehow very unfortunate, broken-down, distressed. To encourage him, I escort him to an armchair, shake his hand and ask him to sit. He sits down reluctantly.

Barely moving his lips, he says:

"If the Red Army moves out, shall we move out with you or remain?"

"And who might you be?" I ask.

"I've come from the colony at 'Krutye ruchi.'[36] That's where we have our colony of lepers."

I feel my heart sink. I rub my hand out of sight on my wadded pants.

"I don't know," I say. "I can't decide this matter alone. Besides, there's no question of our retreating. I don't think the front will extend beyond Yamburg."

Bowing to me, the man leaves. From the window I see him showing his sores to the guard.

I go to the infirmary and wash my hands with carbolic acid.

I didn't catch it. Probably our fear of this disease

is exaggerated.

Bread

I lost consciousness one morning when I came out of headquarters to take a walk in the fresh air.

The guard and telephone man brought me around. For some reason they rubbed my ears and moved my arms up and down as if I had drowned. All the same, I came to.

The regimental commander said to me:

"Go away for a rest at once. I'll give you two weeks leave."

I went to Petrograd.

But in Petrograd I didn't feel any better.

I went to the military hospital for advice. After listening to my heart, they told me I was unfit for the army. And they kept me in the hospital to await a hearing.

And so I have been lying in the ward for two weeks.

Not only do I feel bad, but I'm hungry besides. This is nineteen-nineteen! In the hospital they serve four hundred grams of bread and a bowl of soup. That's not much for a man who is twenty-three years old.

Now and then my mother brings me some smoked carp. I'm ashamed to accept the carp. We have a big family at home.

On the bed across from met sits a young lad in his pants. He has just been brought two loaves of bread from the village. He cuts slices of bread with a pocketknife, spreads butter on them and dispatches them into his mouth. He does this without end.

Some one from among the patients asks:

"Sviderov, give us a little piece."

He says:

"Let me munch first. I'll munch and then give you some."

After doing right by himself, he tosses pieces around to the beds. He asks me:

"What about you, intellect, want some?"

I say:

"Only don't throw it. Put it on my table."

This displeases him. He would rather throw it. That's more interesting.

Sitting in silence, he peers at me. Then he gets out of bed and, acting like a fool, puts the piece of bread on my side table. Doing this, he bows theatrically and makes a face. Laughter in the ward.

I really feel like throwing this offering on the floor. But I restrain myself. I turn to the wall.

At night, lying in bed, I eat the bread.

My thoughts are most bitter.

Brie Cheese

Every day I go over to the fence where "The Red Gazette" is posted.

The paper has a "Mailbox." It prints answers to authors.

I wrote a little story about the village. And sent it to the editors. And now I await an answer with some excitement.

I didn't write this story to earn anything. I'm a telephone man on the border patrol. I'm secure. The story was just written—it seemed necessary to me—to write about the village. I wrote the story under a pseudonym: M. M. Chirkov.

It's drizzling. Cold. I stand at the paper and scan the "Mailbox."

I see: "To M. M. Chirkov. We need rye bread, not brie cheese."

I can't believe my eyes. I'm shocked. Perhaps they didn't understand me?

I begin to recall what I wrote.

No, it appears to have been written correctly, quite all right, rather nicely. A little bit mannered, with some embellishment, with a Latin citation... My God! For whom did I write that way? Is that really the way one should write?... Old Russia is gone... Before me is a new world, new people, new speech...

I go to the station to catch a train for Strelna, where I have duty. I sit in a coach and ride for an hour.

The devil must have inclined me to intellectual work again. This is the last time. Never again. It's my stationary, sedentary work that's to blame. I have too much time to think.

I'm changing my work.

We'll Catch Him

It's night. Dark. I stand in some barren area of Ligovo.

In my coat pocket is a revolver.

Next to me stands the detective agent N. He whispers to me:

"You stand at the window so my bullet won't hit you if I have to shoot... If he jumps out the window... shoot... shoot at his legs..."

Holding my breath, I go up to the little window. It's lit up. I press my back to the wall. Narrowing my eyes, I peer over the short curtains.

I see the kitchen table. A kerosene lamp.

A man and woman are sitting at the table, playing cards.

The man deals out the dirty, ragged cards. He makes a play and slaps the card with his palm. Both laugh.

N. and three detective agents charge the door simultaneously.

This is a mistake. They should have found another way to open the door. It doesn't give in at once to their exertions.

The bandit puts out the lamp. Dark.

The door crashes open. Shots...

I raise my revolver level with the window.

Quiet.

We light the lamp in the cottage. The woman is sitting on a stool—she's pale and trembling. Her partner's gone—he left through another window which was boarded up.

We examine the window. The boards were nailed on so they would fall off at the first touch.

"Never mind," says N., "we'll catch him."

We stop him at dawn, four versts[37] away. He shoots at us. And then shoots at himself.

January the Twelfth

It's cold. Steam blows out of your mouth.

Chunks of my desk lie by the stove. But the room is still not easy to heat.

My mother lies in bed. She's delirious. The doctor said she has "Spanish flu"—a horrible influenza from which people are dying in every home.

I go over to Mother. She's under two blankets and two coats.

I put my hand to her forehead. The heat burns my hand.

The lamp wick goes out. I adjust it. And sit down beside Mother on her bed.

Sit a long time, gazing into her exhausted face.

Quiet all around. My sisters are sleeping. It's two o'clock in the morning already.

"Stop it, stop it... don't do that..." Mother mutters.

I raise some warm water to her lips. She takes a few swallows. Opens her eyes for a second. I lean toward her. No, she's delirious again.

But now her face grows calmer. The breathing more even. Perhaps the crisis is over? She will be better...

I cover her shoulders with the blanket, which has slipped down.

I see: a shadow seems to pass over my mother's face. Fearing to think anything, I slowly raise my hand and touch it to her forehead. She's dead.

For some reason I have no tears. I sit on the bed without moving. Then I rise and, waking my sisters, go off to my room.

I Want Nothing

Wooden sleds on wooden runners.

On the sled rests an unpainted coffin.

Harnessing myself to the sled, I pull it to the cemetery.

Behind the sled walk my sisters and my little brother.

Here's the Smolensk Cemetery already. At the gates stand many such sleds with coffins. The usual wheeled carriages and dressed-up horses are absent. Probably the horses have been eaten, just as their food has been eaten—the oats.

The coffin is borne into the church. I remain on the street. And sit down on the steps of the cathedral. I sit beside the beggars. I myself am a beggar. I have nothing ahead of me. And I want nothing. I have no desires. I am only sorry for my mother.

The coffin is again borne out of the church. And I again pull the sled to a distant lane. There is the grave of my father, who died fourteen years ago.

Beside this grave a new one is dug.

I raise the lid of the coffin and kiss the dead hand of my mother.

A New Path

In the handcart are a small desk, two armchairs, a rug and a set of shelves.

I roll these things to my new apartment.

This is a changing point in my life.

I cannot remain in an apartment where death has been.

A certain woman, who loved me, said to me: "Your mother has died. Move into my place."

I went to the marriage bureau with this woman. And we registered. Now she is my wife.

I roll these things to her apartment, on the Petrograd side.[38]

It's very far. And I push my cart with difficulty.

Before me is a rise leading up to Tuchkov Bridge.

I have no strength left to push my cart. My heart pounds horribly. I look despairingly at the passersby. Perhaps a kind soul can be found—to help me up this incline.

No, the passersby, glancing at me indifferently, pass on by.

To hell with them! I must do it myself... If only there are no heart palpitations... It's stupid to die on a bridge transporting armchairs and a desk.

With my last bit of strength, I wheel the cart onto the bridge.

Now it's easy.

1920-1926

Had I made friends with fortune, no question,
I wouldn't be in my present profession.

The House of Arts

This house stands on the corner of the Moika Canal and Nevsky Prospect.

I walk down a corridor in expectation of a literary evening.

It doesn't mean a thing that I'm a detective agent. I already have two critical articles and four stories. And all of them highly praised.

I walk down the corridor and look at the literati.

Here comes Aleksei Remizov. Little and ugly, like a monkey. His male secretary is with him. A cloth tail sticks out from under the secretary's jacket. This is a symbol. Remizov is the Father Superior of the "Free Chamber of Monkeys."[40] There stands Evgeny Zamyatin. His face is a bit shiny. He smiles. In his hand is a long Russian-style cigarette in an elegant long Mundstück.

He converses with someone in English.[41]

Shklovsky walks by. He wears an Eastern fez. He has an intelligent and impudent face. He argues furiously with someone. He sees nothing—except himself and his opponent.[42]

I greet Zamyatin.

Turning to me, he says:

"Blok's here, he came. You wanted to see him..."

Together with Zamyatin I enter a near-dark room.

A man stands by the window. His face is brown from the sun. A high forehead. And light, wavy, almost curly hair.

He stands surprisingly still. Looks at the lights on Nevsky.

He does not turn around when we enter.

"Aleksandr Aleksandrovich," says Zamyatin.

Turning around slowly, Blok looks at us.

I have never seen such empty, dead eyes. I never thought that a face could reflect such despair and such indifference.

Blok extends his hand—it's flaccid and lifeless.

It makes me feel awkward to disturb a man lost in some sort of oblivion... I mumble my apologies.

In a somewhat hollow voice Blok asks me:

"Will you participate in the evening?"

"No," I say. "I came to listen to the literati."

Zamyatin remains with Blok.

I again walk down the corridor. Some sort of anxiety suffocates me. Now I can almost see my own fate. I see the finale of my life. I see the despair which will certainly suffocate me.

I ask someone: "How old is Blok?" The answer: "About forty."

He's not forty years old! But Byron was thirty when he wrote:

> **Is it that weariness which springs**
> **From all I meet, or hear, or see?**
> **To me no pleasure Beauty brings,**
> **Thine eyes have scarce a charm for me.**[43]

Byron wrote "It is" and did not place a question mark after "see." I mentally ask the question myself. I think to myself—is it really weariness?[44]

The literary evening begins.

"The Twelve" Cafe[45]

This is a cafe at 12 Sadovaya Street. I'm sitting here at a little table with my comrades.

All around, drunken shouts, noise, tavern smoke.

A violin plays.
I mumble the verses of Blok:

> I'll befriend the tavern fiddle...
> I'll drink down the wine once more...
> All the same my strength won't last me,
> Drag me to the very end
> With a wretched sober grin,
> Masking terror of the grave
> And the worry of a corpse.[46]

Toward our table, with an uncertain step, comes a man. He wears a black velvet blouse. On his chest he has a big white muslin ribbon.

This man's face is dusted with powder.

The lips and eyebrows are made up.

The face wears a smile—a drunken and somewhat disconcerted one. Someone says:

"Seryozha, sit down with us."

Now I see that it's Esenin.

He sits down ponderously at our table. Looks angrily at some drunk. Grumbles: "I'll bash your puss in... shove off..."

I rub Esenin's hand. He calms down. Again he smiles somehow disconcertedly and pitifully.

Behind the color of his painted mouth, I see the pale lips.

Someone else comes up to our table.

Someone shouts: "We ought to put the tables together."

They begin to put the tables together.

I go out on the street.

At Gorky's Place

We enter the kitchen. On the stove, big copper pans.

78

We pass through the kitchen into the dining room.

Towards us comes Gorky.

There is something elegant in his noiseless gait, in his movements and gestures.

He does not smile, as befits a host, but his face is receptive.

He sits down at the table in the dining room. We seat ourselves around on chairs and on a small motley-colored divan. I see: Konstantin Fedin, Vsevolod Ivanov in a soldier's overcoat, Mikhail Slonimsky, Ilya Gruzdev...[47]

Coughing, Gorky speaks of literature, the people, the tasks of a writer.

What he says is interesting and even captivating. But I almost fail to listen. I watch how he drums his fingers a bit nervously on the table, how he smiles barely noticeably under his moustaches. I watch his surprising face—intelligent, somewhat crude and by no means simple.

I watch this great man who has legendary fame. Probably it's not so nice, disturbing, oppressive. I wouldn't want it.

As if in answer to my thoughts, Gorky says that far from everyone knows him, that the other day he was riding in a car and was stopped by a patrol. He said that he was "Gorky," but one of the patrol said: "We don't care if you're bitter or sweet. Show your pass."

Gorky barely smiles. Then he again speaks of literature, the people, culture.

Someone behind me notes down what Gorky says.

We rise. Take leave.

Barely touching his hand to my shoulder, Gorky asks:

"Why are you so sullen, so gloomy? What is it?"

In reply I mumble something about my heart.

"That's not good," says Gorky. "It must be cured... Drop by in a day or so—we'll talk over your affairs."

79

We pass through the kitchen again. Go out on the stairway.

We go out onto Kronversky Prospect—now Gorky Prospect.

A Meeting

Up and down the endless stairways I go. In my hands I carry a folder with papers, with blank forms. On these forms I enter information about the tenants. It's the all-union census.

I took up this work in order to see how people live.

I believe only my own eyes. Like Harun Al-Rashid,[48] I go round to other people's houses. I go down corridors, through kitchens, stop in rooms. I see the dim little lamps, the torn wallpaper, the wash on the clothesline, the horribly close quarters, the trash, the rags. Yes, of course, we have recently experienced harsh years, hunger, disruption... But still I did not think I would see what I saw.

I enter a near-dark room. In bed, on a dirty mattress, lies a man. He gives me an unwelcome reception. Doesn't even turn around to me. Stares at the ceiling.

"Where do you work?" I ask.

"Asses and horses work," he says. "I personally do not work and do not plan to work. Write that down in your lousy papers... You can add that I go to the club, play cards..."

He's irritated. Perhaps ill. I want to leave, to get the information from his neighbors. As I leave, I take a look at him. I've seen that face somewhere before.

"Alyosha!" I say.

He sits up in bed. His face is unshaven, sullen.

Before me I see Alyosha N., a comrade in the gimnaziya. He was a grade ahead of me. He was a goodie-goodie, a crammer, a prize student, mama's little boy...

80

"What happened, Alyosha?" I mutter.

"In sum, nothing happened," he says. And I see vexation on his face.

"Maybe I can help you in some way?"

"I need absolutely nothing," he says. "Hey, if you happen to have some money, give me a five spot, I'll go to the club."

I give him considerably more, but he takes only five rubles.

A few minutes later I'm sitting on his bed, and we're chatting the way we once did, ten years ago.

"It's actually the most vulgar sort of story," he says. "My wife ran off with some swindler. I started drinking. Drank up everything I had. Lost my job. Started playing at the club... And now, you understand, I don't feel like returning to what used to be. I could, but don't want to. It's all claptrap, drivel, comedy, nonsense, smoke..."

I get his word that he'll come to see me.

At Night

On my pillow lie letters to the editor of "The Red Gazette." They are complaints about difficulties in the bathhouses. I was given these letters so I could write a feuilleton.

I look through the letters. They're helpless, comical. But at the same time they're serious. I should say so! They concern a human affair of no little importance: the bathhouse.

Drawing up a plan, I set to writing.

The very first lines amuse me. I laugh. Laugh louder and louder. Finally I guffaw so hard that the pencil and notebook fall out of my hands.

Again I write. And again my body shakes with laughter.

No, later on, while copying the story, I won't laugh this way. But the first draft always amuses me to an unbelievable degree.

I feel a pain in my belly from the laughter.

My neighbor knocks on the wall. He's an accountant. He has to get up early tomorrow. I'm disturbing his sleep. Today he knocks with his fist. Must be I woke him up. A shame.

I shout:

"Forgive me, Pyotr Alekseyevich..."

Again I take up my notebook. Again I laugh, this time hiding my face in the pillow.

Twenty minutes later the story is written. I'm sorry I wrote it so quickly.[49]

I go over to my desk and copy the story in a beautiful, even hand. While copying, I continue to laugh softly. But tomorrow, when I read this story in the editorial office, I will no longer laugh. I'll read it somberly and even drearily.

Two o'clock in the morning. I go to bed. But I can't sleep for a long time. I think over themes for new stories.

It's getting light. I take a bromide to go to sleep.

Drivel Again

The editorial office of "The Contemporary," a thick journal.

I submitted five of my best little stories to this journal. And now I have come for an answer.

Before me stands one of the editors: the poet Mikhail Kuzmin.[50] He is exquisitely gracious. He even goes overboard. But from his face I see that he intends to tell me something unpleasant.

He hesitates. I help him out.

"Probably my stories don't fit into the format of the journal?" I say.

He says:

"You understand, we have a thick journal...[51] But

82

your stories... No, they're very funny, very amusing... But they're written... After all, they're..."

"Drivel? You want to say," I ask. And in my brain there flares up the remark at the bottom of my gimnaziya composition: "Drivel."

Kuzmin throws up his hands.

"God forbid. I by no means want to say that. On the contrary. Your stories are very talented... But you must admit, it's a bit of a caricature."

"It's not a caricature," I say.

"Well, just take the language..."

"The language is no caricature. That's the syntax of the streets... the people... Perhaps I exaggerated it a little so it would be satirical, so it would be critical..."

"We won't argue..." he says gently. "You give us one of your ordinary novellas or stories... And believe me... we highly value your creation."

I leave the office. I no longer have the feelings I once had in the gimnaziya. I'm not even irritated.

"God be with them," I think. "I'll make do without the thick journals. They need something 'ordinary.' They need something like a classic. That's what impresses them. That's very easy to do. But I don't plan to write for readers who are gone. The people have another conception of literature.

I bear no regret. I know that I'm right.

In the Beerhouse

Day. Sunshine. I walk down Nevsky. Toward me comes Sergei Esenin.

He wears an elegant blue coat with a belt. No hat.

His face is pale. Eyes burned out. He walks slowly. Mumbles something. I walk over to him.

He's sullen, uncommunicative. His face is full of some sort of dejection.

I want to leave, but he won't let me go.

"Feel bad? Are you ill?" I ask him.

"What do you mean?" he asks in alarm. "Do I look bad?"

And suddenly he laughs. Says:

"Growing old, friend... Soon I'll hit thirty..."

We walk to the Evropeiskaya Hotel.

Esenin stands at the entrance for a minute, then says:

"Let's go across the street. To the beerhouse. For a minute."

We enter the beerhouse.

The poet Vladimir Voinov sits at a table with his friends. He meets us joyfully. We sit down at his table. Someone pours out mugs of beer.

Esenin says something to the waiter. The latter brings him a glass of ashberry brandy.

Closing his eyes, Esenin drinks. And I see how, with each swallow, life returns to him. His cheeks grow brighter. His gestures more certain. His eyes light up.

He wants to call the waiter again. To distract him, I ask him to recite some verses...

For some reason he readily and even joyfully agrees.

Rising from his chair, he recites the poema "The Black Man."[52]

People gather round the table. Someone says: "It's Esenin."

Almost the entire beerhouse surrounds us.

A minute later, and Esenin is standing on the chair, gesticulating, reciting his shorter verses.

He recites wonderfully, and with such feeling, and with such pain, that it moves everyone.

I have seen many poets on the stage. I have seen their extraordinary successes, seen ovations, rapture throughout the entire hall, but I have never seen such feeling and such warmth as are shown to Esenin.

Dozens of hands grab Esenin from the chair and carry him to a table. Everyone wants to clink glasses with him. Everyone wants to touch, embrace, kiss him.

The crowd forms a tight ring around the table where he is sitting.

I walk out of the beerhouse.

It's My Own Fault

Evening. I walk down Nevsky with K.

I made her acquaintance in Kislovodsk.

She's beautiful, witty, gay. She has that joy of life which is lacking in me. And perhaps this quality in her charms me most of all.

We walk along, tenderly holding hands. We come out onto the Neva. Walk along the dark quay.

K. talks without end about something. But I do not dip too deeply into her speech. I listen to her words as to music.

But now I hear some discontent in this music. I listen closely.

"For two weeks I've been walking through the streets with you," she says. "We've walked around all the stupid quays and parks. I simply feel like sitting with you in some living room, chatting, having some tea."

"Let's go to a cafe," I say.

"No, we might be seen there."

Ah, yes. I completely forgot. She has a complicated life. A jealous husband, a very jealous lover. Many enemies to report that they saw us together.

We stop on the quay. Embrace each other. Kiss. She mutters:

"Oh, how stupid that we're on the street."

We walk along again and kiss again. She covers her eyes with her hand. Her head is spinning from these endless kisses.

We walk up to the gateway of some house. K. mutters:

"I must drop in here to see my dressmaker. You

85

wait for me here. She'll just measure me for the dress and I'll return at once."

I walk not far from the house. Walk ten minutes, fifteen, finally she appears. Gay. Laughing.

"Everything's fine," she says. "It'll be a nice dress. It's very modest, no pretensions."

She takes me by the arm, and I escort her home. I see her five days later. She says:

"If you like, we can see each other today in a certain house—of a girlfriend of mine."

We walk up to some house. I recognize the house. Here, by the gateway, I waited twenty minutes for her. It's the house where her dressmaker lives.

We go up to the fourth floor. She opens the apartment with her own key. We enter a room. It's a well-furnished room. Doesn't look like the room of a dressmaker.

By professional habit, I leaf through a little book which I find on the night table. On the title page I see a name familiar to me. It's the name of K.'s beloved.

She laughs.

"Yes, we're in his room," she says. "But don't worry. He's gone to Kronstadt for two days."

"K!" I say, "I'm worried about something else. Does this mean you were with him then?"

"When?" she asks.

"The time I waited twenty minutes for you by the gateway.

She laughs. Closes my mouth with a kiss. Says:

"It was your own fault."

September the Twenty-Third

The window of my room looks out onto the Moika and Nevsky.

I go over to the window. An extraordinary picture:

86

the river has roiled up, turned black. Another half-meter and the water will flow over the banks.

I run out onto the street.

Wind. An unprecedented wind blows from the sea.

I walk down Nevsky. I'm excited and anxious. I walk to the Fontanka Canal. The Fontanka is almost level with the pavement. Here and there the water splashes onto the sidewalk.

I jump on a streetcar and ride to the Petrograd side. My family lives there—my wife and little boy. They live with her relatives. I moved into the House of Arts so the infant's crying wouldn't disturb my work.

Now I'm hurrying to them. They live on Pushkarskaya Street, on the first floor. Maybe they'll have to transfer to the second floor.

The streetcar enters Aleksandrovsky Prospect. We're riding in water. We stop. It's impossible to ride any further. The wooden street-blocks have floated out and prevent the streetcar from going.

The passengers jump off into the water. It's not too deep here—up to your knees.

I walk through the water all the way to Bolshoi Prospect. There's no water as yet on the Prospect.

I almost run to Pushkarskaya. The water has not reached here.

My dear ones are alarmed and anxious. They're very glad that I came and am now with them.

Changing my clothes, I again go out onto the street. I want to see if the water will come.

I walk onto Bolshoi Prospect. Buy some bread in the bakery. Walk over to Vvedenskaya Street. It's dry.

And suddenly, an extraordinary picture: water seeps from all the manholes and speedily floods the pavement. I walk home again through water.

The water is already at the steps.

We transfer to the second floor with bundles.

I make chalk marks on the steps so I can see how the water rises.

At five o'clock in the evening the water splashes at the door.

It's getting dark. I sit by the window and listen to the howling of the wind.

Almost the whole city is under water now. The water has risen almost two sazhens.

On the dark sky there is the glow of some sort of fires.

It's getting light. From the window I see the water gradually subsiding.

I go out onto the street. A horrible spectacle. On the prospect there is a barge full of firewood. Logs. Boats. A small vessel with a mast lies on its side.

Everywhere there is havoc, chaos, destruction.

The Train Was Late

Alya came to me all out of breath. She said:

"He almost wouldn't let me go... I say: 'But Nikolai, be reasonable, I must see my best friend off—she's going to Moscow and who knows when she'll return...' "

I asked Alya:

"When does the train leave with your friend?"

She broke into laughter, clapped her hands.

"You see," she said, "you believed it too... No one's leaving. I thought it up so I could come to see you."

"The train to Moscow leaves at ten-thirty," I said. "That means you should be home around eleven."

It was already twelve when she glanced at her watch. She let out a cry. Ran over to the telephone without even putting on her slippers.

Lifting the receiver, she sat down in the armchair. She shook from the cold and from her anxiety.

I tossed her a small plaid. She covered her legs with the plaid.

She was remarkably beautiful—almost like a Renoir painting.

"Why are you phoning?" I said to her. "It'd be better to get dressed and go."

She waved her hand irritably in my direction.

"Nikolasha," she said into the receiver. "Imagine, the train was late and it just left. I'll be home in ten minutes."

I don't know what her husband said to her, but she answered:

"I'm telling you in plain Russian, the train was late. I'll be home right away."

Her husband must have said it was already twelve.

"Really?" she said. "Well, I don't know what your watch says, but the clock here in the station..."

She tossed up her head and looked at my ceiling.

"The clock here in the station," she repeated, "says exactly eleven."

She squinched her eyes, as if peering at a distant clock in the station.

"Yes," she said, "exactly eleven, or two minutes after. You've got an old churchman's watch..."

Hanging up the receiver, she began to laugh.

Right now this little doll stuffed with sawdust would be a most welcome guest at my place. But then I got angry at her. I said:

"Why must you lie so shamelessly. He'll check his watch and see that you're lying."

"But he believed I was at the station," she said, putting on her lipstick.

After putting on her lipstick, she added:

"But what is this, a lecture? That's not what I want to hear. I know how to act by myself. He runs around with a revolver, threatening to murder my friends and me included... By the way, he doesn't care if you're a writer... I'm sure he'll take a fine shot at you too."

I grumbled something in reply.

Getting dressed, she said:

"What now, are you angry? Maybe I shouldn't come any more?"

"As you like," I answered.

"Yes, I won't come to see you any more," she said. "I see that you don't love me at all."

She left, haughtily tossing up her head at me. She did this magnificently for her nineteen years.

My God, how I would cry now! But then I was quite content. Besides, she came back a month later.

At a Table

Moscow. I sit at a table in some theatrical club. At my table is a second place-setting. Mayakovsky will be dining here. He ordered his meal and went off to play some pool. He'll return shortly.

I hardly know Mayakovsky. We have met only at literary evenings, at the theater, in public.

Here he comes to the table. He breathes heavily. His face is not happy. He's somber. Wipes his forehead with a handkerchief.

He won the game, but it didn't amuse him. He sits down at the table somehow ponderously, heavily.

We are silent. Almost fail to converse. I pour him some beer. He takes a swallow and pushes the glass aside.

I'm also somber. And I don't feel like artificially working up a conversation. But to me Mayakovsky is a master. I'm almost a novice in literature, I've been working five years in all. I'm ashamed somehow to keep silent. I begin mumbling something about pool, about literature.

For some reason I'm remarkably uncomfortable with him.

I speak disconnectedly, lifelessly. And break off in the middle of a word. Unexpectedly Mayakovsky laughs.

"No, listen," he says, "this really gets me. I thought you'd be witty, tell jokes, horse around, but you... No, this is simply great! Absolutely great..."

"Why should I be witty?"

"Well, you're a humorist!... It figures... But you..."

He looks at me with a somewhat heavy gaze. His eyes are surprisingly unhappy. There's a sort of somber fire in them.

"But why are you...like that?" he asks.

"I don't know. I'm looking for the cause myself."

"Is that so?" he asks guardedly. "Do you suppose there is a cause? Are you ill?"

We begin to talk about illnesses. Mayakovsky claims to have a number of indispositions: something's wrong with his lungs, his stomach, his liver. He can't drink and even wants to quit smoking.

I notice one more indisposition of Mayakovsky's: he is even more fastidious than I. He wipes his fork twice with his napkin. Then wipes it with his bread. And finally wipes it with his handkerchief. He also wipes the rim of his glass with his handkerchief.

An actor we know comes over to our table. Our conversation breaks off. Mayakovsky says to me:

"I'll phone you in Leningrad."

I give him my number.

A Reading

I agreed to give readings in several cities. That was an unfortunate day in my life.

My first reading was in Kharkov, then in Rostov.

I was disheartened. They met me with a storm of applause, but left me with barely a clap. That means I don't please the audience somehow, cheat it somehow. But how?

It's true, I don't read like an actor, but monotonously, sometimes lifelessly. But do they really come to my evening as to the evening of a "humorist?" Indeed they do! Maybe they think: if the actors read so amusingly, then the author himself will really do a jig.

91

Every opening becomes a torture for me.

Reluctantly I go out onto the stage. The awareness that in a moment I will cheat the audience spoils my mood even more. I open a book and mumble some story or other.

Someone shouts down from above:

"Give us 'The Bathhouse'...'An Aristocratic Lady'... What rubbish you read us!"

"My God!" I think. "Whyever did I agree to these evenings?"

I look despairingly at my watch.

Notes fly up to the stage. For me, this is a breather. I close the book.

I unfold the first note. Read it aloud.

"If you are the author of these stories, why do you read them?"

I'm irritated. In answer, I shout:

"And if you are a reader of these stories, why in the hobgoblin do you listen to them!"

Laughter in the audience. Applause.

I open up the second note:

"Don't read us what we all know, tell us a comic story about how you got to us tonight."

In a furious voice I shout:

"I caught the train. My family cried, begged me not to go. They said: they'll only torment you with idiotic questions."

A burst of applause. Guffaws.

Ah, if now I were to walk across the stage on my hands or ride a monocycle—then the evening would be quite fine.

The producer of my evenings prompts me from the wings:

"Tell them something about yourself. The audience likes that."

Obediently, I begin to tell my life-story.

Notes fly up to the stage again.

"Are you married?.. How many children do you

92

have?.. Do you know Esenin?.."

Quarter to eleven. I can end.

With a sad sigh, I walk off the stage to light applause.

I console myself with the fact that these are not my readers. I console myself with the fact that these are spectators who would appear with equal enthusiasm for an evening of any comedian or juggler.

Without fulfilling the terms of my contract, I leave for Leningrad.

Animals

I wander down the lanes of the Leningrad zoological park.

In one cage, a magnificent huge tiger. Beside him is a small white bitch—a fox terrier. She nursed the tiger. And now, by her maternal rights, she is kept in the same cage with him.

The tiger glances at her affably.

An amazing sight.

Suddenly I hear a horrifying cry behind me.

All the visitors run to the cage where the brown bears are kept.

We witness a horrible scene. Next to the brown bears is a cage of bear cubs. In addition to the iron bars, the cages are separated by boards.

A little cub has climbed up on these boards and has paw has gotten caught in a crack. And now a brown bear is furiously tearing at this little paw.

Pulling itself away and crying, the cub gets a second paw caught in the crack. Now a second bear goes after that paw.

They both tear at the cub so badly that someone among the visitors falls in a faint.

We try to chase off the bears with dirt and stones. But this only drives them into a greater fury. One paw with little black claws already lies on the floor of the cage.

I take some sort of a long pole and beat the bear with this pole.

The horrible crying and roaring of the bears brings the keepers, the directors.

They pull the cub away from the boards.

The brown bears pace the cage furiously. Their eyes are flooded with blood. And their muzzles are full of blood. Growling, the male mounts the female.

The unfortunate cub is taken into the office. Its front paws are ripped off.

It doesn't cry any more. Probably they'll shoot it now. I begin to understand what animals are. And what is the difference between them and people.

Enemies

Sunday. I walk down the street. Someone cries out: "Misha!"

I see a woman. She's dressed quite simply, a shopping bag with groceries in her hands.

"Misha," repeats the woman, and the tears flow from her eyes.

Before me is the sister of Nadya V.—Katya.

"My God," she mutters. "It's you... it's you..."

My heart pounds horribly.

"Didn't you leave?" I ask. "And where is Nadya? Your family?"

"Nadya and Marusya are in Paris... Come to my place, I'll tell you everything... Only don't be surprised— I live very modestly... My husband's a very good man... He respects and pities me... He's a plain worker..."

We enter a small room.

A man rises up from behind a table. He's about forty years old. After we exchange greetings, he immediately puts on his coat and goes out.

94

"There, you see how good, how tactful he is," says Katya. "He understands at once that we need to talk."

We sit down on the sofa. The excitement overwhelms us. Katya begins to cry. She cries so hard that someone opens the door and asks what happened.

"Nothing," Katya yells shrilly.

She again shakes with sobbing. She is probably crying about what used to be. Probably she sees the past in me. Her youth, her childhood years. I calm her down.

Going over to a wash basin, she wipes her tearstained face, blows her nose loudly.

Then she begins to tell me everything. In nineteen-seventeen they went south to make their way to the Caucasus and from there across the border. But in Rostov the father came down with spotted fever. It was impossible to wait. The days were numbered. The sisters drew lots—who would remain with their father. Katya remained. She lived very poorly when her father died. She worked as a washerwoman, then as a housemaid. Then she managed to get to Leningrad. But here things were no easier for her: she had no apartment and no friends.

"Why didn't you turn to me," I ask. "You must have heard about me..."

"Yes. But I simply didn't think it was you."

Katya began to talk about her sisters. The elder writes, but Nadya doesn't. She hates everything left behind in Russia.

"But what if I write her?" I ask.

Katya says:

"You know Kolya M. You remember how he loved her. He wrote her. She sent him a postcard which contained four words: "Now we are enemies."

Katya and I parted. I promised to drop in on her.

It's Revolting

Alya came. Her face was pale, and her eyes despairing. In silence she unwound a motley-colored scarf

95

from around her neck. Tossed back her head slightly.

On her neck I saw five blue fingers. Someone had evidently strangled her. I gave a shout:

"Alya, what happened?"

She said hoarsely:

"Nikolai found out everything. He tried to strangle me, but I raised such a cry that some people came running."

She began to weep. Through the tears she said:

"Oh, why did I ever come to your place. Now there will be no peace and quiet in my life. I'm not returning to him. I'll move in with Mama and will come to your place now and then."

I put a hot compress on her neck and, taking a cab, took Alya to her mama's.

I was unusually agitated. I don't recall what I had in mind, but that very evening I went to her husband. To my surprise, he met me calmly.

I told him:

"I didn't expect such a vile thing from you. You could have separated from her, left her... But to strangle the little girl... It's revolting..."

I thought he would yell at me, perhaps throw me out. But without moving, sitting in the armchair, he hung his head low.

He said softly:

"She drove me crazy... I suspected that she had been unfaithful to me... But yesterday I found this note in her purse. Here, feast your eyes on this..."

He hurled the note on the floor. It was addressed to the actor N., with whom I had seen Alya on the street several times.

The note left no doubt: she was intimate with him to the fullest extent.

I was so startled, even shaken. I was so shaken that I didn't realize at first that the husband knew nothing about me and the whole thing concerned only the actor.

I glanced distractedly at the husband. No less distractedly he looked at me.

"But exactly what do you have to do with it?" he asked. "What did you do, see her today? She was at your place?.. So she has been at your place before?"

In his eyes I suddenly read his conjecture.

I closed my eyes with my hand.

"My God!" he shouted. "That means she... That means you..." Suddenly he possessed enough irony—to let out a laugh. Almost calmly he said: "That means she deceived you too... That's great..."

We parted coldly. Almost without saying goodbye.

I walked home as if in a delirium. There was chaos in my head. I wanted to decide why she had chosen to come to me with her bruises. Then I calmed down at the thought that, prior to me, she had gone with her bruises to the actor.

All Right

I try to work—can't. Lie down on the sofa—jump up in a minute. I have some sort of nervous condition which does not permit me to be calm for even a few minutes.

I sit down at my desk again. I'll force myself to sit calmly! Force myself to work. As if my life depended on it.

I pick up the pencil. Write. But my thoughts are lifeless. No imagination. Pale phrases. Something has happened in my soul. I've lost something. Some fire has gone out. The music has stopped playing which my life, my work, once danced to...

I sit at the desk, my head hung in my hands.

The lines of Byron come to me:

My days are in the yellow leaf;
The flowers and fruits of love are gone;

97

The worm, the canker, and the grief
Are mine alone![53]

I furiously break the pencil and tear up the paper.
Go out on the street. A marvelous autumn. Yellow leaves.
Blue sky. Maybe a walk will restore my equilibrium.

I walk past a little wooden house. A decrepit old
man sits on the steps. He's sitting in the sun. He sits surprisingly calmly. His eyes are shut. I see a light and
blissful smile on his wrinkled face.

But he can't be any less than eighty years old! He
may have a year in all to live, and yet he sits there so
calmly, so blissfully.

Why must I, a scamp in comparison to him, twitch,
jump up, agitate myself, run. I want to sit on a porch
just as calmly, with just as blissful a soul. Why is this
little bit of happiness inaccessible to me.

The old man opens his eyes. Looks at me.

"All right!" he says.

Downcast, I walk on.

Madness

A man comes into my room. He sits down in the
armchair.

He sits silent for a minute, listening. Then stands
up and shuts the door tightly.

He goes up to the wall and, putting his ear against
it, listens.

I begin to realize that he is insane.

Having listened at the wall, he sits down again in
the armchair and covers his face with both hands. I see
that he's desperate.

"What's wrong?" I ask.

"They're after me," he says. "I was just now riding
on the streetcar and I heard the voices clearly: There he
is... get him... grab him..."

He covers his face with his hands again. Then says softly:

"You alone can save me..."

"In what way?"

"You and me will exchange names. You'll be Gorshkov, and I'll be the poet Zoshchenko." (That's what he said—"the poet.")

"All right. I agree," I say.

He rushes to me and shakes my hand.

But who's after you?" I ask.

"I can't say."

"But I must know, now that I'm bearing your name."

Wringing his hands, he says:

"That's just it, I myself don't know. I only hear voices. And at night I see their hands. They stretch out toward me from all sides. I know—they'll grab me and strangle me."

His nervous chill infects me. I don't feel so good. My head is spinning. Circles in front of my eyes. If he doesn't leave right away, I'll probably lose consciousness. He has a murderous effect on me.

Gathering up strength, I mutter:

"Go. Now you have my name. You can rest easy."

With a radiant face, he leaves.

I lie down on my bed and feel a horrible despair take hold of me.

In a Hotel

Tuapse. A small hotel room. For some reason I am lying on the floor. My arms are thrown out. And my fingers are in water.

It's rainwater. A thunderstorm just passed. I didn't feel like getting up to shut the window. The torrents of rain fell into the room.

I close my eyes again and lie in some sort of stupor until evening.

Probably I should move to the bed. It's more comfortable there. A pillow. But I don't feel like getting up from the floor.

Without getting up, I reach over a suitcase and fetch an apple. I have not eaten anything again today.

I take a bite of the apple. I chew it like straw. Spit it out. It's awful. I lie until morning.

In the morning someone knocks on the door. The door is locked with a key. I don't open it. It's the cleaning woman. She wants to clean the room. At least once every three days. I say:

"I don't need anything. Go away."

At noon I get up with difficulty. Sit down on a chair.

Alarm takes hold of me. I realize that I can't go on like this any more. I'll die in this miserable room if I don't leave here immediately.

Opening my suitcase, I feverishly collect my things. Then I call the maid.

"I've gotten sick," I tell her. Someone will have to take me to the station, get me a ticket... Quickly..."

The maid brings the management and a physician. Rubbing my hand, the physician says:

"Nerves... Only nerves... I'll write you a prescription for brom..."

"I must leave immediately," I mumble.

"You'll leave today," says the hotel director.

Conclusion

And now my recollections are finished.

I have come up to 1926. Right up to the days when I stopped eating and nearly perished.

Before me lie sixty-three episodes. Sixty-three experiences which once agitated me.

I began to re-examine every episode. In one or another of them I hoped to find the cause of my des-

100

pair, my sorrows, my illness.

But I didn't perceive anything in these episodes.

Yes, some of them are burdensome. But no more burdensome than those which people are accustomed to have. Everyone's mother dies. Everyone leaves home at some time. Parts with a sweetheart.

Fights at the front...

No, not in a single one of these episodes did I find what I was seeking.

Then I assembled all these episodes together. I wanted to see the overall picture, the fundamental tone which perhaps had deafened me like a fish yanked out of the water and tossed into a boat.

Yes, of course, tremendous convulsions happened in my lifetime. A change of fate. The downfall of the old world. The birth of a new life, a new people, a country.

But, after all, I saw no catastrophe in this! After all, I strived to see the sunshine in this. After all, despair pursued me even before these events. That means this did not settle the matter. Consequently, this was not the cause. On the contrary, this helped me to see anew the world, the country, the people I had begun to work for... There should have been no despair in my heart now! But there was...

I was discouraged. It seemed I set myself the insuperable task of finding the cause of my despair, of finding the unfortunate experience which had made me into a miserable speck of dust chased about by any wind of life.

Perhaps this experience lies in an earlier period?— I thought. Perhaps my childhood years lay the shaky ground on which I now walk so uncertainly.

Indeed! Why had I banished my childhood years? After all, they represent the first acquaintance with the world, the first impressions, and consequently the deepest. How could I have failed to reckon with them!

Here as well, there is no need to recall everything, I thought. It suffices to recall only the brightest, the strongest things, only things connected with my emotional agitation.

And then with feverish haste I began to recall the experiences of my childhood years. I saw that in my childhood years as well, my emotional agitation cast an unusual light on everything that had occurred.

Again these were snapshots retained in my brain with blinding power.

And so, recalling these childhood episodes, I saw that they agitated me even more than had the episodes of my adult years. I saw that they agitated me considerably more than had even the desire to find the cause of my misfortunes.

IV. THE TERRIBLE WORLD[54]

Only in the tale does the prodigal son
return to his father's home.

And so I began to recall the brightest scenes from my childhood.

Among these scenes, which were connected with an emotional agitation, I hoped to find the unfortunate experience, hoped to find the cause and explanation of my horrible despair.

At what age should I begin?—I wondered.

It's comical to begin at one. Comical to recall what had been at two and at three. And even at four. Just think of the great deeds which took place at that tender age! The rattle was taken away. Dropped the pacifier in the potty. Got scared by a rooster. Mamasha spanked the hiney... Why recall these miserable deeds, about which,

103

by the way, I recall almost nothing.

I should begin at five years of age, I thought.

And then I began to recall what had happened in my life from the age of five to fifteen.

And so, running through the episodes of these years in my mind, I unexpectedly felt fear and even some sort of trepidation. I thought: this means I'm on the right path. This means the wound is somewhere nearby. This means I'll now find the sad experience which ruined my life for me.

From 5 to 15

To cast off more quickly the heavy memory
Of my imaginary hurts...

I Won't Do It Again

On the table, a bowl. In the bowl, preserved figs.

It's fun to chew these figs. They have a lot of seeds. They crunch wonderfully between your teeth. After dinner they gave us only two of these figs each. That's far too few for children.

I climb up on the chair. With a determined gesture I move the bowl toward me. And take a bite out of one fig.

That's right—a lot of seeds. Wonder if it's the same in them all...

Of course, this is naughty, and I shouldn't do it. But then—I don't eat the whole fig. I take only a little bite. Almost the whole fig remains at the disposal of the grown-ups.

Taking a little bite out of all the figs, I get down from the chair and go walking around the table.

Father and Mother come up.

"I didn't eat the figs," I tell them right off. "I only

took a little bite."

Glancing at the bowl, Mother clasps her hands. Father laughs. But he frowns when I look at him.

"Come on, I'm going to give you a little spanking," says Mother, "so you'll remember what you shouldn't do."

She drags me to the bed. And takes up a thin belt.

Crying and sobbing, I yell:

"I won't do it again."

Don't Stand in the Street

I stand at the gate of our home. Not right by the gate, but at the curb.

I go no further than the curb. Can't. A buggy might run over me.

Suddenly I see: a two-wheeled bicycle with a person in a cap rides toward me.

Why doesn't he ring? Bicyclists should ring when they bear down on people.

I run to the side. But the bicycle again rides toward me.

A second—and the man in a cap falls. And I fall. And the bicycle falls on me.

Blood spurts from my nose.

Seeing the blood, I start wailing so loudly that people come running. Even the one-legged paperboy who stands on our corner runs up.

Pushing the people aside, my mother runs up.

Seeing me lying there, she slaps the bicyclist so hard on the cheek that the cap falls off his head.

Then she grabs me in her arms and carries me up the steps.

On the steps she looks me over and feels my body. Nothing broken. Only the blood flows from my nose and there's a scratch on my leg.

Mother says:

"Too bad I didn't know he hurt your leg. I would have torn his head off."

Papa says to me:

"It's your own fault. Don't stand in the street."

Goldfish

On the windowsill, a jar of goldfish.

Two fishies swim in the jar.

I toss them breadcrumbs. So they'll eat. But the fish swim by without interest.

They must feel really bad if they don't eat. No wonder, they're in the water for days on end. But if they just lay on the windowsill. Then maybe they'd get an appetite.

Sticking my hand in the jar, I pull the fishies out and put them on the windowsill. No, they don't feel too good here either. They flap. And also refuse food.

I toss the fishies back in the water.

But they feel even worse in the water. Look, they're even swimming with their bellies up now. Must be asking to get out of the jar.

I pull the fishies out again and put them in a cigarette box.

A half-hour later I open the box. The fishies bit the dust.

Mamasha says angrily:

"Why did you do that?"

I say:

"I wanted them to feel better."

Mother says:

"Don't act like an idiot. Fish were made to live in the water."

I cry bitterly, feeling hurt. I myself know that fish are made to live in the water. But I wanted to spare them this misfortune.

At the Zoo

Mother holds me by the hand. We're walking down a footpath.

Mother says:

"We'll look at the animals later. First there's going to be a contest for children.

We walk to a square. A lot of children are there.

Every child is given a sack. You have to get in the sack and tie it around your chest.

Now the sacks are tied. And the children in the sacks are placed at a white line.

Someone waves a flag and shouts, "Run!"

Stumbling in our sacks, we run. Many children fall down and start bawling. Some of them get up and run on, crying.

I almost fall down too. But then, catching on to the trick, quickly change my position in my sack.

I approach the table first. The music plays. And everyone claps. And they give me a tin of marmalade, a little flag and a little book with pictures.

I walk over to Mother, clutching my gifts to my chest.

Mama tidies me up on a bench. She combs my hair and wipes my soiled face with her handkerchief.

After this we go to look at the monkeys.

Wonder if monkeys eat marmalade? I'll have to give them a treat.

I want to treat the monkeys to marmalade, but suddenly I see that the tin isn't in my hands...

Mama says:

"We probably left the tin on the bench."

I run to the bench. But my tin of marmalade is already gone.

I cry so hard that the monkeys turn and look at me.

Mama says:

"Someone probably stole our tin. Never mind. I'll

buy you another."

"I want that one!" I scream so loudly that the tiger shudders and the elephant raises its trunk.

On the Shore

We're at our dacha. Playing on the shore.
Suddenly my elder sister Lelya screams:
"Hey, everybody, Yulya has drowned."
I look to all sides. That's right, my younger sister Yulya is nowhere to be seen.
Lelya screams:
"It's true! There's her hat floating in the water."
That's right, Yulya's straw hat is floating in the river.
Without stopping for breath, I run to our dacha. Scream:
"Mama! Yulya drowned!"
Mama runs to the river so fast I can hardly keep up with her.
Seeing Yulya's hat floating in the water, Mama falls in a faint.
At this moment Lelya screams:
"No, everybody, Yulya didn't drown. There she is floating in a boat. She's trying to catch up to her hat."
That's right, we see Yulya standing in the boat, paddling with an oar, floating after her hat. But the current is swift. And her hat is far away.
I say:
"Mama, wake up, Yulya didn't drown after all."
Seeing Yulya in the boat, Mama screams:
"Yulya, come back! You'll get carried out to the middle of the river."
Lelya says:
"She'd love to come back, but she can't. She can't manage the oar. Look how far out it's carried her."
We now see that Yulya has been carried far from

the shore.

And she screams in fright: "Help!"

Hearing her scream, Mama again falls in a faint.

Now some man gets in another boat and goes out to Yulya.

I say to Mama:

"Mama, don't be afraid. Yulya's going to be saved. A man is tying Yulya's boat to his boat."

And soon Yulya is on the shore.

Crying and kissing Yulya, Mama carries her home.

Cows are Coming

I shoot at a bird from a slingshot. The bird flies off and lands in a tree rather far from our house.

The order is not to go out of the yard. But at such an exceptional time, it's surely permissible.

And so I run down the road after the bird.

Suddenly I hear mooing behind me.

I look around. My God, a herd of cows is coming.

Retreat is cut off. Too late to run home.

The cows are quite close. After racing about, I climb a tree.

Now the cows are under the tree.

It's interesting to note that they're not leaving.

As if on purpose, they have stopped by the tree and begun to browse in the grass. They pretend they haven't noticed me. I won't leave the tree until the whole herd has gone.

If only the branch I'm sitting on doesn't break off. If the branch breaks off, things will be bad for me. I'd fall right between those two cows there. And then they'd toss me on their horns.

The drover is coming. He snaps a whip.

That's the drover I know, Andryushka. I can make a deal with him.

"Andryushka," I cry, "chase these cows away from under the tree! Let them find another place to do their eating!"

Andryushka snaps the whip. The cows go away unwillingly.

It's not frightening now. I even take aim with my slingshot [55] and release a pebble at the departing cows.

Then I climb down from the tree and, with a guilty walk, return to the yard.

The Thunderstorm[56]

With my sister Lelya I walk through the field picking flowers.

I pick yellow flowers. Lelya picks blue ones.

My little sister Yulya straggles behind us. She picks white flowers.

We pick this way on purpose, so that it will be more interesting to pick them.

Suddenly, Lelya says:

"Hey, everybody, look what a storm cloud."

We look at the sky. A horrible cloud slowly comes up. It's so black that it gets dark all around. It creeps along like a monster, enveloping the whole sky.

Lelya says:

"Quick, let's go home. There's going to be a terrible thunderstorm."

We run home. But run straight for the cloud. Right into the jaws of this monster.

A wind blows unexpectedly. It swirls all around us.

The dust rises. Dry grass flies up. And the bushes and trees bend over.

Without stopping for breath, we run home.

Big drops of rain are already falling on our heads.

Horrible lightning and even more horrible thunder

shake us. I fall down on the ground and, jumping up, run again. I run like a tiger is chasing me.

The house isn't far now.

I look back. Lelya's dragging Yulya by the hand. Yulya's bawling.

A hundred steps more—and I'm on the porch.

On the porch Lelya scolds me for losing my yellow bunch. But I didn't lose it, I threw it away.

I say:

"With such a storm, who needs bunches of flowers?"

Pressing close to each other, we sit on the bed.

Horrible thunder rattles our dacha.

The rain drums on the panes and the roof.

Nothing can be seen for the torrents of rain.

Mad Dog

We run in the house and shut the doors tightly.

I run over to the window and put on the latch.

We look out the window into the yard...

The landlord's daughter Katya walks through the yard.

We rap on the glass and shout at her:

"Katka,[57] you ninny, run home quick! Hide! There's a mad dog on the street."

Instead of running home, Katka walks over to our window. And strikes up a conversation, as if nothing special has happened.

"And where did you see the dog?" she asks. "It might be that it's not mad."

I begin to get angry at Katka. I shout at her:

"It bit two people. And if it bites you, we're not to blame. We warned you."

Katka walks slowly toward her house.

The mad dog runs into our yard. It's black and terrible. Its tail hangs down between its legs. Its jaws hang open. It's foaming at the mouth.

111

Katya grabs a rake and swings it around. And the dog runs off to the side. Katya laughs.

That's unbelievable. The mad dog was scared of Katka. I thought that dogs like that were scared of nothing and bit everyone.

Now people run up with sticks. They want to kill the dog. But the dog runs away. The people run after it. They scream and holler.

Growing bold, we open the window. Then go out into the yard.

Of course, it's not entirely safe in the yard. The dog might come back. Who knows? But sitting on the porch is all right. You can run away in time.

However, the dog doesn't come back. They killed it in the next yard.

Now Go to Sleep

It's dark in the room. Only the icon-lamp is burning. Nannie is sitting by our beds telling us a fairy tale.

Rocking on her chair, Nannie says in a monotone:

"The good fairy stuck her hand under the pillow, and there was a serpent. Stuck her hand under the feather mattress, and there were two serpents and a viper. The fairy looked under the bed, and there were four serpents, three vipers and one hedgehog.

"At this the good fairy didn't say a thing, she only stuck her little feet in her little slippers, but in each little slipper there sat two toads. The fairy took her coat from the nail, to put it on and go away from these parts. She looks, and in each sleeve of her coat there are six vipers and four toads.

"The fairy got all these evil spirits together and says:

" 'Here's the way it is. I don't wish you any harm, so don't you prevent me from leaving these parts.'

"And then all the evil spirits answered the good

fairy, saying:

" 'You won't have any trouble from us, good fairy. Thank you for not killing us.'

"But here thunder sounded. Fire shot up from the bowels of the earth. And before the good fairy there stood the bad fairy.

" 'All those evil spirits' he says, 'I intentionally set on you. But you,' he says, 'made friends with them, and that surprised me. Because of that, I'm going to cast a spell on you and change you into an ordinary cow...' Here thunder sounded again. We look, and instead of the good fairy, an ordinary cow is grazing."

Nannie falls silent. We tremble with fear. My sister Yulya says:

"What about all the other evil spirits?"

Nannie says:

"I don't know about that. Probably at the first sight of the bad fairy they hid themselves away in their usual places."

"That means under the feather mattress and under the pillow?" I ask, moving away from the pillow.

Nannie gets up from the chair and goes away saying:

"Well, that's enough talking. Go to sleep now."

We lie in the beds, afraid to stir. In an intentionally terrible voice, Lelya groans: "Ho-o."

Yulya and I cry out in fear. We beg Lelya not to scare us. But she's already asleep.

I sit up in bed for a long time, not daring to lie down on the pillow.

In the morning I don't drink any milk because it comes from the spellbound fairy.

It's So Simple

We sit in a cart. A little reddish peasant horse runs friskily along the dusty road.

The landlord's son Vasyutka leads it. He holds the reins carelessly in his hands and shouts at the horse from time to time:

"C'mon, c'mon... stop sleeping..."

The horse is certainly not sleeping, it runs very well. But probably this is the way you shout at a horse.

My hands are itching—I want so badly to hold the reins, to lead the horse and to shout at it. But I don't dare ask Vasyutka.

Suddenly Vasyutka himself says:

"Here now, hold the reins. I'm going to smoke."

My sister Lelya says to Vasyutka:

"No, don't give him the reins. He doesn't know how to lead a horse."

Vasyutka says:

"What d'ya mean, doesn't know? It doesn't take any knowing."

And now the reins are in my hands. I hold them with my arms outstretched.

Holding tightly onto the cart, Lelya says:

"Well, this is going to be quite an event—he'll turn us over for sure."

At this moment the cart hits a little bump.

Lelya cries out:

"Well, that's it. Now it'll toss us over."

I also suspect the cart will turn over since the reins are in my inept hands. But no, after hitting the bump, the cart rolls smoothly on.

Proud of my success, I shake the reins at the horse's sides and shout: "C'mon, stop sleeping!"

Suddenly I see: a turn in the road.

Hastily I ask Vasyutka:

"What rein do I pull to make the horse go right?"

Vasyutka says calmly:

"Pull the right one."

"How many times should I pull the right one?" I ask.

Vasyutka shrugs his shoulders:

114

"One time."

I yank the right rein, and suddenly, as in a fairy tale, the horse goes to the right.

For some reason I am saddened, irritated. It's so simple. I thought it was much harder to lead a horse. I thought it was a whole science, requiring years of study. But it's just poppycock.

I hand the reins over to Vasyutka. It's not particularly interesting.

The Terrible World

A house is burning. The flame merrily leaps from the walls to the roof.

Now the shingled roof is burning.

Firemen pump water. One of them, grabbing the hose, squirts the house. A thin stream of water falls on the fire.

No, the firemen won't put out that flame.

Mother holds me by the hand. She's afraid I'll run toward the fire. It's dangerous. Sparks are flying. They spray over the crowd.

Someone in the crowd is crying. It's a fat man with a beard crying. He cries like a little boy. And rubs his eyes with his hand. Maybe a spark got in his eye?

I ask Mama:

"What's he crying about? Did a spark get in his eye?"

Mother says:

"No, he's crying because his house is burning."

"He can build himself a new house," I say. "I wouldn't cry about that."

"You need money to build a new house," says Mother.

"He can work for it."

"You can't build a house with that kind of money."

"Then how are houses ever built?"

Mama says softly:

"I don't know, maybe people steal the money."

Something new enters my conceptions. I look with interest at the bearded man who stole the money, built a house, and now watches it burn.

"Does that mean you have to steal the money?" I ask Mother.

"No, you can't steal. They put you in jail for that."

Now that doesn't make any sense.

I ask:

"Well how then?"

But Mother waves her hand irritably for me to be silent.

I am silent. I'll grow up big and find out how things are done in this world. It must be that the adults messed up somewhere, and now they don't want to tell the children about it.

Someone Drowned

I'm fashioning a little steamboat. It's a board with a smokestack and a mast. The rudder and flag have yet to be done.

Waving her hat, Lelya comes running. She shouts:

"Minka, quick! Let's run. Someone drowned over there."

I run after Lelya. On the way I shout at her:

"I don't want to run. I'm scared."

Lelya says:

"It's not you who drowned. It's someone else who drowned. What's there to be scared of?"

We run along the shore. A crowd stands at the pier.

Pushing people aside, Lelya makes her way through the crowd. I squeeze through behind her.

Someone says:

"He didn't know how to swim. The current's swift. That's how he drowned."

A boy lies on the sandy shore. He's about eighteen. He's white as a sheet. His eyes are closed. Hands tossed out to the sides, and his body covered with green vines.

A woman kneels beside him. She stares steadily into his dead face. Someone says:

"That's his mother. She's not crying because her grief is too great."

I look at the drowned boy out of the corners of my eyes. I want him to move, get up and say:

"No, I didn't drown. It's just me. Just pretend. I was just kidding."

But he lies still. And it becomes so terrible for me that I shut my eyes.

It's Not My Fault

We're sitting at the table and eating pancakes.

Suddenly Father takes my plate and begins eating my cakes. I bawl.

My father has glasses on. He has a serious look. A beard. All the same, he laughs. He says:

"You see how greedy he is. He begrudges his father one pancake."

I say:

"All right, you can eat one pancake. I thought you were going to eat them all."

Soup is served.

I say:

"Papa, do you want my soup?"

Papa says:

"No, I'll wait until dessert is served. Now if you give up your dessert, you are really a good boy."

Thinking that dessert will be a bitter cranberry mash with milk, I say:

"All right. You can eat my dessert."

Suddenly cream, to which I am partial, is served.

Pushing my saucer of cream to father, I say:

"All right, go ahead an eat it, if you're so greedy."
Father frowns and leaves the table.
Mother says:
"Go to Father and tell him you're sorry."
I say:
"I won't go. It's not my fault."
I come out from behind the table without touching my dessert.

That evening, as I lie in bed, Father comes up. In his hands he has my saucer of cream.
Father says:
"Now why didn't you eat your cream?"
I say:
"Papa, let's both eat half. Why should we argue over it?"
Father kisses me and spoons the cream up to me.

In the Water

The kids are swimming and diving. I'm bathing by the shore.
They shout at me:
"Hey, c'mon out. Don't be so scared. We'll teach you how to swim."
I walk slowly into the water. It's cold. Goose bumps crawl up my flesh.
"Dunk all at once, you dummie. Seven times!" the kids shout.
I dunk up to my shoulders. The kids shout:
"Over your head, you goof."
No, I don't think I'll dunk over my head. The water will get in my eyes and ears. That's awful.
"C'mon out! Don't be such a sissy!" the kids shout.
Although it's deep there, I walk forward. I don't want to be a sissy.
I walk forward and suddenly drop in a hole. The green water goes over my head. Could be I drowned.

But no. I float to the top. And paddling like a dog, I swim.

Bravo. It seems I taught myself to swim.

Suddenly someone or something grabs me by the leg. I cry out and sink to the bottom.

This time I drowned for good. I close my eyes.

The kids lug me up to the top. One of them says:

"I pulled him by the leg, I was just kidding. But he near to croaked."

Another says:

"Too bad we dragged him out so soon. He could have stayed there a little longer. Then we could have pumped him."

I lay on the shore spitting out water.

The kids fuss around me like demons. They're angry that I swallowed so little water.

Shut the Doors

Evening. We drink our milk. And go to bed.

I go over to the window. It's dark beyond the window. So dark that you can't even see the flower box.

I peer out the window.

My sisters start playing in the room. They giggle and throw pillows at each other. One of the pillows flies over to me. I angrily toss it aside. It's just the wrong time for such jokes.

Wanting to aggravate me, Lelya says:

"There are definitely going to be burglars tonight. In case you want to know."

Supposing we shut the doors, then there won't be any.

I shout to the grown-ups sitting on the balcony:

"Don't forget to shut the door!"

Mama appears in the doorway.

"What happened?" she asks.

"No, nothing happened," I say, "but Lelya thinks

there will be burglars tonight."

Mama kisses us and walks away with a smile.

I lie in bed with the covers drawn over my head.

It's quiet in the house. Everyone's asleep. But no sleep for me.

The doors, of course, are shut. I myself heard the latches click, but are the windows shut?

I get up from bed. Go over to the window. Try the latch. Shut. Maybe they forgot to shut the window in their room?

Stepping cautiously, I go into the next room. With my fingers I find the latch on the window. Suddenly something falls on the floor with a crash and a bang.

I hear Mama's frightened voice:

"What's that? Who's there?... Burglars!"

"Where, where are the burglars?" I shout to Mother.

Uproar in the house. Everyone runs up. They light the lamp.

A broken flowerpot lies on the floor.

Mother calms me down.

And I go to bed again, pulling the covers over my head.

At Grandmother's

We're visiting Grandmother. Sitting at the table. Dinner is being served.

Our grandmother sits next to our grandfather. Grandfather is fat, ponderous. He looks like a lion. And Grandmother looks like a lioness.

A lion and a lioness sit at the table.

I stare steadily at Grandmother. That's Mama's mama. She has gray hair. And a dark, surprisingly beautiful face. Mama said she was an exceptional beauty in her youth.

A tureen of soup is brought in.

120

That's not interesting. I'll hardly eat that.

But now *pirozhki*[58] are brought in. That's not bad.

Grandather himself dips out the soup.

Handing him my bowl, I say to Grandfather:

"Only a drop for me."

Grandfather holds the ladle over my bowl. One drop of soup falls into my bowl.

I look at the drop in perplexity.

Everyone laughs.

Grandfather says:

"He asked for a drop. So I did what he asked."

I didn't want any soup, but for some reason I feel hurt. I almost cry.

Grandmother says:

"Grandfather was just kidding. Hand me your bowl, I'll fill it up."

I don't hand her my bowl and don't touch the *pirozhki.*

Grandfather says to my mama:

"He's a bad boy. He doesn't understand a joke."

Mama says to me:

"Now give Grandfather a smile. Answer him something."

I look angrily at Grandfather. Say to him softly:

"I'll never come to see you again."

I came to visit Grandmother only after Grandfather had died. He wasn't my real grandfather. And I wasn't sorry he had died.

Mama Cries

Mama lies on the sofa and cries. I go over to her. Mama extends a colored postcard to me. On the card is some beautiful lady wearing a boa and a hat.

Mama asks:

"Really, don't I look like this lady?"

Wishing to comfort Mama, I say:

"Yes, a little bit."

Although I don't see any special likeness.

Mama says:

"In that case, go to Papa, show him this card and say: 'Papa, see how much she looks like our mama'."

I ask glumly:

"What for?"

"Just do it. I can't explain to you what for. You're too little."

I say:

"No, tell me anyway. Or else I won't go."

Mama says:

"Well, how can I explain it to you... Papa will look at the card and say: 'Oh, what an interesting mama we have...'And he will be nicer to me...'"

This explanation brings no clarity to my mind. On the contrary, it seems to me that Papa will see the dissimilarity and become even more angry at Mama.

With great reluctance I go in the room where Papa is working.

Papa's an artist. Before him is an easel. Papa's painting a portrait of my sister Yulya.

I go up to Father and, extending the card, say glumly:

"Seems she looks a little bit like Mother, huh?"

Glancing at the card out of the corners of his eyes, Father says:

"Don't bother me. Go away..."

Well, of course. Nothing came of it. I thought so.

I return to Mother.

"Well, what did he say?"

I say:

"He said: 'Don't bother me, go away...' "

Covering her face with her hands, Mama cries.

My heart is torn with pity. I'm even willing to go a second time to Father with the stupid postcard, but Mother doesn't let me.

Mama Found Some Tickets

In anger, Mama strikes the table with her fist. She says to Grandmother:

"That means while we were at the dacha, he was here having fun... Here are the tickets I found in the pocket of his summer coat."

I know this summer coat of Papa's. It hangs on the coatrack. Quite a bright little coat.

Mama places some tickets on the table.

I go to the table and examine the tickets, read: "Theater Bouffe."

Grandmother says:

"Maybe he went to the Bouffe with an old buddy. How are we to know?"

Mama says:

"No, the tickets are for the first row. I know who he went with. He went with Anna. I've suspected for a long time that she's crazy about..."

Suddenly the door opens, and in walks Papa.

Papa wears a black autumn coat. A hat. He's very tall, handsome. And the beard doesn't spoil him at all.

Smiling, Papa says to Mama:

"I need to talk with you."

They both go into the living room.

Lelya goes over to the doors. Eavesdrops. Then says:

"No, it's all right. There won't be any trouble. I guarantee it..."

I ask Lelya:

"But what happened between them?"

Lelya says:

"All the women are crazy about our papa. That upsets Mama something awful."

Soon our parents come out of the living room.

I see Mama is not especially pleased, but not too discontent either.

Papa kisses Mama's hand goodbye. And goes to spend the night at his studio. It's three houses away from us.

At the Studio

Papa hasn't been at our place for a long time. Mother dresses me. And we go to see Papa at the studio

Mama walks hurriedly. Pulls me by the hand so I can hardly keep up.

We climb up to the seventh floor. Knock. Papa opens the door.

Seeing us, he frowns at first. Then, taking me in his arms, he tosses me up almost to the ceiling. He laughs and kisses me.

Mama smiles. She sits down beside Papa on the sofa. And some sort of mysterious conversation begins between them.

I walk around the studio. On the easels, pictures. On the walls, also pictures. Huge windows. Disorder.

I look over the boxes of paints. Brushes. All sorts of little bottles.

Everything has been looked over, but my parents are still discussing. It's very nice that they're discussing so quietly—without shouting, without arguing.

I don't bother them. I walk around the boxes and pictures a second time.

Finally, Father says to Mother:

"Well, I'm very glad. Everything's fine."

And he kisses Mama goodbye. And Mama kisses him. And they even hug.

Putting on our coats, we leave.

On the way back Mama suddenly begins to scold me. She says:

"Oh, why did you string along with me..."

That strikes me as strange. I didn't string along at all. She herself pulled me to the studio. And now she's not content.

Mama says:

"Oh, how sorry I am that I took you with me. Without you we would have made up completely."

I whine. But I whine because I don't understand where I'm at fault. I behaved quietly. Didn't even run through the studio. And now such injustice.

Mother says:

"No, I'll never take you with me again."

I feel like asking what's wrong, what happened. But I keep quiet. I'll grow up big and then I'll find out everything myself. I'll find out why people are sometimes held at fault even when they're not at fault in any way.

By the Gate

I'm standing by the garden gate. Staring steadily at the road leading to the pier.

Mama's gone to the city. And she hasn't been here since morning. But we've already had dinner. And soon it'll be evening. Oh, my God, where can she be?

I peer into the distance again. No! Some people or other are coming, but she's not there. Probably something has happened to her.

But what could have happened to her? She's not a little kid, after all. A grown-up person. She's thirty years old.

Well, and what of it? All sorts of horrible things happen even to grown-ups. There are dangers lurking at every step for grown-ups too.

Perhaps Mama took a buggy. The horse ran wild. True, buggies have pretty tame horses. They barely crawl along. It's doubtful that such horses might run wild. And if they do run wild, you can always jump out of the carriage.

But what if Mama took a steamship, if a steamship sinks you can't jump off it. Of course, there are life preservers. You can grab one of the life preservers and

save yourself. Still, life preservers are no good if there's a fire, if, for example, our apartment in the city caught fire. Although our house is made of stone and would hardly flare up like a match.

Most likely Mama stopped in a cafe, ate something there and got sick. And a doctor is operating on her right now.

Oh, no! Here comes our mama!

I run to her with a shout. Mama's wearing a huge hat. On her shoulders she has a white boa made of feathers. And a sash with a bow. I don't like Mama to dress this way. I wouldn't put those feathers on for all the money in the world. I'll grow up big and ask Mama not to dress that way. Because it's embarrassing for me to walk with her—everyone turns around.

"You're not glad that I came home, isn't that so?" Mama asks.

"No, I'm glad," I answer without feeling.

It's a Misunderstanding

Kostya Palitsyn and I are sitting at the same desk in the *gimnaziya.*

He's carving some letter or other in the desk with his penknife. I watch how skillfully and secretively from the teacher he carves with his knife.

I've become so engrossed in this matter that I don't hear when I'll called on.

Someone jabs me in the side. And then I stand up and look in bewilderment at the class instructor, who teaches Russian and arithmetic in our preparatory class.

It turns out that for some reason the teacher wants me to recite the poem "Merrily the moon shines o'er the village."[59]

The first line I pronounce smartly, since I just heard it from the teacher. But what comes next, I don't know.

I simply don't know this poem. In fact, it's the first time I ever heard of it.

From all sides they prompt me: "Glistens white the snow."

Haltingly, I pronounce the words I hear.

Looking straight at me, the teacher smiles.

The pupils vie with each other to prompt me. They whisper on every side. With all this, you can't make out what they're whispering... "Cross beneath the clouds, just like a candle burning..."

"Crust beneath the clods," I mumble.

Laughter in the class. The teacher also laughs. And enters a "one" in my workbook.

That's awful. I've been in the *gimnaziya* only five days. And all at once, a one.

I say to Kostya Palitsyn:

"If they give me a one for everything I don't know yet, I'll pile up a lot of ones."

"The poem was assigned," says Kostya. "You were supposed to learn it."

Ah, so it was assigned? I didn't know. In that case it's a misunderstanding.

It weighs more easily on my mind that it's a misunderstanding.

Awful Things Again

I'm wearing my *gimnaziya* coat with silver buttons. My satchel's on my back.

Mama sticks a note with the address of the *gimnaziya* into my coat pocket.

"Mama," I say, "don't you worry, I know the way so well I could make it to the *gimnaziya* with my eyes closed."

Mama says:

"Just don't take it into your head to walk with your eyes closed. I've had enough from you..."

128

I go out on the street.

No, of course, I couldn't find it with my eyes closed. It's dangerous. There are horsecars and buggies on the street. But I can certainly walk from the corner of Bolshoi to the *gimnaziya* with my eyes closed. It's two hundred and ten steps in all. Nothing to it.

Reaching Boilshoi Prospect, I close my eyes and walk like a blind man, knocking into people and grazing the walls and curbstones. All the while I mentally count off the steps... Two hundred. Two hundred and ten...

I pronounce "two hundred and ten" aloud and run into some person with great force. I open my eyes. I'm standing right at the doors of the *gimnaziya*. But the person I bumped into—it's our teacher and class instructor.

"Oh, excuse me," I say. "I didn't notice you."

"You should notice," says the teacher angrily. "That's what you have eyes for."

"They were shut," I say.

"Why do you shut your eyes, you stupid kid?" says the teacher.

I am silent. In the first place, it would take a long time to explain. In the second place, he still wouldn't understand why I closed my eyes.

"Well?" asks the teacher.

"I just shut them. Because of the wind..."

The teacher looks at me with a frown and says angrily:

"Well, why are you standing there like a stump? Move on..."

I am standing because I am a polite person.

I want to let him go in first.

We simultaneously step toward the doors and collide again in the doorway.

The teacher looks at me even more angrily.

A Pood[60] of Iron

I'm busy looking through my pen case. Sorting out the pencils and pens. Admiring my little penknife.

The teacher calls on me. He says:

"Answer this one quickly: which is heavier—a pood of feathers or a pood of iron?"

Failing to see any trap in this, I answer without thinking:

"A pood of iron."

Laughter all around.

The teacher says:

"Tell your mama to come and see me tomorrow. I want to talk to her."

The next day Mama goes to see the teacher and returns home sad. She says:

"The teacher is dissatisfied with you. He says that you're distracted, never listen, don't understand anything and sit at your desk as if what goes on in class doesn't concern you."

"And what else did he say?"

Mama's face becomes quite sad.

Pressing me to herself, she says:

"I thought you were an intelligent and well-developed boy, but he says that your mental development is insufficient."

"What he says is stupid," I shout angrily. "In my opinion, his mental development is insufficient. He asks the pupils stupid questions. And it's harder to answer stupid questions than intelligent ones."

Kissing me, Mama cries:

"Oh, it's going to be difficult for you to live in the world!" she says.

"Why?"

"You're a difficult child. You're like your father. I don't think you're going to be happy."

Mama kisses me again and hugs me, but I break away. I don't like all this mushy stuff.

A Closed Heart

Grandfather came. My father's father. He came from Poltava.

I thought a decrepit old fellow with long moustaches and a Ukrainian blouse would be coming. And he would sing, dance and tell us tales.

On the contrary. A tall, stern man came. Not very old, not very gray. Strikingly handsome. Shaven. In a black frockcoat. In his hands he held a little velvet prayer book and a red ivory rosary.

And I was suprised that we had such a grandfather. And I wanted to talk over things with him. But he wouldn't talk with us children. He only talked a little bit with Papa. And to Mama he said angrily:

"It's your own fault, Ma'm. You gave birth to too many children."

And then Mama began to cry and went off to her room.

And I was even more surprised that we had such a grandfather who was displeased that Mama had given birth to children, among whom was I myself.

And I badly want to find out what Grandfather was doing in his room, which he almost never left and which he permitted no one to enter. Probably he was doing something exceptionally important.

And so I crack open the door and quietly enter the room.

My stern grandfather isn't doing anything. He's sitting in an armchair and simply not doing anything. He looks stock-still at the wall and smokes a long pipe.

Catching sight of me, Grandfather asks:

"What do you want here? And why did you come in to me without knocking?"

And then I got angry at my grandfather and told him:

"In point of fact, this is our apartment, and if you want to know—this is my room, they moved me in

131

with my sisters. Why should I knock at my own room?"

Grandfather threw his rosary at me and shouted. Then he went and complained to my father. And Father complained to Mother.

But Mama didn't start scolding me. She said:

"Ah, if only he would leave soon. He doesn't love anyone. He's like your father. He has a closed heart."

"And do I have a closed heart too?" I ask.

"Yes," says Mother, "I think you also have a closed heart."

"Does that mean I'll be the same as Grandfather?"

Kissing me, Mother says through her tears:

"Yes, you'll probably be the same. It's a great misfortune—not to love anyone."

You Can't Shout It

Disorders in the streets. A policeman was killed on the corner. Gendarmes gallop by on horses. Something extraordinary is happening.

In our *gimnaziya* something strange is also going on. The older pupils gather in groups and quietly discuss something. And the youngsters are much naughtier than usual.

Break between classes. We run down the hall. The second-graders run by shouting: "Revolt." I also join up with them and, waving my hands, shout: "Revolt."

Someone grabs me by the arm. It's the class instructor.

He shakes me by the shoulders and says:

"Repeat what you said."

"I said 'revolt,' " I mutter.

The teacher's face turns to stone. He says:

"Stand by the wall under the clock and stay there until the end of your break. And tomorrow have your mother come and see me."

I stand under the clock. This is something new.

What happened? Why can't you shout this? Everyone was shouting. But he swept down on me like a vulture and grabbed me by the shoulders.

The next day Mama returns from the teacher all upset. She goes to Father and discusses something with him for a long time.

Afterwards, my parents call me into their room.

Father is lying on the bed in trousers and a jacket. He has a dull, glum look. He says to me:

"Probably you didn't know what the word meant, right?"

I say:

"No, I know. It's the imperative of the verb 'to revolt.' But I didn't know that you can't shout it."

Father smiles. Says to Mother:

"Go to the teacher and tell him that our son is a little ninny, he's insufficiently developed... And someday they'll throw him in jail for it."

Hearing about jail, I begin to cry.

Mama says:

"Before, I argued with the teacher about this. But now I'll go and tell him that he was right."

Papa laughs.

"You see," he says, "the teacher's low opinion came in handy."

Papa turns to the wall and doesn't want to talk anymore.

Mama and I leave the room.

A Rupture of the Heart

Softly I open the door and go into Papa's room.

Usually Father lounges on the bed. But today he stands motionless by the window.

Tall, somber, he stands by the window thinking about something.

He looks like Peter the Great. Only with a beard.

Softly I say:

"Papa, I'm taking your little knife to sharpen my pencil."

Without turning around, Father says:

"Take it."

I go over to the desk and begin to sharpen my pencil.

In the corner by the window there is a little round table. On it, a carafe of water.

Father pours a glass of water. Drinks. And suddenly falls.

He falls on the floor. And the chair he knocked against falls.

I scream in horror. My sisters and mother come running.

Seeing father on the floor, Mother throws herself at him with a scream. Shakes him by the shoulders, kisses his face.

I run out of the room and lie down on my bed.

Something horrible has happened. But maybe everything will end all right. Maybe Papa only fainted.

I go to Father's room again.

Father's lying on the bed. Mother's in the doorway. Beside her is the doctor.

Mother screams:

"You're mistaken, Doctor!"

The doctor says:

"In this matter we don't dare to be mistaken, ma'm. He's dead."

"But why was it so sudden? It can't be!"

"A rupture of the heart," says the physician. And he leaves the room.

Lying on my bed, I cry.

Yes, He's Dead

Oh, how unbearable it is to look at Mama! She

cries all the time.

There she is standing by the table on which my father is lying. She has fallen with her face to his face and is crying.

I stand by the door and look at this horrible grief. No, I couldn't cry this way. I must have a closed heart.

I want to calm Mother down, to distract her.

I ask her softly:

"Mama, how old is our papa?"

Wiping away the tears, Mama says:

"Oh, Mishenka, he's quite young. He's forty-nine. No, it can't be that he's dead."

She again shakes him by the shoulders and mumbles:

"Maybe this is a deep faint, a lethargic state..."

Mother unfastens a safety pin from her blouse. Then takes Father's hand. And I see: she wants to stick the pin in his hand.

I scream in horror.

"No need to scream," says Mother. "I want to see, maybe he's not dead."

She sticks the pin all the way through the hand. I scream again.

Mother draws the pin out of the pierced palm.

"Take a look," she says, "not a drop of blood. Yes, he's dead..."

Falling onto Father's chest, Mama again starts crying.

I walk out of the room. A fever comes over me.

At the Cemetery

I'm at the cemetery for the first time. It's not a bit frightening. Only it's very unpleasant.

It's so unpleasant that I can hardly remain standing in the church. If only the service would soon end. I try not to look at the deceased lying on the six catafalques.

135

But my eyes involuntarily rest on them.

They lie there motionless, pale, like wax dolls. Two old women in caps. My father. Someone else's father. A young dead girl. And some fat, pot-bellied man. So pot-bellied, that the coffin will hardly close over that belly. But they'll force it down with the lid. They won't waste time on ceremony. Anyway, he doesn't feel or see anything now.

I don't know if I'll be able to go up to Father and kiss him. Everyone is already going up, kissing him.

Holding my breath, I go up. Barely touch my lips to his dead hand. Then run out of the church.

The coffin is borne in the hands of artists—Papa's comrades. Ahead, on a little velvet cushion, they bear the decoration which Papa received for his picture "Suvorov's Departure." This picture hangs on the wall of the Suvorov Museum. It's done in mosaic. In the left corner of the picture there is a little green fir. The lowest branch of this fir was done by me. It turned out crooked, but Papa was satisfied with my work.

The choir sings. The coffin is lowered into the pit. Mama cries.

They begin filling in the pit. It's all over. The closed heart exists no more. But I exist.

The Days Are Numbered

Mama's brother got consumption. A room was rented for him outside of town. And he started living there.

But the doctor said to Mama:

"He's in a very bad way. His days are numbered."

I went out to see him on a Sunday. I took him *pirozhki* and sour cream.

Uncle Georgy lay on the bed surrounded by pillows. He breathed heavily and hoarsely.

I put what I had brought him on a chair and wanted

to leave. But he said to me:

"I lie here alone for whole days on end. It's horribly boring. Why don't you at least play some cards with me."

Uncle Georgy pulled the cards out from under a pillows. And we started playing sixty-six.

I was terribly lucky. But he wasn't. He lost two hands to me. And then demanded that I play a third with him.

We began to play the third hand. His luck was even worse than before. And then he started getting angry with me. Started yelling and throwing the cards. He was distressed that he was losing, even though we weren't playing for money, but just for fun.

And I was surprised that he was so distressed, seeing that his days were numbered and he would soon die.

So he dealt me the cards. And almost all of them were trumps. And when he saw this, Uncle shook with rage, coughing. He began to moan. And it got so bad for him that he grabbed the oxygen bag and put it over his mouth. He felt stifled. He was afraid he would suffocate.

Afterwards, when he got better, we continued the game.

But I started throwing away my good cards on purpose. Playing the wrong way. I wanted to lose to him so he wouldn't torment himself.

And so I started losing. And this made Uncle so happy that he started joking and laughing. And he flicked the cards on my forehead, saying that I was still too small to play with grown-ups.

I didn't start a fourth hand with him, although he very much wanted to play.

I left with the intention of never coming to see him again.

And I never had the chance to see him again. On the following Sunday he died.

Muza

I'm out visiting. Sitting on a sofa. A girl by the name of Muza is showing me her books.

Showing the books, she suddenly asks me:

"Do you want to be my fiancé?"

"Yes," I answer softly. "Only I'm shorter than you. I don't know if fiancés can be like that."

We go over to a pier glass to check the difference in our height.

We're the same age. Each eleven years and three months old. But Muza is taller than I by almost half a head.

"That's nothing," she says. "There are fiancés who are quite short, and even humpbacked ones. The main thing is for them to be strong. Let's wrestle. I'm sure that you're stronger than I."

We begin to wrestle. Muza is stronger than I. Nimbly as a cat, I slip away from defeat. And we wrestle some more. Fall on the rug. And we lie there for some while, stunned by something we don't understand.

Then Muza says:

"Yes, I'm stronger than you. But that's nothing. Among fiancés there are weak ones and even sick ones. The main thing is for them to be intelligent. How many fives did you get in the first quarter?

My God, what an unfortunate question! If intelligence is to be measured by grades, then things look very bad for me. Three twos. The rest are threes.

"Well, that's nothing," says Muza. "You'll get more intelligent later on. Probably there are fiancés who got four twos and even more."

"I don't know," I say, "it's not likely."

Taking each other by the arm, we walk around the living room. The grown-ups call us to tea in the dining room.

Hugging me around the neck, Muza kisses me on the cheek.

138

"Why did you do that?" I ask, horrified by her action.

"Kisses bind the agreement," she says. "Now we are fiancé and fiancée."

We walk into the dining room.

The History Teacher

The history teacher doesn't call on me the usual way. He pronounces my last name in an unpleasant tone. He purposely whines and squeals when he pronounces my last name. And then all the pupils also begin to whine and squeal, mimicking the teacher.

It's unpleasant for me when I am called on this way. But I don't know what to do to put a stop to it.

I sit at my desk and answer the lesson. I answer rather well. But in the lesson there is the word "Banquet."

"And what is a banquet?" the teacher asks me.

I know perfectly well what a banquet is. It's a supper, a meal, a ceremonious meeting at a table, in a restaurant. But I don't know if such an explanation can be applied to the great people of history. Isn't such an explanation too petty for the scale of historical events?

I am silent.

"Ah-ah?" asks the teacher, whining. And in this "ah-ah" I hear ridicule and contempt for me.

And the pupils, hearing this "ah-ah," also begin to whine.

The history teacher waves me off with his hand. And gives me a two.

When class ends, I run after the teacher. I catch up with him on the stairway. In my agitation I can't utter a word. I break out in a fever.

Seeing me in such a state, the teacher asks:

"At the end of the quarter I'll ask you again. We'll hold a three for you."

139

"It's not about that," I say. "If you call on me that way again, I'll... I'll..."

"What? What is it?" says the teacher.

"Spit on you," I grumble.

"What did you say?" the teacher shouts threateningly. And, grabbing me by the arm, he drags me up to the principal's office. But suddenly he lets me go. Says:

"Go to class."

I go to class and wait for the principal to come and throw me out of the *gimnaziya*. But the principal doesn't come.

A few days later the history teacher calls me up to the board.

He pronounces my name softly. And when the pupils begin to whine by habit, the teacher bangs his fist on the desk and shouts at them:

"Silence!"

Complete quiet over the class. I mumble the assignment, but think about something else. I think about this teacher who didn't complain to the principal and who didn't call on me the same way as before. I look at him, and tears tears well up in my eyes.

The teacher says:

"Don't be nervous. You know enough for a three in any case."

He thought I had tears in my éyes because I knew the lesson poorly.

Chlorophyll

Only two subjects interest me: zoology and botany. The rest don't.

Of course, history also interests me, but not in the book we're using.

I'm very distressed that I study badly. But I don't know what to do to put a stop to it.

Even in botany I get a three. And yet I know this

subject excellently. I've read a lot of books and even made a herbarium—an album in which I paste leaves, flowers and grasses.

The botany teacher relates something in class. Then he says:

"Now, why are leaves green? Who knows?"

Quiet in the class.

"I'll give a five to anyone who knows," says the teacher.

I know why leaves are green, but am silent. I don't want to be a smarty pants. Let the best pupils answer it. Besides, I don't need a five. Why should it stick out all by itself among my twos and threes? It would be comical.

The teacher calls on the best pupil. But this one doesn't know.

Then I carelessly raise my hand.

"Ah, so," says the teacher, "you know. Well, tell us."

"Leaves are green," I say, "because they have the color-producing substance chlorophyll."

The teacher says:

"Before I give you a five, I must know why you didn't raise your hand at first."

I am silent. This is very difficult to answer.

"Perhaps you didn't remember at first?" asks the teacher.

"No, I remembered at first."

"Perhaps you wanted to be above the best pupils?"

I am silent. Shaking his head reproachfully, the teacher enters the five.

It's All Over

The wind is so strong you can't play croquet.

We sit on the grass behind the house and chat.

Besides my sisters, there are Tolya, who goes to trade school, and his little sister Ksenya on the grass.

141

My sisters are teasing me. They think I am not in-different to Ksenya—I keep looking at her and I set up her ball when I play croquet.

Ksenya laughs. She knows that I really do set her up.

Certain of my feelings, she says:

"Could you go to the cemetery at night and pluck some flowers for me?"

"Why?"

"Just because. To do what I ask."

I say softly, so my sisters can't hear:

"For you I could do it."

Suddenly we see—people running behind the fence. We go out of the garden. My God! Water on the highway. Elagin Island[61] is already under water. A bit more, and the water will flood the road we are walking on.

We run to the yacht club. The wind is so strong that we're almost swept off our feet.

Ksenya and I, holding hands, run ahead.

Suddenly Mother's voice is heard:

"Turn back! Come home!"

We turn around. Our garden is under water. The water has rushed in from the field and has inundated everything behind us.

I run toward the house. The ditches are full of water. Boards and logs are floating there.

Wet up to the knee, I run onto the veranda.

But where are Ksenya, my sisters, Tolya?

They're walking through the garden with their shoes off.

On the veranda Ksenya says to me:

"Running on ahead... leaving us behind... Well, what do you know... It's all over between us."

Without a word I go off to my room on the second floor. I lie down on my bed in horrible despair.

The Shot[62]

Morning. We're sitting on the veranda. Drinking tea.

Suddenly we hear a horrible scream. Then a shot. We jump up.

A woman runs onto our veranda. It's our neighbor Anna Petrovna.

She's horribly dishevelled. Almost naked. A robe is tossed around her shoulders. She screams:

"Save me! I beg you! He'll murder me... He murdered Sergei Lvovich..."

Mama wrings her hands.

"You mean the blond student who visited you?"

Saying yes, Anna Petrovna falls on the sofa and goes into hysterics.

I run to our neighbor's dacha, to their window.

When I glanced in the window, I recoiled. There on the bed lay the murdered man. And the blood was dripping from the sheet onto the floor. But there was no one else in the room.

Then I ran into their garden. And there I saw a crowd of people. The people were holding Anna Petrovna's husband by the arms.

He stood peaceably. Without pulling away. And saying nothing. He was silent.

The policeman arrived and started to take him away. But Anna Petrovna's husband said:

"Call my wife to me. I want to say goodbye to her."

And then I rushed to our house and told Anna Petrovna:

"Anna Petrovna, he wants to say goodbye to you. Go out to him. And don't be afraid. The policeman's there."

Anna Petrovna said:

"I'm not accustomed to saying goodbye to murderers. I won't go out to him."

I ran back to the garden to tell them that she

143

wouldn't come out. But Anna Petrovna's husband had already been taken away.

The Remark

I went to a Christmas party at a friend's house. He's my comrade. His parents are very rich people.

All the guests received presents, surprises and all sorts of little things. I myself received two books by Mayne Reid and a pair of beginner's ice skates. Besides this, my comrade's sister Margarita gave me a stamp album, a tiny mother-of-pearl knife and a little gold heart on a watch chain.

Late in the evening the guests began to disperse.

Margarita and her housemaid left to walk me home.

And so I walk ahead with Margarita, and her house-maid walks behind.

We chat merrily and walk all the way to my house without even noticing it.

Saying goodbye, Margarita asks me to meet her to-morrow when she comes home from the *gimnaziya*.

I say goodbye to Margarita and press her hand. Then I say goodbye to Annushka. I also press her hand.

But while I was saying goodbye to Annushka, Margarita flared up and shrugged her shoulders.

The next day I meet Margarita. She says:

"You apparently have only been in democratic homes where it is customary to take a servant's hand when you say goodbye. That's not customary with us. As the English say, it's shocking."

I had never thought about such things. And now I turned red, got flustered. And I couldn't find anything to say for a moment. Then I said:

"I don't see anything wrong with my saying good-bye to Annushka."

Margarita said:

"The only thing lacking was for you to say good-

144

bye to her first, and then to me. You come from a gentry home and that's why you act that way."

We walked two streets in silence. Without any conversation. Then I began to feel out of sorts. I took off my school cap and said goodbye to Margarita.

As I left, she said to me:

"You shouldn't get angry with me. It was because of my good feelings toward you that I made the remark."

My Friend

Every day I go to see Sasha P. He's an intelligent lad. It's interesting for me to be with him. We've become friends. He's my only friend.

Mama said that I'm not capable of making friends with anyone, that I'm a solitary person like my father.

Nothing of the sort. I get lonely if I go only one day without seeing my comrade. I simply need to visit him.

After cleaning my shoes, I hurry to his place. His dacha is on the shore, three streets away.

I walk along the quay and softly hum: "Against my will, to those sad shores..."[63]

I walk into the garden. The whole P. family is on the veranda. Mama, he and his two sweet sisters—Olya and Galya. Olya is fourteen, Galya is sixteen. And I am fifteen.

Everyone is glad that I came. Sasha says to me:

"Today, if you like, we can go down to the beach. Do a bit of philosophizing."

The girls are displeased. They wanted to play croquet with me, sit in the garden.

Sasha says:

"Why don't you chat with the girlies for about an hour. And meanwhile I'll finish this book."

I walk with the girls into the garden. We settle down in the arbor. And we talk about everything imaginable.

Olya attracts me the most, but I attract Galya the

145

most. A dramatic entanglement. It's all terribly interest-in. That's life.

We sit in the arbor for a long time. Then we stroll around the garden. Then we sit on the shore. And finally we settle down in the arbor again.

It's already getting dark. I say goodbye to the sisters. Galya whispers something in my ear. I don't hear it. But she doesn't want to repeat it. We laugh.

Finally I say goodbye for the last time and hurry home in an excellent mood.

And on the way I suddenly remember that I forgot to say goodbye to Sasha and that we were going to the beach together.

I feel terribly awkward. I return to their dacha. Go up to the fence. Sasha is standing by the gate.

He says to me:

"Today I finally realized that you don't come to see me, but my sisters."

I am stricken with grief, try to prove that I come to see only him. And suddenly become convinced myself that it's not him I come to see.

He says:

"Our friendship is founded on sand. I'm convinced of it."

We coldly say goodbye.

The Student With a Stick

Two houses away from us there lived a girl named Irina. She had rather red hair, but she was so good-looking that you could feast your eyes on her for hours.

We kids often went to her fence and looked at her as she lay in the hammock.

She would lie in the hammock almost all the time. But without reading. The book was tossed on the grass, or else lay in her lap.

And in the evening Irina would take a stroll with

Oleg. There was one such student. A railway engineer. Very interesting. With a pince-nez. And a walking stick in his hand.

When he came walking toward her house, we kids would yell:

"Irisha, Oleg is coming!"

Ira would turn red like mad and run toward him.

I don't know what happened between them, but at the end of the summer Irina threw herself from the pier into the water and drowned. And she wasn't found.

All the people in the dacha felt horribly sorry for her. And some even cried. But this student Oleg took her death quite lightly. He walked onto the pier with his stick, just as before. He laughed. Joked with his comrades. And even began to chase after a university student named Simochka.

And we kids were irritated by his behavior. With all our heart we hated this student with a stick.

Once while he was sitting on the pier we began shooting at him from the shore with our slingshots.

He got horribly angry at us. Started yelling. Ran after us. But when he ran after one, the others shot at him.

We shot at him so much that he finally ran home, covering his head with his arms.

For three days we shot up his dacha. We shot at everyone who went into his house. Even shot at his mamasha. And at the cook. And at visitors. And at the dog. And even at the cat which came out to lie in the warm sunshine.

We broke several panes on the veranda. And drove him to such a state that he soon left.

He left with a swollen nose. That was when one of us let go at him with a slingshot, just as he walked onto the pier with his things.

The First Lesson

I have a pupil. He's a clerk in the general staff. I'm preparing him for his examinations.

In two months he'll be taking an examination for the first rank in the staff.

We have an arrangement: if he passes the examination, I'll get his bicycle in return.

This is a magnificent arrangement. And I sit for three hours or more every day with this bonehead who isn't very sharp in the sciences.

I try to pound all my knowledge into his foggy brain. I force him to write, think, count. I end the lesson only when he starts yapping that his head hurts.

And now he got a decent mark on the examination. And came to me beaming.

He looked at me with surprise, saying that he didn't expect it would turn out this way.

We went together to his apartment.

And now the triumphant moment. He rolled his bicycle out into the hallway.

My eyes clouded over when I saw his bike. It was rusty, broken-down, with crumpled handlebars and no tires.

The tears welled up in my eyes, but I was ashamed to say I would not accept such a bike.

Choking with laughter, the clerk said:

"It's nothing. Smear on some kerosene. Rub it off. Buy some tires. And it'll be a decent bike."

With truly great difficulty I managed to roll this heap of rust to the repair shop. Waving his hand, the repairman said:

"Go on, are you in your right mind? You think that can be fixed?"

I sold the bike to a junk collector for a ruble. And he didn't even want to give me a ruble. He gave me eighty-five kopecks. But then he softened when he saw a bell on the rusty handlebars.

Even now, when thirty years have passed, I remember this clerk with revulsion: his duckbilled nose, his yellow teeth and flattened skull, into which I squeezed some of my knowledge.

This first lesson of mine also gave me a certain knowledge of life.

Conclusion

And now the recollections of my childhood are finished.

Before me lie thirty-eight episodes which once agitated and upset me.

I began to re-examine and reshuffle all these episodes. I hoped to find in them the source of my sufferings.

Yet I failed to detect anything special in these episodes.

Yes, of course, certain scenes are extremely sad. But no sadder than what usually takes place.

Everyone's father dies. Everyone sees his mother's tears.

Everyone has disappointments in school. Hurt feelings. Anxious moments. Deceptions. And everyone is frightened by a thunderstorm, floods and tempests.

No, not in a single episode did I find the unfortunate experience which had ruined my life, which had given birth to my melancholy and despair.

Then I assembled all these episodes together. I wanted to see the overall picture, the fundamental tone which perhaps had deafened me as I walked with the uncertain steps of a child down the narrow path of my life.

But in this fundamental tone as well I failed to detect anything special. An ordinary childhood. A somewhat difficult boy. Nervous. Feelings easily hurt. Extremely impressionable. With a gaze turned toward the bad, and not toward the good. Possibly timid because of this. But certainly not delicate, but rather—quite strong.

No, the events of my childhood years could not have ruined my later life.

I was discouraged again. It's an insuperable task— to find the cause of my despair. To remove it. To be happy. Joyful. Rapturous. The way an ordinary man with an open heart should be. Only in the tale does the prodigal son return to his father's home!

But perhaps I am mistaken? Perhaps the unfortunate experience I have been seeking never existed at all? Or, perhaps it occurred at a still earlier age?

Indeed, why had I banished my infant years? After all, the first impressions come not at six and not at seven years of age. The first brush with the world occurs earlier. The first notions arise at two and three years of age. And perhaps even at one.

Then I began to think: what could have happened at this slight age?

Straining my memory, I began to recall myself as a little baby. But here I became convinced that I remembered almost nothing about this. I could not evoke anything complete in my memory. Some snatches or other, pieces, some isolated moments which were sunk in a general gray shroud.

Then I began to recollect these snatches. And while recollecting them, I began to experience a fear even greater than I had experienced when thinking about my childhood.

This means I'm on the right path, I thought. This means the wound is somewhere nearby.

V. BEFORE SUNRISE

It was a world so terrible,
Without a sky, a light, or stars.[64]

And so, I decided to recall my infant years, assuming that the unfortunate experience had happened precisely in this period.

However, recalling these years turned out to be not so easy. They were enveloped by some sort of dim fog.

Straining my memory, I tried to break up this fog. I tried to recall myself as a three-year-old youngster sitting in the high chair or in my mother's lap.

And so, through the distant fog of oblivion, I suddenly started recalling some isolated moments, snatches, disconnected scenes, cast in some strange light.

What could have illuminated these scenes? Fear,[65]

perhaps? Or the emotional agitation of a baby? Yes, probably fear and emotional agitation did break through the dim cloth which shrouded my infant life.

But these were brief moments, this was an instantaneous light. And then once again everything sank in the fog.

And so, recalling these instants, I saw that they pertained to the third and fourth years of my life. Some of them even pertained to two years of age.

And then I began to recall what had happened to me from two to five years of age.

From 2 to 5

What seems so sweet upon our tongue
Produces acid in our stomach.

Open The Mouth

On the blanket, an empty matchbox. The matches, in the mouth.

Someone shouts: "Open the mouth!"

I open the mouth. Spit out matches.

Someone's fingers slip in the mouth. Scoop out some more matches.

Someone's crying. I'm crying louder because it's bitter and because they took them away.

The Slippers are Riding

Little polished slippers. Shiny little slippers of indescribable beauty. They're riding somewhere.

These slippers are on my feet. My feet, on a seat. The seat, blue. Must be a buggy carriage.

The polished slippers are riding in a buggy.

Without stopping, I look at these slippers.
I don't remember any more.

Let Me

A saucer of kasha. The spoon comes straight for my mouth. Someone's hand holds this spoon.

I take away the spoon. Let me.

I swallow the kasha. Hot. I bawl. Swat the saucer angrily with the spoon. Bits of kasha fly in the face, the eyes.

An unbelievable scream. It's me screaming.

Birdie

One man covers himself with a black kerchief. Another man holds a birdie in his hands. It's a big birdie. I stand on the chair and look at it.

The man raises the birdie. What for? So it will fly away? It can't fly. It's not alive. It's on a stick.

Someone says: ready.

I still have this photograph of a little tyke with eyes wide open in surprise. I'm two years and three months old.

Got Lost

A soft, striped sofa. Above the sofa, a little round window. Outside the window, water.

I crawl down off the sofa. Open the door of the cabin. Outside the door there's no water.

I walk down the corridor. Return.

Where's our door? No door. I got lost. I scream and cry.

Mother opens the door. Says:

"Sit here. Don't go away."

Rooster

The yard. Sun. Big flies around.

I sit on the porch steps. Eat something. Must be a roll.

I toss pieces of roll to the chickens.

A rooster comes toward me. Twisting his head around, he looks at me.

I wave my hand for the rooster to go away. But he doesn't go away. He comes nearer to me. And suddenly, hopping up, pecks my roll.

With a scream of horror I run away.

Chase It Away

On the windowsill, flowers. Amid the flowers lies a cat. It gazes at me.

And I gaze at the cat. I'm sitting in a high chair. And eating kasha.

Suddenly a big dog comes up. It puts its paws on the table.

I bawl desperately:

Someone shouts:

"He's afraid of dogs. Chase it away!"

The dog is chased away.

Gazing at the cat, I eat my kasha.

Just Pretend

I'm standing on a fence. Someone holds me from behind.

Suddenly a beggar with a sack walks up.

Someone says to him:

"Here, take this boy."
The beggar stretches out his hand.
I give a horrible scream.
Someone says:
"I won't give you away, I won't give you away. It's just pretend."
The beggar walks away with his sack.

It's Raining

Mother holds me in her arms. She runs. I press to her breast.

The rain drums on my head. Streams of water pour down my collar. I bawl.

Mother covers my head with a kerchief. Runs faster.

We're home already. In the room.

Mother puts me on the bed.

Suddenly lightning flashes. Thunder cracks.

I crawl down from the bed and bawl so loudly that it drowns out the thunder.

I'm Afraid

Mother holds me in her arms. We look at the animals, which are in cages.

Here's a huge elephant. It takes a French roll with its trunk. Gulps it down.

I'm afraid of elephants. We go away from the cage.

Here's a huge tiger. It cuts up the meat with tooth and claw. It eats.

I'm afraid of tigers. I cry.

We leave the zoo.

We're home again. Mama says to Father:
"He's afraid of animals."

Uncle Sasha's Dying

I'm sitting in the high chair. Drinking milk.

There's scum in it. I spit. Bawl. Smear the scum over the table.

Behind the door someone lets out a terrible scream.

Mama comes up. She's crying. Kissing me, she says: "Uncle Sasha's dying."

After smearing the scum over the table, I again drink the milk.

And again behind the door, a terrible scream.

At Night

Night. Dark. I woke up. Scream.

Mother takes me in her arms.

I scream even louder. Look at the wall. The wall is cinnamon. And on the wall hangs a towel.

Mother calms me down. Says:

"Are you afraid of the towel? I'll take it away."

Mother takes the towel away, hides it. Tucks me into bed. I scream again.

And then my little bed is placed alongside my mother's bed.

Weeping, I fall asleep.

Conclusion

And now twelve episodes of a little baby lie before me.

I re-examined these episodes carefully, but failed to detect anything special in them.

Every baby sticks in its mouth whatever comes to hand.

Almost every baby is frightened by animals, dogs. Spits when it gets scum. Burns its mouth. Screams in the dark.

No, it's an ordinary childhood, the normal behavior of a youngster.

Assembled together, these episodes likewise did not solve the riddle for me.

It seemed that I recollected all this childish babble in vain. It seemed that everything I had recalled about my life, I had recalled for nothing.

All these strong impressions must not have been the cause of my unhappiness. But perhaps they were the consequence, and not the cause?

Perhaps the unfortunate experience took place before two years of age?—I thought uncertainly.

Indeed. After all, the first encounters with things, the first brush with the surrounding world took place not at three and not at four years of age, but earlier, at the dawn of life, before sunrise.

It must be that this was an unusual encounter, an unusual first brush. A little animal, unable to speak, unable to think, encountered life. Precisely then, and not later, the unfortunate experience could have occurred.

But how am I to find it? How am I to delve into a world which is devoid of reason, devoid of logic, a world about which I remember nothing?

Before the Age of Two

I saw, as in a grievous dream,
That all was pale, and dark, and dim...[66]

1

Straining my memory, I started thinking about the beginning of my life. Yet I did not succeed in evoking any scenes out of oblivion. I could not catch any distant outlines. The distance merged into one solid, monotonous shade.

A thick gray fog enveloped the first two years of my life. It stood before me like a curtain of smoke and prevented me from delving into the distant mysterious life of a little creature.

And I did not understand how to break up this fog, so I could see the drama which was played out at the dawn of my life, before sunrise.

That the drama was played out precisely then, I no longer had any doubt. Were I searching for something that had never existed, I would not have experienced such an unaccountable fear as I now began to experience, as I tried to delve into a realm which people are not permitted to penetrate, once they have stepped out of the age of infancy.

2

I tried to imagine myself a one-year-old infant, with a pacifier in my mouth, a rattle in my hands, and my little legs cocked up.

But these scenes, artificially drawn in my brain, failed to stir my memory.

And only once, after intense reflection, did some sort of forgotten visions flash through my inflamed mind.

Here are the folds of some sort of a blanket. Some sort of hand from out of the wall. A tall wavering shadow. Another shadow. And another hand. Some sort of white froth. And again a long wavering shadow.

But these were chaotic visions. They resembled dreams. They were almost unreal. Through them I wanted to perceive at least the shadow of my mother, her image, her figure leaning over my bed. No, I did not succeed in doing this. The outlines fused together. The shadows vanished and behind them there was again— emptiness, dark, nothing... As the poet said:

All merged into a murky shade,
It was not night, it was not day,
It was the dark without the darkness,

158

It was a pit of emptiness
Without extent, without confines,
And images with not a face,
It was a world so terrible
Without a sky, a light, or stars.[67]

It was a world of chaos. It disappeared later at the first touch of my reason.

But for now, I could not delve into this world.

Without a doubt, this was another world, another planet, with other, extraordinary laws, which are not controlled by reason.

3

"But how then does the little creature live in this chaos?" I wondered. "How does it defend itself from dangers, since it has no reason, no logic?"

Or is there no defense, and everything is left to chance, to the care of the parents?

Yet even if you have parents, it is not entirely safe to live in this world of wavering shadows.

So I opened the textbooks and studies of physiologists in the desire to see what science had to say about this murky period of human life.

I saw that amazing laws were entered in the books—deduced by scientists from their observations of animals.

These were extraordinarily strict and precise laws, which in their own way protect the little creature.

It's unimportant that there is no reason and no logic. These are replaced by the reaction of the organism— the reflex, that is, the original response of the organism to any irritation which the baby receives from outside. This reaction, this response, represents the organism's defense against dangers.

What does this response consist of?

Two basic nervous processes characterize reflexive activity: excitation and inhibition. A combination of these processes gives one or another response. But all the variety of this cerebral activity can, essentially, be reduced to the simplest function—a muscular movement, or a combination of these movements which are purposeful by their very nature.

And this principle of reflex action pertains in equal measure to a man, to an animal, and to an infant.

Consequently, not chaos, but the strictest order, hallowed by thousands of years, protects the little creature.

And, consequently, the first brush with the world occurs according to this principle of reflex action. And the first encounters with things develop a habit of relating to them in one way or another.

4

I beg your indulgence: I have to speak of subjects which in all likelihood are known to the informed reader.

I have to speak of elementary things just in case not all my readers know these things firmly. Perhaps they have forgotten something about this and need to be reminded. Other informed readers, it must be assumed, know nothing about this, since they have never been interested in digging into formulas drawn from the life of dogs.

And those who know everything and remember everything, and perhaps even work in this area—may they not rail at me, may they run their eyes through two rather short chapters without irritation.

I will be speaking of a higher psychic function, more precisely, about its sources—about reflexes.

This is the same thing as speaking about the primal matter from which the world was created. It is equally important, for in it lie the sources of reason, the sources of consciousness, the sources of good and evil.

Once the great scientist Newton worked out the law of gravitation after he had seen an apple fall from a tree. A scene no less simple permitted the great Russian scientist to work out the law of conditioned reflexes.

The scientist noticed that a dog reacted in equal measure both to food and to the footsteps of the attendant who brought the food. Both to the food and to the footsteps the dog salivated. Consequently, thought the scientist, two nidi of excitation had arisen in the dog's brain, and these nidi were conditionally connected.

The scientist substituted a flash of light, the tick of a metronome, a musical note for the attendant's footsteps, and the dog's salivary glands functioned in the same way. In the event, of course, that these new stimuli coincided at least a few times with the moment of feeding.

These new stimuli (light, sound, musical scale), repeated several times (at the moment of feeding), created new neural connections, highly conditional in their nature.

In other words, the conditioned tick (or any other stimulus) elicited the notion of food in the dog. And the dog reacted to this conditioned signal exactly as it reacted to food.

This conditioned neural connection, which arose in the cerebral cortex between two nidi of excitation, was called a "temporary connection" by the scientist. It was a temporary connection, for it disappeared if the experiments were not repeated.

This was an amazing discovery.

5

Then the scientist made his experiments more complicated.

He sent an electric shock through the dog's paw. This procedure was accompanied by the tick of a metronome.

This procedure was repeated several times. And subsequently the tick of the metronome alone elicited a painful reaction in the dog.

In other words, the conditioned stimulus (the metronome) created a nidus of excitation in the cerebral cortex, and this nidus "ignited" the second nidus (pain), although the stimulus for this second nidus was absent. The neural connection between the two nidi continued to exist.

Then the scientist saw that one may interfere in the work of the central nervous system by purely material means, that one may establish whatever neural connections he likes.

The scientist obtained the possibility of directing the behavior of an animal, of creating new mechanisms in its brain.

A general physiological law was found, the basis of which was the simplest function of higher psychic activity—the reflex.

The law pertained in like measure both to the normal and to the pathological states.

This was a great discovery, for it dispelled obscurity in an area where there should be absolute clarity above all—the area of consciousness.

Only clarity in this area permitted human reason to proceed further, without turning back to savagery, to barbarianism, to obscurity.

This was a truly great discovery, for it pertained in equal measure to a man, to an animal, and especially to an infant, whose behavior is not controlled by consciousness or logic.

And in the light of this law the behavior of an infant becomes quite clear.

An infant becomes acquainted with the world, with things surrounding it, according to the principle of the conditioned reflex.

Every new object, every new thing creates new neural connections, new relationships, in the infant's cerebral cortex. These neural connections, just as in the dog, are extremely conditional.

The tick of the metronome elicited a painful reaction in the dog. A shout, the slamming of a door, a shot, a flash of light, any stimulus which accidentally corresponded (let us say) with the moment of feeding the baby and was repeated several times, might create complex neural connections in the infant's brain.

The sight of a hypodermic syringe elicited vomiting from the dog. The sight of any object which accidentally caused the baby pain might later have caused him suffering.

True, in order for this reflex to have arisen, repetition was necessary. But so what! Repetition could have occurred.

But then these neural connections were called temporary. They lapsed if the experiments were not repeated.

Here was a question which required careful consideration. The scientist proposed only the simplest principle, which he had tested on dogs. The psyche of man is more complex. The mental development of man does not remain on one level: it changes, progresses. And consequently the neural connections also change: they may be extremely complex and entangled.

Death prevented the scientist from continuing his experiments on animals closer to man—on monkeys. Such experiments had been begun.

Experiments on man were not conducted to the extent that they should have been.

6

This great discovery—the law of conditioned reflexes, the law of temporary neural connections—I wanted to apply to my own life.

I wanted to see this law in action, applied to examples from my infant life.

It seemed to me that my unhappiness might have arisen because untruthful conditioned connections had been established in my infant brain and had later frightened me. It seemed to me that I was frightened of a hypodermic syringe which once had squirted poison.

I wanted to destroy the mistaken mechanism which had arisen in my brain.

But again an obstacle lay before me: I couldn't recall anything about my infant life.

If only I could recollect at least one scene, one experience—I would unravel whatever followed. But no, all was enveloped by the fog of oblivion.

But someone told me that you must go to the place where something was forgotten, and then you would be able to recall this forgotten thing.

I asked my relatives where we had lived when I was a child. And my relatives told me where I had lived the first years of my life.

There were three houses. But one house had burned down. I had lived in another house when I was two. In the third house I had spent no less than five years, beginning at the age of four.

And there was still another house. This house was in the country, where my parents had gone every summer.

I wrote down the addresses and with unusual agitation went to look over these houses of long ago.

I looked for a long time at the house where I had lived at the age of three. But I could recall positively nothing.

And then I went to the house where I had lived five years.

My heart sank when I approached the gateway to this house.

My God! How familiar everything was to me here. I recognized the stairway, the little garden, the gateway, the courtyard.

I recognized almost everything. But how little it

resembled what had been in my memory.

Once the house had seemed a huge colossus, a sky-scraper. Now there stood before me a shabby little three-story affair.

Once the garden had seemed fabulous, mysterious. Now I saw a miserable little plot.

It had seemed that a massive, high, cast-iron fence had enclosed this garden like a belt. Now I touched miserable iron bars no higher than my own belt.

How different were my eyes then and now!

I went up to the third floor and found the door to our apartment.

My heart contracted with incomprehensible pain. I felt bad. And clutched the railings convulsively, not knowing what was wrong with me, why I was so agitated.

I went back down and sat for a long time on the curb by the gateway. I sat until the janitor came up. Looking at me suspiciously, he ordered me to leave.

7

I returned home thoroughly ill, crushed, distraught by I knew not what.

In horrible despair, I returned home. And now this despair would not leave me by day or by night.

By day I shuffled about my room—I could neither lie down nor remain seated. And by night I was torment-ed by some sort of horrible dreams.

Previously I had not had dreams. More precisely, I had had them, but forgotten them. They were brief and incomprehensible. I usually had them toward morning.

Now they appeared as soon as I lowered my lids.

These were not even dreams. They were night-mares, horrible visions from which I woke up in terror.

I started taking bromides to still these nightmares, to calm myself. But bromides were little help to me.

Then I called on a certain physician and asked him

165

to give me something to stop these nightmares.

On learning that I was taking bromides, the physician said:

"What are you doing! On the contrary, you need to have dreams. They come to you because you are thinking of your childhood. Only through these dreams will you manage to deal with your illness. Only in your dreams will you see those scenes of infancy you are seeking. Only by means of the dream will you delve into that distant forgotten world."

And then I related my latest dream to the physician, and he began to interpret it. But he interpreted it in such a way that I became indignant and did not believe him.

I said that in my dreams I saw tigers and some sort of a hand from out of a wall.

The physician said:

"That's patently clear. Your parents took you to the zoological park too early. You saw an elephant there. It scared you with its trunk. The hand—is the trunk. The trunk—is a phallus. You have a sexual trauma."

I did not believe the physician and became indignant. And he, feeling insulted, answered me:

"I interpreted your dream according to Freud. I am a disciple of his. And there is no more reliable science which can help you."

Then I called on several more physicians. Some laughed, saying that dream interpretation is nonsense. Others, on the contrary, attributed great significance to dreams.

Among these physicians there was one extremely intelligent physician. He explained and related a great deal to me. And I was very grateful. And even wanted to become his disciple. But then I decided not to. It seemed to me that he was not right. I did not believe in his treatment.

He was a violent opponent of Pavlov. Except for experiments of a zoological nature, he saw nothing in

166

his works. He was an orthodox Freudian. In every act of a child and an adult he saw the sexual element. Every dream he deciphered as the dream of an erotomaniac.

This interpretation did not coincide with what I considered infallible, it did not coincide with the method of Pavlov, with the principle of conditioned reflexes.

8

However, this method of treatment did amaze me.

There is something comical about interpreting dreams. It seemed to me that this was the occupation of old feebleminded hags and mystically inclined people.

It seemed to me that this was incompatible with science. I was very surprised when I learned that all of medicine had arisen, essentially, from one source, from one cult—from the science of dreams. All of the ancient, so-called temple medicine had been developed and cultivated on one basis—on the interpretation of dreams. This was the basis of the cult of Asclepius—the son of Apollo and god of healing[68] among the Greeks—Aesculapius.

Why was such significance attributed to dreams? What were the motives behind this? Were there really only religious and mystical motives? Was there really nothing reasonable in this? After all, the ancient world was not barbarian. The ancient world gave us remarkable philosophers, writers, scientists. And finally, remarkable physicians—Hippocrates, Galenus.

How did these physicians heal? The history of medicine tells us of the ancient method of treatment.

The sick person was left for the night in the temple. There he had a dream. And in the morning he related it to the priests and scientists. And these men made a diagnosis as to the type of indisposition suffered by the sick person. And, by interpreting his dream, they freed the supposed sick person from his suffering.

This ancient medicine, of course, was closely connected with the priests and religious mystical devices.

167

Sacrifices were made to the god of healing. All the ceremonious and mysterious trappings of the treatment undoubtedly could act on the imagination of the sick person, could inspire his belief in the might of the god of healing. Might not the cure have been founded on this self-hypnosis?

Without a doubt, this was significant, but it was not the sole cause of the cure.

The history of medicine says that the religious rites connected with the treatment were later abandoned. Something like sanataria were set up in the temples. At the same time, medical schools and corporations of physicians began to appear in the temples. It was from precisely such temple schools that Hippocrates and Galenus came.

But how did this idea of dream interpretation arise? Why did this idea form the basis of ancient medicine? Why did it cease to be a science? And why have many physicians and scientists in modern times, including Freud, tried to make it into a scientific discipline?

I could not provide myself the answers to these questions.

And so I opened the textbooks of medicine and the studies of the physiologists to see what modern science had to say about dreams, and about dreaming, and about the possibility of using the dream to delve into the distant forgotten world of an infant.

9

What is a dream from the viewpoint of modern science?

Above all, it is a physiological condition in which all the external manifestations of consciousness are absent. More precisely, all the higher psychic functions are excluded, and the lower functions—released.

Pavlov held that at night a man disengages from the external world. And during sleep the inhibited forces, suppressed feelings and stifled desires come to life.

This occurs because there is an inhibition in the mechanism of dreaming. But this inhibition is partial: it does not encompass our brain entirely, does not encompass all the points of the great hemispheres. This inhibition does not descend below the subcortical centers.

Our brain, in the opinion of physiologists, has, as it were, two stories. The upper story is the cortex of the brain. Here lie the centers of control, logic, critical judgement, the centers of acquired reflexes, here lies the experience of life. And the lower story is the source of inherited reflexes, the source of animal traits, animal forces.

These two stories are united by neural connections, which we have already mentioned.

At night the upper story subsides in sleep. As a result, consciousness is absent. Absent also are control, critical judgement, conditioned traits.

The lower story continues in the waking state. However, the absence of control permits its occupants to come manifest themselves to a greater or lesser degree.

Let us assume that logic or mental development inhibits or expels a fear which once awakened in a child. When control is absent, this fear might appear again. Only it appears in dreams.

Consequently, dreaming is a continuation of the spiritual life, a continuation of a man's psychic activity, minus control.

And consequently dreaming can explain what kind of forces inhibit a man, what frightens him, and what can be expelled by the light of logic, the light of consciousness.[69]

It now becomes clear why ancient medicine attributed such significane to dreams.

At the same time we may be surprised: modern science has only recently managed to sort out the mechanism of our brain. Yet it was at the dawn of human culture, several thousands of years ago, that the idea arose—to find what was not controlled during sleep.

We do not know who deserves the credit for creating ancient medicine. It was a shining idea, the brilliant thought of a genius, which formed the basis for this ancient science.

From the hands of a genius, this idea passed into the hands of talentless, mediocre people. And with their abilities they brought it down to their own level, to the level of charlatanry.

Something comical began to accompany this idea. Modern man cannot look on the ancient dream interpretors, the ancient oneirocritics, without a smile. Nonsense and babbling are found on every page of these ancient books.

A correct idea was vulgarized to such a degree that it no longer became possible to make any sense of it.

And only in the light of modern physiology does this idea—to delve into the psyche of a sick man, to understand what provokes inhibitions—become clear.

This is why scientists in recent times have tried once again to approach dreams, to see the source of a psychoneurosis through dreams, to understand something that may seem to be a tragedy of human reason.

10

And so, our brain has two stories: the upper and the lower.

The experience of life and the conditioned traits room together with inherited experience, with the traits of our ancestors, with the traits of animals.

Two worlds, as it were, are enclosed in the complex apparatus of our brain: the civilized world and the animal world.

It might seem that the source of many nervous disorders lay precisely in this struggle.

Yet the miseries lie somewhere else entirely.

I do not want to rush ahead of myself, but I will

say a brief word. Even if we assume that the conflict between the higher and lower is a cause of nervous disorders, still this cause is not all-encompassing, it is only a partial cause, by no means the main one or the basic one.

This conflict of the higher with the lower may (let us assume) lead to certain sexual psychoneuroses. And should science perceive in this conflict, in this struggle, the sole cause—it would not proceed any further than the discovery of sexual inhibitions.

A struggle in this area is to a certain degree normal, and not pathological.

It seems to me that Freud's system is faulty on precisely this point.

This fault, this mistake was easy to make since the mechanisms discovered by Pavlov were not taken into account.

Inaccuracy in the initial premises, plus nebulousness in the formulation of the struggle between the higher and the lower forces, produced an inaccurate conclusion, in one direction, in the direction of sexual deviations. But this did not decide the matter. It was only a part of the whole.

11

Freud saw the source of nervous disorders in the conflict of the higher forces with the lower, in the collision of atavistic drives with the feelings of modern civilized man. Freud wrote: "Prohibited by the course of cultural life and repressed to the depths of the unconscious, these drives exist and make themselves known by bursting into our consciousness in a distorted form..." Consequently, the cause of the tragedy was perceived in the conquest of reason over the animal instincts. In other words, higher reason is brought into doubt.

The history of human thought knows numerous instances where miseries were attributed to reason, where higher consciousness was brought under attack and, consequently, people saw the tragedy of human reason in higher consciousness, in the conflict of the higher forces with the lower. It seemed to them that the conquest of consciousness over the lower instincts produced misery, illness, nervous disorders, weakness of the spirit, psychoneurosis.

This seemed a tragedy from which there was only one way out—a return to the past, a return to nature, a departure from civilization. It seemed that the paths of human reason were mistaken, artificial, unnecessary.

I do not consider this philosophy identical to the philosophy of fascism. Fascism has other roots, another nature, but in respect to reason fascism has drawn something from this philosophy, distorting it, simplifying it, bringing it down to the level of dull-witted people.

A return to barbarism—this is not a formula proposed by fascism merely for the needs of war. From the fascist point of view, this is one of the basic premises for the future cast of man.

Better barbarism, savagery, animal instincts, than the further progress of consciousness.

How ridiculous!

People artificially thrown back into barbarianism would by no means get rid of the nervous disorders which alarm them. The earth would be populated by scoundrels relieved of the responsibility for their base deeds. But still they would be scoundrels who had not gotten rid of their previous sufferings. They would be suffering scoundrels, even more unhealthy than before.

The return to a harmonious barbarianism, which people have fantasized about, was not possible even thousands of years ago. And even should such a possibility exist—the source of sufferings would remain. For the mechanisms of the brain would remain. We are not capable of destroying them. We can only learn how to deal with them. And we should learn to do this with an art worthy of higher consciousness.

We should thoroughly study these mechanisms discovered by Pavlov. The knowledge of how to deal with them will free us from the tremendous sufferings which people endure with barbarian submissiveness.

The tragedy of human reason does not come from the high level of consciousness, but from its insufficiency.

12

Science has not been perfected. Truth is the daughter of time. Other, more exact paths will be found. In the meantime, we can use a careful analysis of dreams to glimpse the distant world of an infant, that world not controlled by reason, that world of oblivion where our miseries sometimes have their source.

Thus dreams may explain the cause of a pathological inhibition, and the Pavlovian system of conditioned reflexes, when applied to these dreams, may eliminate the miseries. Whatever is inhibited may be released.

This inhibition can be removed by the light of logic, the light of higher consciousness, and not by the dim light of barbarianism.

And so, having pondered all this, I understood that I could now attempt to delve into that locked-up world of the infant. The keys were in my hands.

At night the doors of the lower story would open. The watchmen of my consciousness would fall asleep. And then the shades of the past, languishing in the cellar, would appear in my dreams.

I wanted to meet these shades at once, to see them, so that I could finally understand the tragedy or mistake I had made at the dawn of my life, before sunrise.

I wanted to recall some dream or other from among the great many dreams I had recently had. Yet I could not remember a single dream in its entirety. I had forgotten.

So I began to think what kind of dreams I had most frequently, what they were about.

And here I remembered that most frequently I dreamt about tigers coming into my room, about beggars standing at my door, and about bathing in the sea.

VI. BLACK WATER

Like a hunk of lead—black water
In it—oblivion forever.

1

I went by chance to the village where I had spent
my childhood.

I had been planning to go there for some time. And
then, while strolling along the quay, I saw a steamship
standing at the pier. Almost mechanically I got on the
steamship and went to the village.

This was the village called "Peski."[70] There was no
pier there now. I crossed the Neva in a rowboat.

Oh, with what anxiety I stepped out onto the
shore. I immediately recognized the little round chapel.

175

It was still standing. I immediately remembered the cottages just opposite, the village street and the steep rise from the shore where there was once a pier.

Everything now seemed miserable, miniature in comparison to the grandiose world left in my memory.

I walked down the street, and everything here was so well-known to me it hurt. Except the people. Not one person did I recognize among those I met.

Then I stopped in the yard of the house where we had once lived.

A not so young woman was standing in the yard. She had an oar in her hands. She had just chased some calf or other out of the yard. And there she stood angered and inflamed.

She didn't want to talk to me. But I named several village dwellers I remembered.

No, all these names belonged to people who had already died.

Then I gave my own name, the name of my parents. And the woman smiled. She said that she had been a young girl then, but she remembered my late parents well. And then she began to give the names of our relatives who had lived here, the names of our acquaintances. No, all the names she gave belonged to people who had died.

Sorrowfully I went back to my boat.

Sorrowfully I walked down the village street. Only the street and the houses were the same. The residents were all different. The former ones had lived here like guests, and had left, vanished, never again to return. They had died.

It seemed to me on that day that I understood what life is, what death is, and how one must live.

2

With the greatest sorrow I returned home. And at home I did not even begin to think about my searches,

176

about my childhood. Everything had become of no interest to me.

Everything seemed to be nonsense, trivia, compared to the picture of brief life which I had witnessed today.

Is it really worth thinking, struggling, searching, defending yourself. Is it really worth setting yourself up like a landlord in a life which passes so precipitously, with such insulting, even comical speed.

Isn't it better to live your life without complaining, and then relinquish your miserable spot to other scions of the earth.

Someone started laughing in the next room while I thought about these things. And it seemed to me strange and savage that people were able to laugh, joke, even speak when everything was so stupid, senseless, insulting.

It seemed to me that it was easier and simpler to die than to wait submissively and obtusely for the fate which awaits everyone. In this decision I suddenly saw courage. How amazed I would have been had I been told then what I know now—that this was by no means courage, this was an extreme degree of infantility. It had been dictated by the infant's fear of the thing I wanted to find. It was resistance. It was flight.

I decided to give up my searches. And with this decision I went to sleep.

That night I awoke in fear from some sort of horrible dream. The fear was so strong that I continued to shiver even after I was awake.

I put on the lamp and wrote down my dream so I could think about it in the morning, if only out of curiosity.

However, I could not fall asleep and began to think about this dream.

Actually, it was an extremely stupid dream. A stormy dark river. Murky, almost black water. Something white floats in the water—a piece of paper or a rag. I'm on the shore. Without stopping for breath, I run away from the shore. Run through a field. The field is blue for some reason. And someone is chasing me. And just now he tries to grab me by the shoulder. The hand of this person is already touching me. Lunging forward, I run away.

I began to ponder this dream, but understood nothing.

Then I began to think that once again I had seen water in a dream. That dark, black water... And suddenly I recalled the verses of Blok:

> **Old, old dream... Out of the gloom**
> **Streetlamps swim—where to?**
> **Ahead—only black water,**
> **Ahead—oblivion forever.**[71]

This dream was like my dream.
I ran from the black water, from "oblivion forever."

3

I began to remember dreams connected with water. Now I am bathing in a stormy sea. Struggling with the waves. Now I wander somewhere up to my knees in water. Or sit on the shore, and the water splashes at my feet. Or walk along the very edge of the quay. And suddenly the water rises higher and higher. Fear grips me. I run away.

I recalled one more dream. I'm sitting in my room. Suddenly water begins to seep from all the cracks in the floor. Another minute, and the room is filled with water.

After such dreams I usually woke up oppressed, ill, in a bad disposition. My despair was usually strengthened after such dreams.

Perhaps the frequent floods in Leningrad had had an influence on my psyche? Or perhaps something else was connected with water?

I began to recollect those scenes I had written down in my search for the unfortunate experience. I again recalled the story of the drowned boy, the story of the flood, the scenes where I almost drowned, my sister almost drowned.

Without a doubt, water was connected with some strong sensation. But what sensation?

Perhaps I fear water in general? No. On the contrary. I love water excessively. I can admire the sea for hours. I can sit beside the river for hours. I usually travel only to places where there is a sea, a river. I always try to find a room with windows looking out on the water. I always dreamed of living somewhere on the shore, quite near the water, so that the waves would be right at the porch of my house.

The sea or the river frequently restored my peace of mind when I suffered despair which so often visited me.

But what if this is not love of the water, but fear?

What if underneath this exaggerated love there lies respectful fear?

Perhaps I do not admire the water but look out for it? Perhaps I admire it when it is quiet, when it is not about to swallow me up?

Perhaps I look out for it from the shore, from the window of my room? Maybe I situate myself nearer to it so as to be on guard, so it will not catch me unawares?

Perhaps this fear is that fear which does not reach my consciousness, which nestles on the lower story of my psyche, forced down there by logic, by the control of reason?

I laughed: how comical this was and yet, evidently, how true.

Not a doubt remained: a fear of water was present in my mind. But it was deformed. It was not in the form by which we understand it.

179

Then it seemed to me that I understood my dream. It undoubtedly related to my infant days. In order to understand it, I would have to depart from my usual conceptions, I would have to think with the images of an infant, look through its eyes.

Of course, not entirely with its images: they were undoubtedly too poor. They had changed along with the infant's development. But their symbolism evidently had remained as before.

A murky, stormy river: this is a bathtub or a basin of water. The blue shore: a blanket. The white rag: a swaddling band left in the basin. The baby was pulled out of the water in which it bathed. The baby was "saved." But the threat remained.

I laughed again. This was comical, but credible. This was naive, but no more naive than it should have been.

But how could it have happened? All infants are bathed. All babies are plunged into water. No fear remains with them. Why then was I frightened?

"This means water was not the first cause," I thought."This means there were some other objects of fear connected with water."

Here I recalled the principle of conditioned reflexes.

One stimulus may elicit two nidi of excitation, for a conditioned neural connection may have been made between them.

Water alone, the water in which I had been plunged, could not have produced anxiety to such a degree as I had. This means that the water was conditionally connected with something else. This means there was no fear of the water itself, but the water elicited fear, for the neural connections combined it with some other danger. It was in such a complex arrangement as this that the matter was decided. And this was why water was able to frighten me.

Yet what was water connected with? What kind of "poison" did it contain? In what did the second unfortunate stimulus consist, the stimulus which had "ignited" the combination of such a violent response?

I had not yet begun to guess about the second stimulus, about the second nidus of excitation to which the neural connections so obviously inclined.

In fact, this stimulus was already partially visible in that very same dream. The infant's world is poor, the objects are extremely limited in number. The stimuli are not numerous. But my lack of experience did not permit me to ferret out the second stimulus right away.

The riddle was not solved, but the keys to it were in my hands.

Further events showed that I had not been mistaken in principle. I was mistaken only in the number of nidi of excitation: there turned out to be not two, but several of them. And they were intertwined in a most complex network of conditioned connections.

By a combination of these nidi of excitation, one or another response was given.

5

The principle of conditioned reflexes states that neural connections have a temporary character. The experience must be repeated for them to be established and confirmed. Without such experience they lapse or disappear altogether.

But so what. In the present case water was an excellent and frequent stimulus in the infant's life. There undoubtedly was repetition. I did not know yet what kind of stimulus this second one was, but I understood that its conditioned connection with water could have been established.

But then this connection should have vanished later, with the development of the child. After all, repetition

181

could not have continued forever. After all, if not the child and not the youth, then the mature man should have finally severed this incorrect, false connection. And it was incorrect, mistaken—that was obvious.

A person's mental development truly struggles with untruthful, false, illogical notions. Yet the child, while developing, might encounter other, more logical proofs of the danger of the thing he fears.

Again I began to examine my recollections connected with water.

Proofs of the danger of water were found at every step.

People drown in the water. I could drown. Water floods the city. People throw themselves in the water to die.

What weighty proofs of the danger of water.

Without a doubt, this could have frightened a child, proved to him that his infant notion was correct.

Such "false" proofs could have accompanied me all through life. Such was undoubtedly the case. Water contained elements of fear, abetted the infant fear. The newly formed temporary connections with water might not have vanished, they might have grown stronger and established themselves more firmly.

This means a man's mental development does not destroy the temporary conditioned connections, it only rearranges them, raises these false proofs to the level of its development. And perhaps willingly seeks out these proofs, without testing them too carefully, for without testing they can dwell together with logic, since they fall on painful soil.

These false proofs frequently become fused with genuine proofs. Water really is dangerous. But a neurotic regards this danger, and likewise reacts to this danger, in a manner which is not normal.

6

But if this is so, if water was one of the elements of fear, one of the stimuli in the combination of my psychoneurosis, then what a sad and pitiful picture lay open to my gaze.

For it was precisely with water that they treated me. Precisely with water they tried to rid me of despair.

I was prescribed water, both inside and outside. They sat me in bathtubs, wrapped me in wet sheets, prescribed sprays. Sent me to the sea—to travel by water and to bathe.

My God! From this treatment alone my despair could have arisen.

This treatment could have reinforced the conflict, could have created an inescapable situation.

But then water was only a part of the trouble, perhaps a negligible part.

The treatment, in fact, did not create an inescapable situation. It was possible to avoid this treatment. And that is what I did. I stopped the treatment.

In order not to be treated, I conceived a ridiculous theory whereby a man should work all the time, without ceasing, to maintain perfect health. I stopped going to resorts, considering this a superfluous luxury.

Thus I freed myself from the treatment.

But I could not free myself from the constant collisions with the thing that frightened me. The fear continued to exist.

This fear was not yet conscious. I did not suspect its existence, for it had been forced down onto the lower story of my psyche. The watchmen of my reason did not give it freedom. It had the right to come out only at night, when my consciousness was not in control.

This fear lived a nocturnal life, in dreams. But during the day, in my collisions with an object of fear, it appeared only obliquely—in incomprehensible symptoms which could confuse any physician.

We know what fear is, we know its effect on the working of our body. We know its protective reflexes. Their basis is the urge to avoid danger.

The symptoms of fear are varied. They depend on the strength of the fear. They are expressed in a constriction of the blood vessels, intestinal spasms, convulsive muscular contractions, heart palpitations, and so on. An extreme degree of fear causes complete or partial paralysis.

Precisely such symptoms were created by the unconscious fear which I experienced. To one degree or another they were expressed in heart seizures, loss of breath, spasms, convulsive muscular twitchings.

Such were the major symptoms of fear. The chronic presence of fear undermined the normal functioning of the body, created steadfast inhibitions, led to chronic indispositions.

At the root of these symptoms there was a "purposefulness": they blocked my path to "danger," they precipitated flight.

An animal which is unable to avoid danger pretends to be dead.

On occasion I pretended to be dead, ill, weak, when it was impossible to get away from the "danger."

All this was a response to an irritation from outside. This was a complex response for the conditioned neural connections, as we shall later see, were extremely complex.

7

We may assume that a child acts this way when it wants to avoid a "danger." But how does an adult act?

How did I act? Did I really fail to struggle with this nonsense? Did I really save myself only by flight? Was I really and truly a wretched speck of dust, driven about by any coincidence?

No, I struggled with it, defended myself against

this unconscious misery. But this defense corresponded to my development every time.

In my childhood years, my behavior inclined mainly toward flight and, to a certain degree, toward the desire to master water, to "overcome" it. I tried to learn how to swim. But I could not learn. Fear held me fast in its grip.

I learned to swim only as a young man, after subduing this fear.

This was my first victory and possibly my only one. I remember how proud I was of this.

Later on, my consciousness did not direct me away from this struggle. On the contrary, my consciousness directed me toward this struggle. I strove every time to meet my mighty opponent as soon as possible, so that once again I could measure my strength against his.

Right here lay the contradiction which masked my fear.

I did not avoid steamships, boats, I did not avoid visits to the sea. In defiance of my fear, I went almost on purpose into this single combat. My consciousness did not want to admit defeat, nor even faint-heartedness.

I remember an incident at the front. I was leading a battalion to its positions. A river turned up before us. For a minute I was disconcerted. The crossing would not have been difficult, but nevertheless I sent scouts out to the left and right to find an easier crossing. I sent them with the secret desire of finding some dried-out path across the river.

It was the beginning of summer, and no such paths could have existed.

I was disconcerted for only a minute. I ordered the scouts called back. And led the battalion across the river.

I remember my anxiety as we entered the water. I remember my heart palpitations which I could barely endure.

It turned out that I had acted rightly. The crossings

were the same everywhere. And I was glad that I had not procrastinated, that I had acted decisively.

This meant I was not a blind instrument in the hands of my fear. My behavior was dictated every time by duty, conscience, consciousness. But the conflict which arose from this frequently caused me an indisposition.

Fear acted outside of my reason. The violent response to an irritation was outside my consciousness. But the unhealthy symptoms were only too obvious. I did not know their origin. The physicians defined them roughly as neuroses caused by overexertion, weariness.

Sensing the inequality in forces, I nevertheless continued to wage a struggle with the unconscious fear. But how strangely the struggle proceeded. What strange paths were taken for a dubious victory.

8

A thirty-year-old man intended to free himself from fear by studying water. The struggle proceeded along the lines of knowledge, along the lines of science.

This was astonishing, for consciousness took part in this struggle. I do not fully understand how these paths were taken. Consciousness was not familiar with the mechanisms of unhappiness, and perhaps therefore a path was chosen which seemed reliable, but which in the present case was mistaken, even comical.

All my notebooks, writing pads began to be filled with data on water.

These notebooks now lie before me. I look through them with a smile. Here are some entries on the most powerful storms and floods in world history. Here are the most detailed figures—on the depth of the seas and the oceans. Here are data on the most stormy waters. On rocky coasts which cannot be approached by ships. On waterfalls.

Here are data on drowned people. On first aid to

186

drowned people.

Here is an entry underlined in red pencil:

"71 percent of the earth's surface lies under water, and only twenty-nine percent is dry land."

A tragic entry! In red pencil is added:

"3/4 of the globe is water!"

Here are some more tragic entries which show the percentage of water in the bodies of people, animals, plants:

"Fish—70-80%, jellyfish—96%, potatoes—75%, bones—50%..."

What a gigantic task I undertook! What a senseless one.

Here is a whole little notebook full of scribblings on the winds. This is understandable: wind is the cause of floods, the cause of storms, tempests.

A bit of one entry:

"3 meters a second—leaves rustle,

"10 meters a second—large branches shake,

"20 meters a second—a strong wind,

"30 meters a second—a storm,

"35 meters a second—a storm turning into a hurricane,

"40 meters a second—a hurricane destroying houses."

A note under the entry: "ty—excessive, phoon—wind. The typhoon of 1892 (island of Mauritius)—54 meters a second!"

Here is still another notebook on floods in Leningrad.

Leafing through these notebooks of mine, I smiled at first. Then my smile turned to grief. What a tragic struggle. What an intellectual, and at the same time barbarian, path consciousness had found so that, through knowledge, it might "overcome" its opponent, destroy the fear, gain the victory.

What a tragic path had been found. It corresponded to my mental development.

187

This path also found a reflection in my literature.

But here I should make a reservation. I by no means intend to say that this path—fear and the desire to destroy it—predetermined my life, my steps, my behavior, my melancholy, my literary designs.

By no means. My behavior would have been exactly the same had the fear been absent. But the fear complicated the steps, intensified the indisposition, increased the melancholy which might have existed even without it, due to other causes, due to other circumstances which equally pertain to all people.

Fear did not predetermine the paths, but it was one of the units in the complex sum of forces which act on man.

It would be a mistake not to take this unit into account. But it would be an even greater mistake—to take this unit as the sum itself, as the single factor acting on man.

Only in a complex accounting is the matter decided.

We have seen this complexity in my behavior. The basic activator was not fear, but other forces—duty, reason, conscience. These forces proved to be considerably higher than the base forces.

My behavior was basically reasonable. Fear did not lead me by the hand like a blind man. But it was present in me, undermined the correct working of my body, forced me to avoid "dangers," if there were no higher feelings or obligations.

It clamped down on me and, most of all, affected my physical condition.

My consciousness was determined to eliminate it. My mental development chose the path of knowledge. The professional skills of a literary man likewise took part in this struggle. Among the many themes which occupied me was the theme connected with water. For this theme I had a great predilection.

I spent a half-year on materials from Epron,[72] studying the history of the wreck of "The Black Prince."

While working on this book, I carefully researched everything that related to it. I traveled out to the place of operations, acquainted myself with deep-sea diving, collected literature on all the inventions in this field.

After finishing the book *The Black Prince*,[73] I immediately set about collecting materials on the wreck of the submarine "55."[74] I did not complete this book. The theme ceased to engage me, for at about this time I found a more reasonable path for the struggle.

And so, by studying water in all of its properties, I intended to free myself from unhappiness, from my unconscious fear. This fear did not even pertain to water. But water elicited the fear, for water was conditionally connected with another object of fear.

The struggle against this fear, I repeat, corresponded to my mental development.

What a tragic struggle. What woe and what a defeat it promised me. What blows were predestined for my pitiful body.

What miseries, then, can we speak of which come from our higher consciousness?

For the time being, we can only speak of a reason which lacks sufficient knowledge. We can speak of a little unhappy savage who wanders down a narrow mountain trail, barely lit by the first rays of the morning sun.

10

And so, the first steps in search of the unfortunate experience have been taken.

The unfortunate experience arose on my first brush with the surrounding world. It occurred in the pre-dawn twilight, before sunrise.

It was not even an experience. It was a mistake, an

189

unfortunate incident, a striking combination of coincidences.

This coincidence created untruthful, unhealthy notions about certain things, including water.

This was a drama in which my guilt was nothing more than the act of suffering.

However, this drama has not yet been played out to the end.

> **We have scotch'd the snake, not kill'd it;**
> **She'll close, and be herself...**[75]

It would be necessary to find the conditioned neural connections, which led from water to something unknown, to something perhaps even more terrible. Without this, water would not have been an object of horror.

And now, confident of my strength, I proceeded further in search of my unfortunate experience.

VII. SHUT THE DOORS

We have scotch'd the snake, not kill'd it;
She'll close, and be herself...

1

I often saw beggars in my dreams. Dirty ones. Ragged ones. In tatters.

They knocked at the door to my room. Or appeared suddenly on the road.

I would wake up in fear, and sometimes in horror.

I began to think: why do I dream about beggars? What is it about them that frightens me? Could it be that the Beggar is a conditioned stimulus for me?

I leafed through my recollections, hoping to find scenes among them which had terrified me.

No, the image of the beggar was absent from my re-collections. Except for one brief scene from my third year of life: my mother, in jest, held me out to a beggar.[76]

Perhaps that beggar had frightened me? Perhaps there remained an infantile fear which came to life in my dreams?

I recalled all the beggars I had met on the street. No, I felt no fear of them. I experienced no anxiety.

But this fear should be present in the daytime as well, if only to the slightest degree. I have already written that I experienced such a distorted fear of water. And in the daytime this fear expressed itself in strange symptoms. It found a reflection throughout my whole life. I struggled with this unconscious fear by making it conscious. It was a real struggle. Traces of this tragic struggle were left in my notebooks, in my literature. Water was the first conditioned stimulus for me; the beggar, in all likelihood,—the second.

So I opened my notebooks, expecting to find traces of this new struggle, traces of new skirmishes with my unconscious opponent.

Yet this time I did not find what I sought in my notebooks. There were no ciphers, no notes. There was nothing to account for my intense interest in this object.

Then I leafed through my works, my books.

Without a doubt, the theme of the beggar interested me greatly. But it was the normal interest of a literary man in a social phenomenon.

This theme was present only to the degree that it deserved to be present in the works of a satirical writer. It even seemed to me that this theme was taken with insufficient fullness and breadth.

I was disconcerted. How could this be? I saw beggars in my dreams. Beggars frightened me. This much was obvious. Yet the night passed, the sun arose, and all trace of the beggars disappeared in the rays of its light.

192

2

So I began to think over my life again, trying to remember scenes connected in some way with a beggar.

Yet I failed to recall anything of consequence in this regard. I could not evoke any beggars from out of oblivion.

And then I had a ridiculous sort of dream.

A steamship. A crowd of passengers on board. The crowd is applauding me. Out of the crowd walks an old man with an extremely youthful look. He is blooming in health, smart in appearance, rosy-cheeked. A flower in his buttonhole.

Bowing respectfully to me, the old man declares:

"Oh, thank you, young man! Remember what a decrepit thing I was at eighty? Now that I have turned sixty I feel really splendid."

I answer:

"I'm very happy, Pavel Petrovich, that I was able to help you."

The old man takes me by the arm. We march off together ceremoniously. We come up to some door. The door opens. The old man vanishes.

That's the whole dream. It seems absurd, senseless. At first I didn't even want to think about it.

But it must be said that this dream dates from the time when I began collecting material for my book *Youth Restored.* It must be that some old man thanked me for my future book, which restored his youth to him.

I began to think about my snoutish old man— whether I had even seen him in life. No, never before had I chanced to see those crimson cheeks.

But why then, if such were the case, did I call him Pavel Petrovich? You can only address someone you know this way.

I began to run through the forgotten first names in my memory. Such a first name I did not recall.

But here my attention stopped at the door to which

I had led the old man. Where had I seen that heavy engraved oak door? Without a doubt, I had seen it somewhere. I remember it perfectly. I even remember the copper plate on it. And the surname on the plate: Chistyakov.

What Chistyakov is this?

I began to run through the surnames in my memory. No, this one was not found among the surnames known to me.

There was a very famous artist Chistyakov. But what did he have to do with me?

For the sake of curiosity, I opened an encyclopedic dictionary to see by what names this artist was called.[77] And to my surprise I saw that the first name and patronymic corresponded to those I had pronounced in my dream.

This was the renowned Russian artist Pavel Petrovich Chistyakov.[78]

Unexpectedly I remembered: he was my father's director at the Academy of Arts.

And suddenly, with unusual clarity, I recalled a forgotten scene.

3

Winter. Snow. Vasilevsky Island.[79]

I walk with mother along the street. We stop at a door with a copper plate: *Pavel Petrovich Chistyakov.*

I ring. A doorman answers. Mother says:

"Tell his excellency that the widow of Zoshchenko has come."

The doorman leaves and says on returning:

"His excellency requests that you wait here."

We sit down on a wooden settee. For a long time we sit looking at the exquisite broad staircase. We wait a very long time. I begin to whine. I'm bored. It's unpleasant to wait so long. I tell my mother.

"Since he hasn't come for such a long time, it

means he doesn't need us. Mama, let's go."

Mama tells me softly:

"It's not he, but we who need him. Now that Papa has died we should receive a pension. How much we receive will depend on Pavel Petrovich."

An hour passes. Finally an old man in a black frock-coat comes down the staircase. He's extremely old, emaciated, pale.

Mama bows respectfully to him. And asks about something.

The old man answers something with distaste, heavily stressing his o's.

The conversation continues three minutes.

We leave.

Mama takes me by the hand. And again we walk along the street. I say:

"Mama, I wouldn't have spoken to him so politely as you spoke to him."

Mama answers:

"What can you do, Mishenka, we're dependent on him."

"All the same. He talked badly to you. And he said goodbye badly—he immediately turned away."

Mama begins to cry.

I tell Mama:

"Yes, but he treated me still worse than you. He didn't even say hello or goodbye. And yet I'm not crying."

Mama cries still harder.

To console her I say:

"I have twenty kopecks. If you like, I'll hire a buggy and we can ride home."

I hire a buggy, and Mama and I sit down in the carriage.

4

It seemed to me this scene in the antechamber held

some significance in my life.

It seemed to me this scene had frightened me.

Indeed. The image of a beggar again stood before me. Yet this time the beggar was I myself.

I stood in an antechamber with an outstretched hand. I begged. And something was given to me. Perhaps I was afraid of becoming a beggar? Afraid of finding myself in the position of a miserable pauper? And that is why the image of a beggar frightened me?

I began to think about the beggars who roamed in great numbers down the old roads of my country. And of the great revolution which set itself the task of eliminating this poverty.

I began to think of that past world in which I had been born and had lived. Of that world which had created beggars, paupers, people who bow, bum, debase themselves.

Probably this world had frightened me. Instilled uncertainty. Created a bogeyman in the image of a beggar.

I remembered this world. Remembered people who used to surround me. Remembered our relationships.

Without a doubt, this was an unhappy world. It bore illnesses no less dangerous than those I describe in this book. It could have instilled apprehension, fear. Without a doubt, it could have created a bogeyman in the image of a beggar.

And so I remembered the world in which I had been born. The world of rich men and beggars. The world of paupers and almsgivers. The world which had frightened me.

What a strange and mixed feeling I experienced! And suddenly I understood that I would never see this world again. And I felt regret such as one often may feel for anything that has passed—especially the time of his own childhood. And what joy I experienced in this regret!

But what did I have to regret? What had I left behind in that past world? And why did I feel a tinge of regret for something which had frightened me?

I couldn't understand it. Couldn't find the words to express the cause of my regret. And then I related these feelings to a certain lonely woman. She was my coeval. But she considered herself to know more about the past world.

She said:

"I experience the same feelings. But they're not accidental, as with you. I have not ceased mourning for the past world, although eight years have gone by since we lost it."

I said:

"But look, the past world was a horrible world. It was a world of rich men and beggars. It could frighten people. It was an unjust world."

"Unjust it may have been," the woman answered, "but I still prefer to see rich men and beggars instead of these dreary, boring and humdrum scenes we see today, even if they are just. The new world is a crude, cloddish world. It lacks that decorative quality we are accustomed to. That sense of beauty which pleases our sight, our hearing, our imagination. And that's the source of our pain and our regret. As regards justice, I have no argument with you, though I suspect the shoe will wear down in time."

As I left this woman I began to think—could what she said be so?

I felt like recalling some exquisite scenes from the past. I fell to thinking of silken fabrics, of music in drawing rooms, of genteel words said upon meeting, of lacquered carriages driving through the streets.

I recalled a few scenes. No, they were not connected with my emotional agitation. They had not formed part of my recollections. It must be that they were a customary sight to me. It must be that they were not the slightest bit surprising, completely quotidian.

197

5

I would probably not have remembered these scenes if I had not thought what I am thinking now, if I had not tried to understand where this pain came from, this joy and regret.

At the Seashore

In a student uniform,[80] with a walking stick in hand, I go along the seashore.

The beach at Sestroretsky.[81] It's hot. Summer. A symphony orchestra is playing.

People have taken their places on the burning sand. Chic women in hats, with umbrellas in hand. Tubercular looking men in pince-nez, in pea-jackets.

Cute little kids stroll by. They're in hats, in socks, in shoes.

A pretty little girl is whining.

"Mommie," she says, "please let me take off my socks."

"No, that's not nice," says the mother. "We will take off our socks when we go swimming."

Everything is quite proper, boring. Hardly any suntanned bodies to be seen. Hardly any shouts, screams, laughter to be heard. Someone squeals going into the water. Someone reads poetry in a sing-song voice. Someone is brought beer on a tray.

My God, how unbearably boring...

"The Spirit is Higher, Young Man"

Tapping my stick against my tight pants, I go up to some acquaintances of mine. It's the renowned lawyer N. and his wife Madam N. N.

I like this lawyer's wife. I chase after her a bit.

Madam N. N. smiles as I come up. Modestly covers her body, forced skintight into a chic bathing suit. Waves a white fan made of ostrich feathers.

I sit down beside them.

Madam N. N. plays the coquette with me. But the conversation doesn't catch on. The husband is right beside us. It's stuffy.

"Sergei," she says to her spouse, "you really should go into the water. You don't have to swim, but you ought at least take a dip, my friend. It's good for your health."

Sergei, without a murmur, strips off his tussore jacket. Unfastens his silk suspenders. Undresses.

I see his wasted body. A caved-in, consumptive chest. And the pitiful arms, devoid of muscles.

Catching my gaze upon him, the courtroom laborer mutters:

"The spirit is higher, young man. The spirit, and not the body—therein lies our concern, our beauty."

Stepping gingerly on the sand, Sergei, as if over nails, walks toward the water.

His arms, thin and lifeless, dangle like lashes.

We Listen to a Poema

An elegant drawing room. Silken furniture. Lacework. Tulle. Porcelain knickknacks. French patter.

The host: pale, languid, weary. Something decadent in his face.

Softly gesticulating, he reads his verses. He reads a poem about some "primogenitive" beauty which all people should strive for, about a refined suffering soul astray in the crude world, the world of vile passions. The reading is interrupted by a shout of some kind in the antechamber.

The host frowns. His brow furrowed with suffering, he listens as the housemaid quietly reports something to him.

Unexpectedly a woman appears at the threshold of the drawing room. She's not young. Poorly dressed. Gray hair sticks out from under her small hat.

"What kind of game are you playing with me, Pierre?" she says. And catching sight of the guests, she continues: "No, I don't care if you do have guests. Let everyone know what a scoundrel you are. Your late father, my own brother, ordered you to give me one hundred rubles a month. But what are you doing? What are you doing, you despot, making fun of me?"

Frowning all over as if from a toothache, the host says quietly:

"Go away, Aunt Lizet. Father didn't tell me that. Take it to court."

Maid and host show the aunt out. Unexpectedly she falls at the threshold.

"She's faking," says the host. And pulling paper money out of his pocket, he throws it at the aunt.

The door to the drawing room closes. We do not see the continuation.

Covering his eyes with his hand, the host begs his guests' forgiveness for an unavoidable scene. One of the guests says:

"How well your poema matches what happened! What a crude world! And what good fortune that we can avoid it, shut ourselves off from it with poetry, with spiritual solitude..."

The host continues to read his interrupted poema.

On the Back Stairs

On the slats of the stairs sit some workers. They're dirty, ragged. Some of them wearing bast shoes.

These are seasonal workers. They're making an extension of the house into the courtyard. And today, on Sunday, they've come to the owner to receive their weekly wages.

200

One of them says:

"No, they don't like to pay right away. They keep people waiting, and only then they pay."

One of the workers rises, goes up to the door and knocks uncertainly.

The housemaid appears at the door. She's in a little white apron. On her head is a starched white headdress.

The maid says:

"Now why are you knocking, you devils... Seems you were told the master was busy. Come this evening."

The worker says:

"If we come this evening they'll say—come in the morning. We get the same runaround every week. Be so good, inform the master that, you know, the people are waiting..."

The maid answers spitefully:

"The master is busy. He won't pay you today. Go ask the goblin in the wood."

The door slams shut.

I sit at the windowsill with Valya. Valya is the owner's daughter. We are both fifteen. We like to flirt with each other. For the last hour we have been sitting at the windowsill and chatting about something.

I ask Valya:

"Valechka, what is your papa doing?"

Lowering her eyes in embarrassment, Valya says:

"Annelle has come to him again. When Mama was alive she didn't dare come. Now she's been coming. I'm afraid Papa's going to marry her. She's been with him since morning. They're getting ready to go to the races."

I look at the seasonal workers seated up and down the stairs. Some of them are smoking. Others drink and have a bite to eat.

Valya and I look out the window...

6

Like lost visions these little scenes from my past

life flash before me. What unpleasant scenes, what bitter memories! What a beggarly beauty!

That's why I'm glad I will no longer see the world which has departed, the world of unprecedented injustice, indigence and undeserved wealth! That's why I'm glad I will no longer see weak-chested, consumptive men whose hearts shelter both refined, higher feelings and barbarian designs!

So I have no cause for regret. But it did exist, this regret, and this pain did remain. And again I could not understand where this pain came from.

Perhaps it came from the sad scenes I had seen of people parting with this world. I was a witness to how this world departed, how this flimsy beauty, this decoration, this elegance slipped from its shoulders.

I remembered a certain poet: A. T-v.[82]

He had the misfortune to live longer than he should have I remember him well before the Revolution, in 1912. And then I saw him ten years later.

What a terrible change I observed. What a horrible example I saw.

All the tinsel had vanished, gone. All the elevated words were forgotten. All the high-flown thoughts were lost.

Before me was an animal more terrible than any other, for it dragged the seasoned professional abilities of a poet after itself.

I met him on the street. I remembered the little smile which used to slide over his lips—slightly ironic, enigmatic. Now the smile was replaced by a predatory grin.

Digging into his torn briefcase, he pulled out a thin little book, just off the press. Making an inscription on the book, the poet, with a ceremonious bow, made me a gift of it.

My God, what the little book contained!

For at one time the poet had written:

Like maidens, recently betrayed,
The flowers looked so sad and meek.
Like bitter tears, the foamy drops
Descended from their waxen cheeks.

Now, ten years later, the same hand had written:

Wide the hips, and red the lips,
Smartly plink the ivories.
Darling little prostitutes,
You'll do anything to please...

All in place, and all to work,
Each one offers goods for gold:
Prostitute—her ample flesh,
I—my talent and my soul.

In this little book, published privately by the
author (1922), all the verses were extraordinary. First of
all, they were talented. But at the same time they were
so horrible that it was impossible not to shudder when
you read them.

In this little book there was a certain poem entitled
"Prayer for Food." Here is what this poem had to say:

Food so tasty, food so sweet,
O my fate, provide for me—
And in turn I will perform
Any base and loathsome deed.

I'll throw smut in a pure heart.
Wings of thought I'll gladly trim.
I'll steal this, and I'll rob that,
Kiss my worst foe's feet for him.

These lines were written with extraordinary power.
This Smerdyakovian-inspired poem is nearly touched
with genius. At the same time the history of our litera-

203

ture surely does not know any comparable cynicism, any comparable human decline.

But then this was not a decline, a collapse, a death in one's lifetime, a rotting away. The poet remained healthy, flourishing, strong as before. With exceptional zeal he pursued the joys of life. But he no longer wished to lie. He had stopped faking. Stopped babbling words like waxen cheeks, maidens, bosoms. He exchanged these words for others closer to his heart. He tossed off all the tinsel he had draped over himself before the Revolution. He became what he was in actual fact—a naked, disgusting beggar.

7

And this poet T. really did become a beggar. He chose a well-deserved path for himself.

I caught sight of him once on the corner of Liteiny.[83] He stood with his head bared. Bowed lowly to all who passed by.

He was beautiful. His graying head was almost magnificent. He looked like Jesus Christ. And only a keen eye could detect in his aspect something horrible, disgusting—a puss with the frozen little smile of a man who had nothing more to lose.

For some reason I felt ashamed to go up to him. But he called out to me himself. Called out loudly, by my surname.[84] Laughing and snickering, he began to relate how much he earned in a day. Oh, this was much more than the earnings of a literary man! No, he did not regret the changes. What difference did it make how you live in the world before you die like a dog!

I gave the poet almost everything I had in my pockets. And for this he wanted to kiss my hand.

I began to shame him for these debasing acts he had chosen for himself.

The poet cackled. Debasing acts? What are they? It's debasing not to feed your face. Debasing to die like a dog before your appointed time. Everything else—is not debasing. Everything else is in keeping with the present life which fate handed him in exchange for the past.

An hour later I went by the same street again. To my surprise, the poet stood on the corner as before, bowing and asking for handouts.

It turned out that he had not left, even though I had given him a considerable sum of money. To the present day I still don't understand it—why didn't he leave? Why didn't he rush immediately to a beerhouse, a restaurant, home? No, he remained standing and bowing. It must be that this did not weigh on him. Perhaps it even afforded him a certain interest. Or was it not yet time for his lunch, and the poet remained on the street merely for the exercise.

I met T. a year later. By now he had lost all resemblance to a human being. He was dirty, drunken, ragged. Tufts of gray hair stuck out from under his hat. On his chest hung a cardboard box with the sign: *Give to a former poet.*

Grasping at the arms of the passersby and cursing foully, T. demanded money.

I do not know his eventual fate.

The image of this poet, the image of a beggar, remained in my memory as the most horrible thing I had ever seen in my lifetime.

I could have been frightened by such a fate. Could have been frightened by such feelings. Such poetry.

I could have been frightened by the image of a beggar.

8

And so, thinking about this unhappy poet, I involuntarily began to remember the poetry of my time.

I remembered the touching and sorrowful romances which were sung then: *O, this is but a dream; Burn, burn, my star; Chrysanthemums in the garden.*

I will not conceal from you—tears appeared in my eyes when I suddenly recalled these forgotten sounds.

"So that's where my regret comes from," I thought. "That means I mourn not the 'beautiful world' of rich men and beggars, I mourn the sad poetry which was in my blood. Perhaps it really was good—this poetry?"

I began to recall the verses of my time.

They were superb verses, superb poetry. The poetry of Blok, Esenin, Akhmatova.

But what pain one felt in it! What sad melodies these poets sang! Why?

And suddenly I remembered the verses of Valery Bryusov:

> **But you, who come to destroy me,**
> **I meet with a hymn of greeting.**[85]

Why did he speak this way? Why did he not say that he meets with a hymn of greeting those who will destroy injustice, crying inequality, penury. No, we know that the poet welcomed the Revolution. He aligned himself with it and followed in its wake so as to see the new world, the new people. But why then had he applied such cruel words to himself?

I began to leaf through Bryusov's verses, his diaries, letters.

I saw that he was no minor poet. But how uneven he was! What melancholy came over him at times!

What hysterical notes one heard in his music, in his thoughts! What catastrophe dwelt in his heart!

Without a doubt, he did not consider himself a healthy, full-fledged human being. And that is why he spoke that way.

It must be that he did not want art to rest in the trembling hands of neurasthenics. He did not want it to inculcate the same old feelings, the same old people.

What cruel words were pronounced! What a hellish

206

way out was found!

But perhaps this catastrophe, hysteria and melancholy were peculiar to only the great poets by virtue of their higher mission, higher sensitivity, higher consciousness?

Perhaps all the other poets sang triumphant hymns to nature with bravura voices?

I began to leaf through the verses of my time.

No. The same thing again. Only worse. More pallid. More horrible.

Blok had united all the feelings of his time in himself, as in a focal point. But he was a genius. He ennobled with his genius everything that he thought, wrote.

The lines of the lesser poets, denied this nobility and taste, were horrible:

> The fairy's eyes are emerald,
> These eyes she turns down to the grass.
> Her tresses are a miracle:
> Now opal, chrysolite, topaz.[86]

What a flowery, beggarly language! What an operatic fantasy in a poet who was, in fact, not all that bad!

> My princess, she has a palace so high,
> And seven gold columns it has,
> My princess, she has a garland so fine
> With jewels in all seven sides.[87]

No, it is unpleasant to read these verses. Unbearable to hear this impoverished, infantile music. Disgusting to see this tinsel, these pitiful, mannered symbols.

I am leafing through the poetic anthologies of my time.

With a cold heart, without a drop of excitement, I read what we used to read and, it must be, used to love.

I don't trust myself, I only trust
The remote and scintillating stars.
For these stars send trusty dreams to me,
Dreams that spread throughout the milky way,
And there blossom in a timeless desert
Flowers of another world for me.

No. I feel no pity for this forfeited poetry. No pity
for these lost "flowers of another world."
I feel no pity either for the lost bravura which I
encounter in some other poems:

I trust the principle of light,
I know the dark's dismal truth.
In the gloom I was rocked by the Night
So I could beflower the Depth.

God be with it, this bravura poetry. It's disgusting:

I'll break your sweet little fingers
In my tender, fiery grasp
And then smother you with kisses,
Crush you to death in my clasp.

I leaf through the luxurious journals of my time.
Here is Balmont writing poetically about the girlfriend
of Edgar Allan Poe:
"Sorceress and slave of her feminine fears, a
woman who loved an angel, a demon, a spirit, someone
more than a man, and therefore a woman who knew
fear—tender Sybil, enticing both herself and another
soul into the enchantment of love..."
And still more:
"Harbinger of the Unbounded, herald of the depths
and bearer of the mysteries—deathless Edgar, who in his
term of service on earth took on the great necessary
burden of showing us how alone the soul of Man may be
among people..."

The tears have long since dried in my eyes. No, I no longer regret anything. I don't regret the loss of that world.

9

"But where have I strayed?" I thought. "What psychological jungle has the beggar led me into, the beggar whom I obediently followed in the hope of finding the cause of my fear of him?"

I don't know what new steps lie before me, nor what disappointment awaits me should I proceed further along this path.

But I caught myself in time. I understood that I was reasoning incorrectly, proceeding incorrectly.

For I had to find the cause of my infant fear of the beggar, and not the cause of my adult fear.

But could my apprehensions, anxieties, feelings, verses and the past world with which I had parted be understood by an infant?

But could the beggar-image be understood by an infant?

No, the beggar-image is not an image understood by an infant.

If such is the case, how did it arise? How come it appeared in my dreams?

I remembered the principle of dreaming. Remembered what a dream is from the viewpoint of science.

I shall repeat it, if only in brief. This is of primary importance.

Our brain has two stories. The upper story is the cortex of the brain and the subcortical centers—here lie the sources of acquired traits, the centers of conditioned reflexes, the centers of our logic, speech. Here lies our consciousness. The lower story is the source of inherited reflexes, the source of animal traits, animal instincts.

These two stories, as we have said, frequently come

into conflict. The upper forces struggle with the lower, conquer them, press them down still lower or expel them altogether.

At night the upper story subsides in sleep.

Consciousness fades out, control is weakened.

But since the inhibition of consciousness descends no lower than the subcortical centers, the lower forces come to life and, taking advantage of the weakened control, appear in dreams. Fears come to life which were inhibited or suppressed by consciousness.

Such, in outline, is the general picture of dreaming. And such are the mechanisms which form the basis for our dreams.

It would appear quite simple by means of a dream to reveal the cause of a pathological inhibition, to detect this or that suppressed feeling, to understand the image arising in dreams.

Yes, it would be quite simple if the upper and lower stories "spoke" to each other in the same language. However, the "occupants" of these stories do not speak in the same tongue. The upper story thinks in words. The lower story thinks in images. It may be assumed that this imaginal thinking is peculiar to animals and in equal measure to infants.

Due to this imaginal thinking, the dream frequently acquires a symbolic character. This makes sense: the simplest images, combined together, may create a symbol. And the complexity of these symbols is not always the same. The complexity is dependent upon the subject's development.

More than once we have seen how conditioned neural connections change and become complex along with one's mental development. In equal measure dreams change their meaning, change their significance in proportion to the growth of a man's consciousness, his character, his individuality.

Therefore, in order to understand an image from the lower story, one must speak in the language of an infant, one must look through its eyes. And at the same time he must decipher the symbolism which arises by virtue of the infant's imaginal thinking, taking into consideration, of course, the subject's growth and development.

This means the beggar-image is a symbolic image. This image was able to arise only by virtue of the infant's later mental development. And without a doubt more primitive images, understood by an infant, formed the basis for this image.

This means I should break down the beggar-image into its simplest components.

What components could create the beggar-image as an object of fear? It may be assumed that the symbol arose from the specific actions of a beggar.

What does a beggar do? He stands with an outstretched hand. He begs. His outstretched hand takes something.

Now here is something accessible to the understanding of an infant. The hand which takes something could frighten an infant. Out of these components the symbolic image of a beggar might eventually arise.

10

With perfect clarity I suddenly understood that I feared not the beggar, but his hand. I feared not the beggar who would take something from me, but the hand which would deprive me of something.

At once I understood that this hand was what I had been seeking. I understood that this hand which frightened me was the second conditioned stimulus in the complex combination of my infant psychoneurosis.

Some sort of hand was trying to seize me as I ran in a dream through a blue field, trying to save myself from the black water. Precisely this hand wanted to take, remove, steal something.

This hand of a thieving beggar and perhaps a murderer possessed the simple components which later helped create the symbolic image of a beggar, so horrible to me.

Thus: water and hand.

What conditioned connection could have been firmly established by the two stimuli I had found? What fateful repetition could have occurred in the life of a child?

And what exactly did this hand signify? And what did it want to take from me?

What does a beggar take, or rather his hand? It takes what people give: money, bread, food—handouts.

Without a doubt, a baby could regret that a beggar's hand would take something which belonged to him, the baby. But why was this regret accompanied by fear? This I could not understand. Then I began to remember the details of a dream in which a beggar had figured. I sit at some sort of a big table. The bell rings. Then there's a knock. I run to the door meaning not to open it, but to check to see if it is shut tight. A beggar stands behind the door. He pulls it toward him. Making a great effort, I prevent the beggar from opening the door. A struggle ensues. My heart is pounding from the fear and the physical exertion.

Horror seizes me when the door cracks open. But I make an effort and pull the door shut. I fasten the latch, on a chain. With relief I return to the table.

Was it really a beggar behind the door? Perhaps it was a thief? No, a thief would not knock and ring. It was definitely a beggar who wanted to take something from me.

What was it he wanted to take?

Again I could not understand. But then I understood that I experienced this fear not only in my dreams. I experienced it in the daytime as well. For I—as a boy, then as a youth, and finally as a man—would shout: "Shut the doors!" And every night I would check the latches and bolts on the doors, the windows. I could not fall asleep if the door was open. If the door had no latch or bolt, I put a chair in front of it and rested a suitcase or some other things on the chair, hoping that they would fall and awaken me should someone try to enter my room.

It must be that this dream was based on fact. It must be that this fear was present not only in my dreams.

What was this fear related to? What did the beggar want to remove from me? After all, I never regretted the loss of anything. On the contrary, I was even glad when something or other of mine got lost. It seemed easier and simpler to me to live without things.

In this case, what could have frightened me? What loss seemed irretrievable to me? What was I defending with such fear and trembling?

And finally, what did this frightening hand want to take, this hand which plunged an infant into water, punished it and made its unhappy little heart pound in fear?

VIII. TIGERS ARE COMING

He jests at scars that never felt a wound. **88**

1

When I first wondered what the hand signified and what it intended to take from me, I began to experience exceptional fear.

I had not previously experienced such powerful fear, not even at night. Now it arose in the broad daylight, especially on the street, in streetcars, when meeting people.

I understood that this fear arose because I was probing the deepest wounds, but still this fear shook me every time. Seeking escape, I began to flee from it.

It was ridiculous, unbelievable, even comical, but the fear vanished when I reached home, reached the stairs.

It left me right at the street entrance.

I wanted to struggle with it. Wanted to crush it, annihilate it—by will power, by irony. But it would not submit to me. It rose to an even higher level.

So I began to flee the street, people. Nearly stopped going out of the house.

But soon the fear penetrated my room as well. I began to be frightened of the night, darkness, food. Stopped sleeping in bed. Slept on the floor, on a mattress. Nearly stopped eating. The piece of bread I forced myself to swallow would bring on nausea, vomiting.

It seemed it was all over. It seemed the conclusion was fast approaching—a meaningless, brutal, shameful one.

By now nothing interested me. The game, it seemed, was lost. The struggle had ended in defeat. I was at the complete mercy of my fear. Darkness had descended around my head. Ruin more terrible than I had anticipated was at hand.[89]

Days came when I could neither lie down nor remain seated. Extraordinarily weak, I reeled from corner to corner, gasping from horrible heart seizures and unbearable spasms all over my body.

On my writing desk lay a small leaflet. In it were entered the dreams which had disturbed me. From time to time I turned to these dreams in the feeble hope of making some sense out of them. But they were incomprehensible to me.

I sought the hand, its significance, its connection with whatever had frightened me so badly. But the dreams said nothing about a hand. They spoke of tigers coming into my room.

I had had such dreams before. But now they were

unusually realistic. Tigers came into my room and, twitching their tails, followed my every movement.

I felt the hot breath of these tigers, saw their flaming bright eyes and terrible crimson maws.

The tigers did not always come into the room. Sometimes they remained outside the door. And then their horrible thunderous roaring was heard. The roaring shook the room. The dishes rattled, furniture fell, the curtains and pictures quivered on the walls.

No, these tigers did not tear me to pieces. After standing a while in the room or behind the door, they went away clattering their claws sharply on the floor.

One day a conjecture crossed my mind.

"What if," I thought, "the tiger is a symbol? A symbol just like the beggar-image?"

For the principle of all dreams is the same. The imaginal thinking on the lower story of the psyche and the further development of the baby create a symbolic system.

In the beggar-image I had detected the simplest components. I had detected the hand and the action of this hand—it takes, removes. It must be that in the tiger-image one should detect something more primitive, more accessible to the understanding of a small child.

The tiger is a predatory animal. What does it do? Leaps on its prey, seizes it, carries it away, tears it to pieces. It gulps it down. Rips its flesh with tooth and claw.

Unexpectedly associations were made with a hand. With that terrible greedy hand which also takes, removes, seizes something.

Without a doubt, these images were of the same order.

The hand of a beggar, a thief took on new qualities, qualities belonging to a savage beast—a tiger, a predator, a murderer.

217

2

I remembered a dream from long ago. Perhaps it was not even a dream. Perhaps my memory had retained something that had occurred when I was awake. But it stayed in my memory as a dream.

Through the distant fog of oblivion I remembered a confining room.

From out of the wall, toward me, there stretched a huge hand. The hand is already over me. I scream. Awake in horror. Want to jump out of bed. But I can't. The bed is covered by a net.

If this is a dream, then it refers to a time long ago. The little bed covered by a net indicates the period of infancy. Indeed, this dream is too primitive, too simple. It must have been dreamed at some time by the infant.

The baby dreamed about a hand. This hand, judging by its flared fingers, was about to take, to seize the baby. It is unlikely that the dream repeated a daytime occurrence. The daytime fear was evidently of a lesser intensity. Otherwise the dream would not have arisen.

In this case, what actually occurred in the daytime?

Evidently in the daytime a hand took, seized, removed something from the infant.

What is it that would have been so frightening for a hand to take, seize? Probably something extremely dear, valuable, almost as valuable as the infant itself.

What could be so valuable in the life of an infant? A toy? A baby bottle? The mother's breast? Nourishment?

It must be nourishment. Most likely, the mother's breast, the breast which feeds the infant, gives it life, nourishment, joy.

It must be that this breast had been removed by a hand.

If a hand had removed the breast, had withdrawn nourishment, then from the viewpoint of infant logic, this terrible hand could commit a new, even more heinous crime. The dream speaks of precisely this crime. The hand of a beggar, a thief, appeared at night in its new guise: it came after the infant itself. It wanted to take it, seize it, carry it away.

But then what was the source of the daytime fear, which became so magnified and complicated at night? What exactly took place in the daytime?

It could very well be that nothing special occurred in the daytime. Perhaps there was only that ordinary, everyday event in the life of every infant: the mother's hand removed the breast.

Perhaps the greedy little youngster, frightened by this frequent repetition, anxiously followed the hand which removed the nourishment, the breast, life. Perhaps the father's hand, placed on the mother's breast, frightened the baby still more.

But surely the same thing is repeated in every baby's life—a hand removes the breast, punishes, bathes. Why does this occur to others without leaving a trace, without traumatizing them, without causing a wound? Well, let's face it: we are dealing with an exceptional case. We have before us an extremely sensitive infant psyche— the psyche of a future artist, a fantasist. We have an instance in which such a sensitive psyche promotes the inception of illness.

In the present case we are not speaking of a normal development.

3

And so the hand removed the breast, nourishment. The hand came for the baby, to take it, seize it, carry it away.

But why was this hand associated with a tiger? Does this mean something else occurred?

And here, while analyzing the symbolic image of a tiger, I had a dream which confirmed the precision and

219

soundness of this symbol.

I saw a long corridor. Very bright. With a great number of windows. I go running down the corridor without stopping for breath. Someone is chasing me. Turning slightly back, I see a man with a knife in his hand. A long shiny, sparkling knife. The knife is borne above me.

Lunging forward, I run out of the corridor. A courtyard. Stones. I fall on the stones. Above me is the blue sky, the sun. Silence...

I immediately understood this dream. The windows of the corridor gave me a precise reference point. These were the huge bright windows of a hospital—evidently the operating room.

Without a doubt: the hand with a knife was the hand of a physician, a surgeon.

Unexpectedly I remembered a story my mother had told me a long time ago. My mother told of an operation when I was two years old. The operation was performed without chloroform, hastily, unexpectedly, my blood was infected.

I vaguely remember this story. The main thing I retained was that my mother spoke of her own suffering. She heard my horrible cry. And lost consciousness.

That is all I retained of my mother's story.

I began to examine my body, hoping to find some sort of scar, cut, left by the surgeon's knife.

I found the scar. It was almost three centimeters in length. It must have been a very deep cut if the scar remained for life.

Poor little thing. You can imagine his horror when the terrible hand which had brought him so much misfortune and anxiety armed itself with a knife and began to cut his pitiful little body. Without a doubt, this hand, or rather the possessor of the hand with these qualities, could be equated to a tiger. This was the hand of a predator, the paw of a bloodthirsty beast.

The poor little thing could not even imagine what

was being cut, why. He lay with his puny little legs cocked up, felt a hellish pain and saw the hand with a knife—the familiar hand of a beggar, a thief, a predator, a murderer.

What a striking and fateful correspondence!

What a confirmation of trauma! What a psychic castration! What a violent response might be made in the future to the conditioned stumulus!

But could such a violent response be made only to the second conditioned stimulus—the hand? No. Such a response could be made in equal measure to the third conditioned stimulus. This third stimulus was the breast. The mother's breast. The breast which had combined with the hand in a conditioned neural connection.

I again remembered the principle of conditioned reflexes. One stimulus conditionally connected with others (even in the absence of the second) creates two nidi of excitation which are equal in strength, for a conditioned neural connection has been made between the two nidi.

It must be that the breast seen by the infant created in him a second nidus of excitation, that nidus which was formed by the sight of a hand—the hand of a thief, a beggar, a predator, a murderer.

What a terrible perspective spread out before me! What a miserable life awaited the baby, the youth, the man! How much my character and behavior were already determined...

4

I began to remember my mother's stories. More than once she had told me of my childhood, my infancy. She smiled every time she related what a difficult, complex and capricious little boy I had been.

And well I might have been! Almost from my very first days a hellish conflict was present. I should have refused the breast, given up nursing, so as not to experience that constant fear, constant anxiety. But I could

221

not do this. I could not refuse the breast. Mother told me with a smile that she weaned me from the breast when I was two years and two months old.

"It was already becoming indecent," Mother said with a smile. "You already walked, ran, babbled verses from memory. But still you didn't want to give up the breast for anything."

Mother smeared her nipple with quinine so that finally I would be repulsed by this mode of feeding. Shivering with revulsion and horrified that the breast concealed new misfortunes, I continued to nurse.

It makes sense. It was a struggle. The struggle raged all the more violently the greater became the possibility of losing the thing I defended.

My poor mother, with a smile, related my childhood to me. But she stopped laughing every time the subject turned to my various peculiar habits.

I could not fall asleep while lying in bed with Mother. I would fall asleep only when alone in bed. And then only in complete darkness. Even the light from the little icon lamp would disturb me. Blankets were draped around my little bed.

Recalling these peculiar habits, Mother said that all this probably stemmed from her. Once when she breast-fed me, she experienced exceptional fear, exceptional anxiety, apprehension.

Perhaps, said Mother, these feelings were "sucked in with the milk."

In the summer there were horrible thunder storms. These storms, she said, occurred almost every day. And one day a most powerful storm blew up. Lightning struck in the yard of our dacha. A cow was killed. The barn caught fire.

Horrible thunder shook our whole dacha. This coincided with the very moment when mother had begun to breast-feed me. The clap of thunder was so strong and unexpected that Mother lost consciousness for a minute and released me from her hands. I fell on the bed. But awkwardly. Hurt my hand. Mother immediately came to herself. But all night long she could not calm me down.

You can imagine the unhappy youngster's new tribulation. The clap of thunder perhaps occurred at the very moment the baby took the nipple in its lips. Probably the baby approached and touched the breast with caution, for it concealed these dangers: a hand might come, might take, carry away, punish... And then the hellish clap of thunder, falling, the mother's senseless body. What a new proof of the danger of the breast!

What thunder was, what a storm was—the infant did not know. For it was becoming acquainted with the world for the first time, beginning to encounter things for the first time. That thunder could have occurred because its lips touched the breast. Who would prove it the contrary?

Mother said that the storms continued all summer. Therefore the claps of thunder could have coincided several times with the infant's nursing. Therefore a conditioned reflex could easily have been established in the infant's sensitive psyche, in that psyche already prepared for new miseries from hand and breast.

5

At night I heard a tiger roaring. The roaring recalled the distant rumblings of thunder. Perhaps these thunderous rumblings echoed a storm, a clap, thunder. Perhaps in some fantastic way they combined in the infant's consciousness with the mother's breast and imparted extraordinary new properties to this object.

The reader should not smile at these thoughts. For we are dealing here with an infant. We are dealing with the beginning of life, when the light of reason is still absent, when there is no logic, no consciousness We are dealing with a little animal become acquainted with the surrounding world, this terrible world where you must defend yourself from dangers at every step.

The symbolic image of a tiger, as it were, united all these dangers in itself.

The roar of a tiger or lion once heard by the little boy at the zoo added the final touch to this symbolic image.

I opened my notebooks intending to locate the corresponding entries, hoping to detect traces of a new duel—a struggle against predators with the aid of the knowledge corresponding to my mental development.

Yet I discovered no references to tigers in my notebooks.

Well, what of it! In life I had never encountered any tigers. I had seen them only in cages. I had been perfectly safe from them.

But then, while searching my notebooks for references to tigers, I came upon a whole series of singular entries.

These entries greatly surprised me. They were of a medical nature and touched mainly upon paralysis, stroke,[90] brain hemorrhage.

There were many medical references in my notebooks, but references to strokes were repeated with uncommon frequency. Here were explanations of causes, listings of symptoms, methods of treatment and prophylactics.

It looked as though I had sought to guard myself against brain hemorrhage. But I am not plethoric. More likely, emaciated. And young. It would seem I had had no reason to fear such a dismal end.

And here, while, pondering the causes of my worry, I unexpectedly associated this affliction—stroke, paralysis, hemorrhage—with the clap of thunder, with that "stroke" which had once frightened me.

Could this actually be that forgotten clap of thunder? Could it actually have undergone such changes as I developed that it degenerated into a new bogeyman?

Unexpectedly I remembered my book *Youth Restored*. My hand was still blind when I wrote it. I still did not understand a lot at that time. My searches then were directed mainly at consciousness. I gave too little attention to what lay beyond the threshold of consciousness.

What had guided my hand through this book?

This book, as it were, had served as protection. I was defending myself from dangers. I submitted the proofs of the dangers and showed how to struggle against them.

The ancient professor in this novella marries a young woman. For precisely this reason the professor is stricken by paralysis. He suffers a stroke, brain hemorrhage.

It must be that this thought—a stroke—had persistently clung to me. And I had been giving proof of its substance. It must be that the neural connections, as before, had conditionally combined two objects of fear.

I did not yet begin to unravel the whole chain of thoughts around these "painful" objects. But it became perfectly clear to me that the fourth conditioned stimulus in the complex combination of my psychoneurosis was undoubtedly—thunder, a stroke, a shot.

6

And so the unfortunate experience is found.

The thoughtless little creature, becoming acquainted with the surrounding world, made a mistake, taking things to be dangerous which were not dangerous.

Water and hand became objects of fear.

The breast and food in general began to cause the baby anxiety, fear, sometimes horror.

A conflict arose on the threshold of infant life.

A striking concurrence of circumstances reinforced this conflict, confirmed the soundness of these fears.

The sensitive infant psyche gave proof of their conditioned nature.

Water. Hand. Breast. Stroke.

The tiger became a symbol of danger.

An incomprehensible gulf, it seemed, arose between the strength of the stimulus and that of the response. It was all the more incomprehensible because a contradiction lay in the response itself: rejection and simultaneous longing, fear and love, flight and defense.

Four highly conditioned stimuli began to accompany the little boy down the unsteady roads of his life.

They acted on the infant with tremendous, overwhelming force, for frequently they communicated, sometimes simultaneously, closely linked temporary conditioned connections.

Temporary connections? Yes, they might have been temporary had they been established in the primitive psyche of a dog. Probably they would have been severed and extinguished had the mind remained unchanged. But the mind did change, consciousness developed and, concomitantly, the proofs of danger changed and rearranged themselves. The interaction was intense: the proofs were also highly conditional.

Yet it would seem this hand could be a bogeyman only in the period of childhood. No! Imaginal thinking elevated this hand into a symbol. The hand became a chastising hand, an imaginary, symbolic one. This symbol was level with the subject's mental development.

For what thing did this hand begin to chastise?

It began to chastise for precisely the same thing it had chastised in infant life—for food, the breast...

The conditioned proofs—genuine, logical and nevertheless conditioned—were always attached to the food!

Once the mother smeared her nipple with quinine so the baby would lose his urge for the breast. Food seemed toxic, poisonous. This was confirmed. Food frequently brought poisoning, pain, sickness.

226

Once a clap of thunder, a "stroke," coincided with the nursing. And this also had a confirmation. Food, it would appear, caused plethora—induced a stroke, brain hemorrhage.

Did this mean I should have avoided food? But it is impossible to avoid it. If so—death.

In this case, how should I have acted? I had to eat and suffer for the food. It seemed to me that this was the normal way.

I remember how I used to eat. Almost always standing, with extreme haste (it could be removed), carelessly, without interest. I expected retribution for the food, and it came, this retribution—illnesses, spasms, nausea.

I gulped powders to neutralize the danger of food. It seemed to me that science, medicine would relieve me of this danger.

I gulped down medicines in huge numbers, poisoning myself still further.

The final stage, however, was miserable, disastrous. I stopped eating. The abundance of conditioned proofs must have convinced me that food was a deadly danger.

This rejection of food came twice in my life. And I did not understand where it came from. And only now does the picture become clear, distinct, terrible. The conditioned neural connections were increasing in strength.

7

The chastising hand meted out punishment for the food. But the mother's breast was food only in the period of infancy. In the future the mother's breast came to personify woman, the feminine principle in general.

Does this mean that the image of a woman represented the chastising hand for me? Does this mean that I should fear woman in equal measure, avoid her, expect retribution, punishment?

Trembling, I leafed through my recollections. Trembling, I remembered my youthful life. My first steps. My first love encounters. Yes, without a doubt, I fled from woman. I fled from her and simultaneously drew toward her. I drew toward her in order to flee from her in fear of the expected retribution.

Scenes from my infant life acted themselves out in my adult years.

But surely I did not always flee from her? Yes, not always. Not every woman frightened me. I was frightened by whatever had frightened the infant.

But what exactly did I fear as an adult? What retribution did I expect? What chagrin did woman promise me?

I remembered a murder I had seen in my childhood ("The Shot").[91] A husband shot to death the lover of his wife. The chastising hand, armed with thunder, a stroke, a shot, meted out retribution for the woman who ran almost naked to us on the veranda.

Was this not proof positive of the danger of woman? Did there not follow on her heels—a shot, a stroke, a knife?

I remembered a young woman who had thrown herself in the water because of love.[92] I remembered Uncle Georgy who had gotten consumption because (as Mama said) he had loved many women.[93]

I remembered books which described murders because of love, horrible punishments, poisonings, duels.

The conditioned proofs of deadly danger were everywhere attached to love, woman.

The chastising hand—of a husband, brother, father—accompanied this image.

A shot, a stroke, consumption, illnesses, tragedies—here is the retribution for loving a woman, for doing what is not permitted.

There was something genuine in these proofs. Logic was not shaken. The conditioned situation seemed to be the truth. Nevertheless, the perception of it was unhealthy, conditioned. The strength of the sensation and the strength of the response did not correspond to the stimulation.

An extraordinary picture began to unfold before my gaze.

In an instant I understood everything I had failed to understand before. In an instant I saw myself as I really was—a dark little savage frightened of every shadow. Holding my breath, looking around, listening to the bellowing of tigers, I walked and ran through the overgrowth of the jungle. And what could there be in my heart besides despair and exhaustion!

No, I was not simply upset by what I had seen, understood. I was horrified, jolted, driven to desperation.

I remembered someone's words:

O my bitter experiments! And why did I want to know everything?
Now I will not die as quietly as I had hoped.[94]

But this was a momentary weakness, a momentary desperation. It arose from the shame that I had previously known nothing, that I had not previously guessed what nonsense, what bunk held me firmly in its grip.

With cold calculation I continued to think out the dire consequences of my unfortunate experience.

8

I remembered the story of my first heart seizure ("Finale").[95] What had happened then? There was a party, a banquet. The nurse Klava led me into her room. We kissed there. Then I went to the village, to my regiment. Got in bed by morning, probably around five o'clock. And at six o'clock the first bombs fell on

229

the village.

I remember exactly. I drifted off to sleep with memories of this woman. And hardly had I fallen asleep than the terrible explosion of a bomb shook the house.

My brain, perhaps weakened by alcohol that morning, understood the blow as my due. The infantile conceptions of long ago came to life. I would have to avoid subsequent "blows," subsequent meetings with this woman.

I felt ill. I grew short of breath. The response of my organism was neurotic, violent. And at the same time purposeful—I abandoned the "dangerous" places, severed the dangerous connection.

No, duty and conscience were not forgotten. I left for heart treatment, so that I could return to the ranks again. I left with precisely this firm intention.

I remembered the story of how I fell ill the last time ("In Tuapse").[96]

What happened then? I sat in a chaise lounge aboard a motorboat. I felt splendid. With pleasure I looked forward to Moscow, where I would meet my friends and the woman who loved me and whom I liked.

I remember exactly how I thought with chagrin of her husband. I sympathized with him. And I felt ashamed for deceiving him. He was very fond of me. He was very kind to me. It seemed he even had a condescending attitude toward my "romance" with his wife. What frightened me in this case? The little revolver stuck in his belt? More than once that thought had flashed through my mind. But did it arise perhaps from the dark cellars of my psyche?

I sat on the chaise lounge and admired the sea. I looked closely at the surface of the water. Perhaps beyond the threshold of consciousness old associations arose, old connections with water, hand, woman.

In the miserable hotel of Tuapse I sprawled out

on the floor. I remember exactly how I got up from the bed and moved to the floor. I moved at the moment a clap of thunder sounded and a storm began. Did I perhaps want to avoid the bed on which the infant drama was once enacted? There is no other way to explain this savage, ridiculous move. Without severing the connections, I moved away from the connections, fled from them.

9

Thus scenes of infancy acted themselves out with a force great enough to shock me. But wasn't I fully conscious? Yes, I was fully conscious. But my consciousness did not know the source of my miseries. It did not correct my actions, for it did not understand them. I was at the complete mercy of my fears. They seemed to be an illness, to be symptoms of those illnesses I suffered.

This unhealthy response arose with such violent strength at that time, because all four stimuli appeared almost simultaneously before me.

There was something purposeful in this response. I wanted to leave Tuapse for Moscow, but my miserable condition and especially my heart seizures blocked my path.[97] I refused the trip to Moscow. I returned home.

This was a flight—the simplest, most vulgar protective reflex.

This was a flight and a deceit.

But let me repeat, I did not flee every time and did not feign illness every time. I fled and feigned only when to a greater or lesser degree I encountered "painful" objects.

I remembered one surprising incident. Even now, fifteen years later, the color comes to my face.

I was walking arm in arm with a certain woman. In Peterhof.[98] We walked out to the sea. Unexpectedly I

231

felt bad. It seemed—my heart was stopping. I began to catch my breath.

My companion was frightened by the strength of my attack. She wanted to help me. But I asked her to go away, to leave me alone, saying that usually it gets better when I remain alone. Not without offense, she went away and two days later, with exceptional cruelty, told me that I had purposely acted out a heart seizure so as to part with her, so as to get rid of her.

I was irritated, shocked by her pettiness. I argued with her.

And only now do I understand that she was right.

Without a doubt, I had "acted out" that seizure, feigned an illness. But I had no idea that this was the case.

I refer to Nadya V., of whom I have written so much in my recollections.

Does this mean I fled from her? No, it couldn't be. I loved her. It's nonsense.

No, it's not nonsense. I really did flee from her.

10

No, I lack the strength to describe my life any further. And not simply because it makes me sad to remember it. It's irritating and humiliating for me to admit that such bunk held me firmly in its grip.

I refer the reader to my scanty recollections. To the little stories about my life. Now these stories are cast in an entirely different light. Now you can see almost everything in them.

In them you can see the four conditioned stimuli which acted on me with tremendous, overwhelming force.

In them you can see my unconscious fear. You can see my defense, fakery, flight. And that bitterness which darkened my life.

And that attitude toward women which they

did not deserve.

What a bitter and sorrowful life I experienced!

What a closed heart I would have to lay open again!

IX. DANGEROUS CONNECTIONS[99]

For thou dost fear the soft and tender fork
Of a poor worm... [100]

1

So then, this was a sexual psychoneurosis?

No, it was not a sexual psychoneurosis, but sexual motives did enter into the complex combination of the psychoneurosis. Yet they entered only at the time and to the degree corresponding to the subject's growth and development.

These sexual motives were not present in the original source of the psychoneurosis.

We have seen how the mechanisms of the psychoneurosis were established. They were established according to the principle of conditioned reflexes. The conditioned neural connections combined four "painful objects." One of these objects was the mother's breast. But this was also the breast of nourishment, of food. This object was bound up with the feeling of hunger, and not of eros. The loss of the object threatened the infant with death, destruction. His struggle and emotional conflict did not extend beyond the instinct of self-preservation.

Freud holds that all our impulses may be reduced to sexual drives, that eros forms the basis for our feelings, even an infant's feelings. But the present example, not to mention many others, points to something different. The sexual element is lacking in the mechanism of this psychoneurosis. And only the further development of the little boy introduced this motive.

Granted that this motive may have arisen in childhood, it was nevertheless absent at the time when the conditioned mechanisms were established.

The baby's fear and emotional conflict were based on cruder, more material, more substantial grounds. Objects whose conditioned nature was misunderstood by the infant: this is what caused the psychoneurosis and this is what inspired fear and joylessness.

The joy of satisfying hunger began to be accompanied by fear. The conditioned neural connections combined the joy with misery. It was precisely this conditioned connection which eliminated the joy and effected a castration.

The feeling of hunger and the fear of losing nourishment: this is what found a lively response and a well-prepared soil beyond the threshold of consciousness.

Our unconscious world is formed not only by inherent properties. Without a doubt, this world has constantly experienced and continues to experience pressures of another sort, pressures from without. The struggle for existence, the obtaining of food, labor: this is what exerts a tremendous influence on the subconscious.

Fears arise in precisely this area—the fear of losing nourishment, the fear of perishing, the fear of being deprived of food...

Consequently, by no means all of our impulses may be reduced to sexual drives. Fears based on social motives are no less potent. On occasion they may even prevail in the depths of our subconscious. And in any case they help prepare the soil for unhealthy conceptions.

The unconscious world is a world more extensive and more varied than the world one can imagine while gazing only at sexual impulses. To be sure, sexual motives also exert a tremendous force in this world. But they are by no means alone. And pathological inhibitions pertaining to sex form only a component part of the pathological inhibitions which characterize psychoneuroses.

The mechanisms of the brain discovered by Pavlov confirm this with mathematical precision.

2

It is impossible to discover the precise causes of nervous disorders without considering the laws of conditioned reflexes.

Without considering the established mechanisms, Freud saw the actions of other forces both in the normal and the pathological states—the conflict of the higher with the lower, the collision of atavistic drives with the feelings of modern civilized man.

Freud located the cause of psychoneurosis in the prohibition of these drives.

But then the prohibition of these animal drives and the entire struggle in this sphere is nothing but a moral category. This should oblige the theory to seek out moral disorders.

And this is precisely what happened. But not only this. When the theory encountered forces of a non-sexual nature, it began to subordinate them to forces of a sexual nature. Even in the feeling of hunger the theory described eros. In the fear of losing nourishment the theory discovered the fear of castration.

The theory was compelled to do this. Otherwise the "ends would not meet," the idealistic formulation would not be justified.

The theory confined itself to seeking out sexual disturbances. I by no means deny their tremendous force, their significance and influence in the development of a psychoneurosis. I suspect that most miseries derive from these forces. But it would be wrong to locate all of the misery in this alone.

I encountered this mistake at my very first practical session. The Freudian physician did not understand the significance of the hand which the baby had seen in its dreams. It seemed to him that the baby had associated the hand with an elephant's trunk. And that the trunk was supposedly a phallus.

The hand of a beggar, the hand of a thief which removes nourishment, the paw of a predator, a beast, a tiger, was transformed into that fabulous attribute which was certainly not dangerous, not frightening and in any event not comprehensible to an infant.

This example shows how the theory attempts to subordinate everything to the sexual element. The mistake is revealed here with striking clarity.

But then practice demonstrates that the Freudian method of psychoanalysis may effect a cure. Without a doubt, sometimes it may effect a cure. Any knowledge in this area, any control of the lower forces by reason, even a partial control, brings about a relief.

The light of logic expels or excludes these forces.

Freudian psychoanalysis, which is worked out so meticulously, should effect a cure in those cases in which sexual stimuli occupy an important place. Or rather in those cases in which the original conditioned stimuli were transformed into conditioned sexual stimuli.

But one may suspect that this cure will be incomplete, or rather not final. For the physician and the patient continue to encounter moral categories and fail to detect in them the mechanisms which must be corrected. They fail to see the neural connections which must be severed.

These conditioned neural connections continue to exist and to function. This promises a return to the illness and no doubt a tremendous resistance.

The essence of effecting a cure consists in locating these connections and severing them, disuniting the objects of fear, showing their actual negligibility.

3

And so, beyond the threshold of consciousness there appeared an extensive, rarely investigated world, the lower world, the world of an animal.

The infant's first impressions were received and retained with tremendous force. They happened to be mistaken, untruthful. And as a result they produced an illness, created a conflict, inhibited the subject's development and complicated his behavior and character.

The subject's mental development did not correct these mistakes. On the contrary, it reinforced them, proved their logic and elevated "painful" objects into symbols.

The conditioned connections continued to exist. The conditioned proofs—both false and genuine—continued to nourish and strengthen the neural connections.

This was an illness, an illness against logic, against common sense. This was a psychoneurosis which was none too easy to discover at first.

The subject's behavior remained reasonable for the most part. His actions in no way differed from the actions of a normal healthy man. Forces of another order—social, communal forces—exerted the primary influence and determined the manner of his behavior. And only on occasion did some sort of "eccentricity," some sort of oddity reveal itself in his actions.

This eccentricity was especially noticeable in the trifles of everyday life.

It was more convenient to sleep on a bed, but I most often slept on a sofa.

It was more convenient to eat at a table. But I ate standing up, hastily, sometimes on the way. I washed myself hastily, standing in the bathtub. I carefully shut the doors to my room, frightened of something or other.

I performed dozens of strange actions. They seemed nonsensical, illogical. But they contained their own iron logic, the logic of a man who wishes to avoid contact with "painful" objects. Only in such contact was it possible to discover the illness.

Perhaps in the future physicians will be able to reconstruct the picture of a patient's illness, to locate the sources of his delirium, by interpreting his strange actions and eccentricities. Perhaps this will prove easier than seeking the cause in his dreams. For all the actions of an "eccentric" are infantile, and they reproduce scenes from his infant life almost to perfection.

There was a time when the street frightened me. I began to avoid it. Stopped going by foot. At first this seemed an eccentricity. But beneath this eccentricity there lay a "purpose." At home there is less danger. On the street there are cows, dogs, children who might hurt you. On the street you might get lost. You might disappear, vanish. Gypsies, streetcleaners might abduct you. Carriages, cars might run over you. Outside the house are water, war, gas, bombs, airplanes...

The neural connections linked the street with dozens of misfortunes.

The conditioned proofs of the street's danger were numerous. Street and danger were made synonymous.

239

The connection between them was inseparable. The abundance of proofs led to the final stage—fear and the desire to avoid the street. It was on the street that I first experienced fear.

4

The street presented numerous proofs of danger. The conditioned neural connections linked woman as well with a great number of misfortunes.

Here the struggle and the resistance in the realm of feelings were even more intense. But the struggle and the resistance by no means proceeded along moral lines.

Freud holds that we usually see our mother or sister in other women. And this is the cause of taboos and inhibitions. Civilization and morality: these are supposedly the misfortunes which cause man to suffer. Without a doubt, a boy's first impressions, his first aroused sensations may relate to his mother and sister. This is natural. But the conflict is created not only by this moral category and not only by the fear of punishment: the conflict arises on contact with "painful" objects. The painful objects personify the mother and later, woman. It is not eros and the concomitant moral struggle that produce an inhibition. An inhibition arises from a fear which is conditionally connected with painful objects.[101]

It is not the Oedipus complex, but something more simple and more primitive which is present in our unconscious decisions.

Without a doubt, the moral struggle does exist, and it may be great, but it does not create this unhealthy conflict, it alone does not determine the nature of the illness, the nature of one's behavior.

Conditioned connections and conditioned proofs of danger: this is what decides the matter. The abundance and precision of conditioned proofs: this is what induces and compounds the illness.

240

At the same time these proofs, attaining maximum power, make the subject refuse contact with the "painful" objects.

That is why a catastrophe most often occurs not in one's youthful years, but in maturity, at 35-40 years of age. Up to this point, the subject somehow circumnavigates, maneuvers around the painful objects. They have not yet frightened him to the final degree.

But the abundance of "proofs" eventually deprives him of his last hopes.

Just as in sclerosis calx is deposited in our arteries and ruptures them, so these proofs, deposited on our psyche and weighing it down, frighten us, isolate us from life, deaden our tissues, castrate us and bring us to ruin.

Here perhaps is one of the causes of an early fading, an early death, decrepitude.

5

Without a doubt, this was a very severe case of psychoneurosis. The main arteries, through which life streamed, were affected.

Food and love, water and the chastising hand, foretold a most pitiful finale. Disaster, it seemed, was unavoidable. Disaster from cold, from fear and perhaps even from thirst. The fear of punishment and the mania of persecution might take part in the finale.

This finale could easily have been called a psychic illness. But at the same time it was nothing but a violent response (more correctly, a complex of responses) to conditioned stimuli. Moreover, the response was purposeful from the viewpoint of the unconscious animal psyche. The protective reflex formed the basis for this response. Defense against danger was the basis...

Reason did not control this response. Logic had been broken. And fear acted on me with pernicious intensity.

This fear held me fast in its grip. And it did not soon leave me. It squeezed me ever tighter the deeper I delved into that astonishing world whose laws I could not understand for such a long time.

But I managed to cross the threshold of this world. The light of my reason lit up the horrible slums where the fears were lurking, where barbarian forces found refuge, forces which had so darkened my life.

These forces did not retreat when I came upon them. They took up the battle. But the battle was uneven. I had already suffered defeat in the darkness. Without knowing with whom I struggled, without understanding how I should struggle. But now, as the sun lit up the dueling place, I spied the miserable, barbarian snout of my enemy. I spied his naive ruses. I heard his bellicose cries which previously had so frightened me. But now that I had learned the enemy's tongue these cries ceased to frighten me.

And then step by step I began to crowd my opponent. And he, in retreat, found the strength in himself to continue struggling, making convulsive efforts to remain, to live, to function.

But now my consciousness controlled his actions. Now I could parry his blows with ease. Now I met his resistance with a smile.

And then the grip of fear began to weaken. And finally stopped. The enemy fled.

But what this struggle had cost me!

I rolled around in my bed. My weaponry—paper and pencil—lay beside me. And sometimes I even lacked the strength to pick them up again.

It seemed that life was leaving me.

As it is said in Goethe:

Whoever wants to study something living
Must always kill it first of all.[102]

242

I was slain, torn apart, cut to pieces, so that I might rise again from the ashes.

I lay almost without breathing, expecting that my opponent would return again and then all would be over. But he did not return.

From time to time the customary symptoms appeared, but they were not accompanied by fear.

Life began to return to me. And it returned with such speed and force that I was startled and even perplexed.

I got up from the bed a completely new man. Unusually healthy, strong, with a great joy in my heart, I arose from my bed.

Every hour, every minute of my life was filled with some sort of rapture, happiness, exultation.

I had not known this before.

My head became unusually clear, my heart opened up, my will was free.

Almost stunned, I followed my every movement, action, wish. Everything was remarkably new, amazing, strange.

For the first time I perceived the taste of food, the smell of bread. For the first time I knew what sleep was like, tranquility, rest.

I nearly ran in circles, not knowing how to direct my barbarian forces, so uncustomary for me, so unfettered.

Like a tank I moved through the fields of my life, overcoming all obstacles, all barriers with ease.

I very nearly caused myself many misfortunes by not keeping my new steps and actions within bounds.

And then I thought over my new life. And it seemed to me less attractive than at first. It seemed to me that I had begun to bring people more grief than before, when I was fettered, feeble. Yes, this was the case.

And then new tears came in my eye,

> And I felt troubled and would fain
> I had not left my recent chain.[103]

The choice stood before me: to go back without consolidating what I had won, or to go forward. Or to turn my new forces over to art—to that which I had previously taken up by necessity, because I was unable to realize my feelings fully other than on paper.

But now my reason was free. I was at liberty to do whatever I wanted.

I again took up what my hands had once held—art. But now I took it up without trembling hands, with no despair in my heart, with no sorrow in my gaze.

An unusual path spread open before me. I have been walking this path now for many years. And for many years I have not know gloominess, melancholy, despair. I have forgotten what color they are.

I make only this reservation: I do not feel despair without cause. I still know, of course, what a lousy mood is: it comes from external causes.

6

Yet what was the source of my cure? What mechanisms were corrected? Why did the old fears take leave of my person?

They took leave of me simply because the light of my reason had cast light on the illogical nature of their existence.

These fears were linked to objects which were not so dangerous as the infant had supposed.

To sever these false, conditioned, illogical connections: this was the task at hand.

I severed these connections. Separated the true misfortunes from the conditioned objects of fear. Assigned these objects of fear their proper significance. And the cure consisted in this. The absence of logic was cured by logic.

Yet it was not always a simple matter to sever these conditioned neural connections. Some connections were unusually complicated, entangled, contradictory. There was something so absurd, even comical about them that it seemed they could have no significance. But every time it was necessary to consider the position of the infant, it was necessary to look through its eyes, to think with its images, to fear its fears.

Thunder, water and hand varied in many ways. Sometimes the neural connections extended from these objects to other objects. Sometimes the imaginary dangers from these objects were ludicrous. And nevertheless, no matter how ludicrous these dangers may have been, the fears took root and affected me throughout my whole life.

The chastising hand pertained equally to food, and to woman, and to work. And to my entire behavior. A stroke, a shot, brain hemorrhage: this was the expected retribution. Obviously the strength of the sensation did not correspond to the stimulus.

I have already related the dream in which water filled my room, seeped from all the cracks in the floor and began to rise and threaten me with disaster. Even in this ridiculous dream one must see the infant's fear and the consequences of this fear, its conditioned symbolism.

I do not consider it possible here to enumerate everything I have encountered. This book is not a manual of medicine...

Still, as regards conditioned connections, it is necessary to say the following.

Every time I severed these conditioned neural connections, I was startled, dumbfounded: how could they have functioned? But they did function, and to a degree inimical to my existence. And every time it was necessary to "get down on all fours" in order to destroy them.

I severed and destroyed the neural connections

245

which had brought me so many miseries.

And once these conditioned connections were severed, I was freed from inhibition, from that pathological inhibition which arose on every contact with a "painful" object.

The ordinary protective reflex had formed the basis for this inhibition.

I cannot say that this reflex vanished entirely. Certain symptoms of a mechanical nature remained. But their logic was rendered entirely harmless—they ceased to be accompanied by fear. And as a result they gradually began to die out...

7

I promised my friend the physiologist not to make any generalizations in my work.

I remember well his warning: "Don't promise people anything."

All right, then! I am speaking only of my own life, my own sad days and the days of my emancipation.

I do not go beyond the confines of my own illness, which I successfully abolished.

Yet there can be no doubt that people with my qualities, my sensitive psyche, could suffer similar miseries. And here, it occurs to me, one can make a generalization—within the confines of those illnesses grouped together under the general term of "psychoneurosis."

Yet if science does not agree with me or find any generalization too bold, I will not insist on it.

So, I thought, my illness was something exceptional. And Allah helped me to save my hide, contrary to all the existing laws, by which I should have ended my transitory path on earth in such a lamentable manner.

But another generalization was forced upon me. The laws of conditioned connection pertain to all people. Not in equal measure, but to a greater or lesser degree, they are dangerous even to people who do not possess my sensitive psyche.

These conditioned connections are dangerous to all people who are not controlled by their reason. I remembered one unusual case. And immediately after it, I remembered a whole series of such cases. And now I will tell you some of them.

The Case of a Young Woman

In a dispassionate tone, without raising her voice, a young woman told me of her grief.

She wanted to have a baby. Then she and her husband would be happy. Only in a baby did they see the complete embodiment of their love.

But fate persecuted them. She was pregnant for the third time. And for the third time, evidently, she would not give birth. The pregnancy proceeded very irregularly and with such abnormal developments that the physicians again would insist on an abortion. For the third time she would have to lie on the operating table.

I look at the tormented, uncommonly weary face of the young woman. The tears have probably already been shed. What remains—indifference, resignation, almost equanimity. And only by her convulsively clenched hands can I see her internal commotion, the hell and uneven struggle which will end in defeat.

I am shocked somewhat by the force of her grief.

Suddenly it seemed to me that the reaction to this grief did not correspond to its true dimensions.

And so I asked the woman whether her first pregnancy had been connected with some sort of distress.

"No," said the woman, looking calmly at me.

Then, becoming embarrassed and blushing, the woman said:

"My first pregnancy? My very first? But that one was not now, not with my husband."

Extremely embarrassed, the woman said that she first became pregnant when she was 17 years old. She was

247

a school girl. She had to hide her pregnancy from her parents, from the school. She hid it until the last month. Then she went to a girlfriend's place outside of town and there gave birth to a dead baby. She had completely forgotten about this, which is why she said that there had been no distress. Of course there had been. Tremendous distress.

Immediately everything became clear. She had hidden her pregnancy, had been horrified by it, frightened, desperate. Her protest had been great, her grief extraordinary. Pregnancy and grief had been connected with one another, identified with one another.

The conditioned reflex remained. The neural connections were not severed even when the situation changed. The brain did not take note of the change in her fate. The new pregnancy was again perceived as grief. The response of the organism was violent.

I said nothing more to the woman, but she herself suddenly understood what was wrong with her. Wringing her hands, she said:

"Could that really be it? Could it really come from that?"

I told the woman:

"Yes, that is it. You have to sever these conditioned connections. Separate the past from the present. Control your actions and your condition."

I read embarrassment and then triumph on the face of this woman.

A week later she phoned me to say that she was better. A month later she said that she was nearly well and would give birth to the baby.

She actually had a successful delivery.

The Case of a Young Man

An extremely handsome young man came into my room.

248

He was tall, healthy, even flourishing. Yet in his eyes there was something surprisingly sad. I read some sort of woe in his gaze. Dark, almost black shadows showed beneath his eyes.

He said:

"Please listen to me. I know that you are not a physician. But for some reason it seems to me that you can help me."

With complete candor I said that I could barely cope with my own miseries, and I categorically refused to inquire into the indispositions of others.

Then he began to cry. I'm not exaggerating. The tears gushed from his eyes. And like a child he began to rub his eyes with his fists.

There was something extremely infantile, babyish, in this gesture.

Wishing to console him, I asked him to relate what was wrong with him.

He began to tell me all about his illness. He had a neurosis of the stomach so intense that he had to isolate himself more and more from people. He had been treating it for a long time, traveling to health resorts. But there was no improvement. On the contrary, he was worse. He was unhappy. He avoided society. He had lost all the joys of life. Nausea, vomiting, spasms of the stomach and intestines—such was his pitiful lot.

I asked if an analysis had been made.

The young man said:

"Yes. They found excessive acidity. The diagnosis was a serious form of stomach neurosis."

I asked:

"When are your attacks most violent? Under what conditions?"

"They are most violent," he said, "when I'm around people, in society."

"And do you have these attacks at home?"

"Very rarely at home."

"But when? When you are waiting for someone? A

249

woman?"

He nodded his head in silence. And I began to ask him questions, excusing myself for intruding into his private life.

Turning pale and flushing, he gave his answers.

Then I began to question him about his childhood. He remembered little of it. But suddenly he related a story he had heard from his mother. His mother once fell asleep while he was at the breast. She came out of her slumber when the baby was nearly blue. They revived him only with difficulty.

I did not question the young man any further. The neural connections were quite obvious. The response of the organism was obvious. The desire to avoid disaster lay in the infantile response. The conditioned connections were not severed.

However, a careful, thoroughgoing analysis was required. I wrote a note with my deduction and directed the young man to a physician.

Sated

In the days of my youth I once met an amazing woman.

She was exceptionally attractive. But it seemed she was created only for love and nothing more.

All of her ideas and intentions were directed toward love. Nothing else interested her or touched her. She was, as it were, concentrated solely in one direction.

There was something stormy in her temperament. Like a meteor she coursed through other people's lives.

Many men who had an affair with her were scorched by her passion.

Some of them were ruined by their love for her. One hanged himself from the porch of her home. Another shot at her. And she was wounded. A third nearly strangled her. A fourth spent huge sums of

250

money on her, was sentenced and sent away.

Her unhappy husband did not have the strength to give her up. He looked spellbound on her affairs. Forgave her all her transgressions. He considered her an exception, one of a kind. He did not see any promiscuity in her behavior. He supposed that this was her normal way.

When he learned I was seeing her, he came to me and silently placed a sheet of paper on my desk: it was a list of her lovers. This was the way he warned me about her. This was the way he wanted to save her for himself.

No, she did not bring me any unhappiness. In those years, the years of my melancholy, it seemed that nothing could touch me.

Almost indifferent, I parted with her, and she was offended that I did not hang myself and did not even cry. And was apparently even glad.

She went to the Urals. And from there to the Far East. And I did not see her for eleven years.

And then I once met her on the street. It turned out that she had returned to her native city a long time ago. Well, it was not so surprising that I had not heard anything about her: she lived very quietly, did not go about. Everything bored her—both people and feelings.

I looked at her closely. No, she was as attractive as before. Her stormy life found no reflection in her aspect. It even seemed to me that she had become more beautiful than before. And all the same—what a monstrous change had taken place in her!

"Bored with everything?" I asked her. "Don't love anyone?"

Shrugging her shoulders, she said:

"No one. Bored with everything. Except for loathing, I have no feelings."

"Are you sated?"[104]

"I must be," she said. And her eyes clouded over with unusual sadness.

251

"Did something happen, occur during these last years?"

"No," she said. "Nothing occurred. It's the same old thing as before..."

"Yes, but that was no small thing," I said. "There were dramas, scandals, a shooting, abortions three times a year..."

With a sad laugh she said:

"Of course, once this brings only distress, what use is it to me?"

And in this answer of hers, said quite artlessly, I suddenly saw everything, saw the cause of her "sated" condition.

All the time, without ceasing, her love, her desires were connected with unhappiness. When would the end ever come? Come it did. Love and unhappiness became synonymous. The conditioned connections bound them firmly together. Better there should be no more desires than misfortune all over again.

I looked again at the young woman. I was about to tell her the causes of her unhappiness. But I kept silent. And not because she would not have understood me. No, it seemed to me that she was better off the way she was.

We began to say goodbye. She extended a flaccid hand toward me. An indifferent gaze slid over me. And with slow strides she wandered down the street.

I began to feel sorry for her. I wanted to shout to her, to stop her, to tell her what was wrong with her. But I didn't do it.

Let her stay the way she is, I thought.

8

No, I do not gaze good-naturedly on everything that takes place around me—I do not make a habit of analysing other people's actions and do not take any special delight in concerning myself with other people's affairs.

I live as it befits a man to live: thinking within good measure and not turning my head into an instrument for inquiring into other people's miseries.

But in those years when I first came upon these matters, I observed people with interest and excitement.

I was especially excited by the unhealthy "responses" of people which occurred beyond the control of their reason. These responses were sometimes so monstrous and ridiculous that it seemed their significance was unfathomable. But on reflection I became convinced every time of the purposefulness of these responses. Of course, from the viewpoint of common sense this purposefulness was ridiculous. But I immediately found sense in it if I translated what was ridiculous into the language of an animal or an infant.

In a neurotic's every action and sometimes even in his death one could see flight, the desire to get away from "painful" objects, the impotence to sever the conditioned connections.

I will tell you a few astonishing stories. They are true.

An Unexpected Finale

A girl from the university came into my room. She was a very young woman of pleasing appearance.

She was taking her final examinations. And she needed some material on my literary work.

She conversed with me almost without ever raising her eyes. But at the end of the conversation she made bold. And even became coquettish with me.

Everything was already said, and it was time to go, but she did not go.

She went only after obtaining permission to come the next day to consult further on her work.

She came the next day. And she was a bit sad. She began to relate that she was married to a student, that

253

they had a little baby. Only the baby and her studies filled her life. And this was very good. It would have been horrible if someone attracted her, if she loved someone. That would have been a catastrophe, because she could not deceive her husband. She would have to break off her life, her studies, her fate and the fate of her husband.

I listened to her declarations in amazement. I told her that she should not admit such feelings.

In a barely audible voice she replied:

"It seems to be too late. I'm afraid I've already fallen in love."

No, she did not say that she loved me. But I could see it in her eyes, in her whole aspect, in her gestures.

She was extremely embarrassed. There really was something awkward in this feeling of hers. Yes, I was somewhat younger, handsomer, but still something unnatural lay in this impetuosity of hers. One could suspect adventurism in such a swift action. She was afraid I might think this.

I saw her internal struggle: she wanted to go, but did not go, because she understood that I would not take a step to meet her again.

She wanted to come two days later. But she did not come. I was sincerely glad of this.

She came two weeks later. She came pale, changed. She came leaning on a cane.

She said that she had become seriously ill. That a year ago she had fallen in a track and field meet. Injured her leg. And now the injury was making itself felt again. She had a swollen knee. She could hardly walk. She came only to tell me of her feeling, which would now probably die out in her heart.

I immediately understood the cause of her illness.

I told her:

"Get me out of your head. And you will be well right away. You became ill to prevent yourself from coming to see me. Your legs stopped serving you, for

254

you yourself said that it would be a catastrophe if you fell in love with someone. The illness defended you. It chose the most vulnerable spot."

She was an intelligent woman. She listened to my words with a faint smile. Then she began to laugh. And she laughed so hard that the cane fell out of her hands.

In the midst of the laughter she said:

"It's astonishing. But that's undoubtedly the way it is."

We parted as friends. And when she left she forgot her cane in my room.

Poor Fedya

This is a story from very long ago. I might not have remembered it. But the conclusions I have drawn unexpectedly revived this story in my memory.

Kislovodsk. The whistle-stop "Minutka." Two houses away from me lives the student Fedya Kh. He is here in the Caucasus for the same reason as I—for practical experience.

Fedya is a university math student. A nice fellow. A bit shy. Sings and plays guitar magnificently.

He comes to my place almost every day. And I listen to his music.

After playing, he begins to talk about girls. He has no luck. All the other students have managed to find "sympathetic" friends, but he has no one. When will his turn finally come?

It came toward the end of summer. Fedya fell in love with his own pupil. He had been giving lessons in physics to a girl in the final year of the *gimnaziya*.

He loved her. And she, evidently, was attracted to him. We began to see them together in the lounge and on the park benches.

Unexpectedly, a misfortune occurred: Fedya was afflicted. He was afflicted with eczema. The eczema began on his chin and spread up onto his cheeks.

For Fedya this was the worst kind of luck. He was already a shy person, but now the blisters completely disheartened him. He stopped meeting with his pupil. He was ashamed for her to see the horrible scarlet spots.

This was a nervous eczema. But the physicians began treating Fedya with ointments and ultraviolet light. And the affliction got worse. The suspicion arose that the patient had a blood infection, sepsis. Fedya hardly ever went out of the house. He cried, saying that only to someone with his lousy luck could such a thing happen. For this thing had happened on the day after his pupil had confessed her feeling for him.

At the end of August I returned with Fedya to Petersburg. We traveled together in the same coach. On the second day of the trip Fedya was already better. The crimson spots on his cheeks began to grow pale. By the end of the trip Fedya's face had almost completely cleared up.

Fedya would not part with his mirror. With rapture he observed that the affliction really was leaving him. With a sad smile he spoke of his bad luck. What good was his health to him now, since the one he loved was not with him?

Again I say: I might not have remembered this story. But I did remember it, because I could see how conspicuous was the cause of his affliction: it was a defense, a protection, flight.

A fear which should have been deciphered impeded his steps. A fear which had not become conscious impaired the functioning of his glands. The chemical activity of his body was unquestionably disordered. The poisoning could therefore have occurred from internal causes, rather than from external ones.

"Better I Go Blind"

I would not have remembered this story either had my conclusions not matched it so closely.

An acquaintance of mine lay dying. He was alone. And his death was terrible, even horrible.

This was in the nineteenth year of the century.

He was an old journalist. Educated by the old life, he was a bitter enemy of the new life.

Grief and deprivations embittered him all the more. Flaming with hatred, he wrote articles which, of course, were not published anywhere. He sent these articles abroad, entrusting them to chance travelers.

I argued a lot with him, demonstrating that he was wrong, that he did not see Russia, did not understand the people, believed that the people were only a small layer of the intelligentsia. That he had no call to identify his thoughts with the thoughts of the people. Precisely in this lay his mistake. And the mistake of many.

We had an argument. And I stopped visiting him.

But I came to see him again when I learned of his condition.

He had a nervous paralysis. The right side of his body was immobile. Yet he was as intractable as before.

He dictated his articles to a stenographer he knew. And as before he sent them abroad, knowing that the affair would end badly for him, that he would be found out. But he courted this danger. His embitterment, it seemed, was greater than his fear.

A month before death he went blind.

I stopped by his place. He lay immobile, blind, helpless. I began talking to him. And he answered briefly, meekly, crushed by his new misfortune. Above all, he regretted that he had finally lost the ability to work—he could not even read what was written.

An unexpected smile crossed his lips. He said:

"But now I am out of danger. Who would want me now in this condition?"

He died. And I forgot about him. And only now do I remember him. I remember his smile, in which I perceived some sort of relief. It seems to me now that he went blind to prevent himself from writing. This is the way he warded off the danger.

No, I realize that there are other, "real" illnesses which can paralyse and blind a man according to all the rules of medicine. But in the present instance it seems to me that the downfall and ruination of this man did not follow the established rules of science.

I remembered a whole series of such cases.

9

I remembered a great number of cases. And all of them convinced me that my conclusions were justified.

These were cases of conditioned connections, which were not severed, cases of the most serious illnesses, catastrophes, dramas.

But I also remembered cases of connections which were severed in time and rendered innocuous.

I remembered a certain circus performer. He kept failing his stunt. Three times he fell in the net. It happened during the actual performances. It nearly caused a scandal. The audience smiled. The performers shook their heads, saying that now he would never be able to do this stunt.

Immediately after the third failure, when the audience had left, the acrobat took away the net stretched under the big top and twice executed the stunt.

He severed something that had begun to be connected. He severed the conditioned connection: stunt and failure. The stunt was once again linked with success.

I remembered still another striking instance of connections which were severed, disallowed.

When a certain famous pilot was buried, the radio

announcer made a slip. Instead of the surname of the deceased pilot he gave the surname of another famous pilot who was present at the funeral.

This pilot blanched slightly and was flustered when he heard his own name. Immediately after the funeral, he set off for the airfield, got in a plane and flew up in the sky. He set a new record for height, greatly excelling his previous attempts. He proved to himself that the slip was nonsense, an accident. And this accident would not be linked to his further fate.

At the very outset he severed neural connections which might have been confirmed. This was a courageous decision.

I remembered a great many cases concerning severed and unsevered connections. And all of them confirmed with mathematical precision the laws discovered by Pavlov.

In both the normal and the pathological states the laws of conditioned reflexes were infallible.

They held the key to many sufferings.

10

And then I thought about people who had already died. About people who died without ever knowing the causes of their sufferings.

Excitedly I remembered the notes I had taken in the days of my horrible gloom. For I had noted down everything relating to melancholy, to illnesses.

My rough list included great and remarkable men, glorified for their creative works, their deeds. Had they too been at the mercy of these laws? Had such nonsense also held them firmly in its grip?

And I wanted at once to learn the cause of their sufferings. the cause of their melancholy, their downfall. Trembling, I began to leaf through my materials. No, I saw that all the main facts remained in their place. All the causes of their downfall were those causes which historians, sociologists had found. Nothing fundamental was shaken here. Their actions and behavior were pre-determined by other pressures—from outside. But in the sum total of their sufferings I again detected a new item which had not previously been reckoned. And on occasion it was great. On occasion it pressed with a force that was deadly.

Excitedly I leaf through my materials.

And now the shades of the past come to life, magnificent shades before whom we all bow.

X. "WOE TO WIT"[105]

When one stands tall he knows what threats are,
And when he falls he breaks to pieces...

1

What compels me to write this book? Why, in these difficult and dreadful days of war, do I mumble about my own and others' indispositions, which took place ages ago?

Why speak of wounds not received on the battle-field?

Perhaps this is a book for after the war? And it is designed for people who will need such salutary material once they have ended the war?

No. I write my book with a full awareness of our

days. I equate it to a bomb destined to explode in the camp of the foe and to destroy the despicable ideas scattered everywhere.

But certainly Hitlerism does not have its own philosophy. It has plundered others' ideas from both field and stream. What despicable ideas, then, do I mean? I mean precisely the ideas which were plundered—and then distorted, simplified, reduced to the level of beastlike people.

It was no great crime when people chatted in salons about the misfortunes which stem from the mind. It was only a half-crime when from the ranks of the verbal battalions esteemed literati spoke of the happiness one finds living in forests and in caves. And there, far from the bustle of the city, to seek salvation from machines, from civilization, from the progressive growth of consciousness.

But it is a great crime when such words are piously recited by a soldier with pretensions to world domination.

And he piously recites these words, distorting them, exaggerating them without any restraint. Hearing the bell ring, but not knowing where he is, he exclaims: "Education cripples people... the intelligentsia is the refuse of the nation... I want my young men to be like savage beasts... consciousness causes people innumerable misfortunes..."

At the dawn of human consciousness he sees the sunset, and he desires it! What a gloomy desire, and what a dark and vile soul gave birth to it!

The world will cloud over for a thousand years if this Gefreiter[106] on the gray horse of a conqueror rides onto the spring fields so little furrowed by the plow of science.

This did not happen. And it cannot happen! Nevertheless, "in defense of reason and its rights" one must continue to write.

And this is one reason why I write my work in these

262

dreadful days of war.

2

But I am not writing my book for this reason alone.

I am writing it in the hope that it will be useful to people.

Perhaps one may detect in this desire of mine a certain naivete, a futile aim, false premises. I have not forgotten the words of the physiologist: "Don't promise people anything."

But I promise only within measure.

For some, perhaps, my book will afford relaxation, entertainment. Others it will leave completely unaffected. Still others it will anger, force them to think. Force them to descend from Olympus and listen to what an ignoramus has to say, an ignoramus who experienced something that only dogs experience.

"My God!" they will exclaim. "A dog has begun to speak! It swears that it experienced all this with its own hide. Gentlemen, let's see if everything is the way this dog says!"

And then, perhaps, turning away for a time from dogs, they will concern themselves with infants, who afford science such inconceivable difficulties and anxieties as they grow into mature beings.

These delightful scenes of attending to people regale my sight, turned to the distant heavens.

It is precisely these scenes from the future which compel me to write my book, compel me to leave the path strewn with roses.

Yes, my path would be strewn with roses if I finished my book in poetical form. Ah, what a glorious little tome it would be, composed of exquisite little novellas drawn from life!

With a radiant smile the reader would hold this book in his hands.

Yes, and it would be so much easier, so much simpler for me. For I have written these exquisite little novellas without any effort, almost blindfolded, almost with divine ease...

And now in their place you will see something of an investigation with dry, unearthly words: reflex, symptoms, neural connections...

O no, who needs it! Why throw away a cuckoo in the hand for a falcon soaring in the sky? Why does the writer have to be a Feldscherer[107] as well? Gentlemen, order him to write the way he began!

With the greatest of pleasure I would carry out this legitimate demand. But the subject does not permit it. It does not fit the exquisite frames of belles lettres, although out of respect for the reader I have been trying to squeeze it in somehow.

I cannot ignore the subject itself. It is of exceptional importance, at least to me personally. For its sake I took up this composition. For its sake I chose this dolorous path.

The dolorous path! Yes, I anticipate the pious comments, the morose looks, the caustic words.

I can almost hear the voices screeching that it's not necessary to pay so much attention to your own body, that it's harmful to have excessive control over yourself. What good does it do, they will say, to keep such a vigilant mind, especially in this new and dubious capacity.

I anticipate this. Yet I hope that the finale of my book will dispel all these doubts.

3

And so, where had we stopped? Was it not to dwell upon the words of Byron:

> Count o'er the joys thine hours have seen,
> Count o'er thy days from anguish free,
> And know, whatever thou hast been,

'T is something better not to be.[108]

No, we had not stopped to dwell upon these dismal words.

We had stopped to dwell upon a list of remarkable and celebrated men. Astounded by the unhappiness and gloominess of these people, I wanted to learn the causes of their unhappiness. Might they not be the same as with me?

You have seen how my suffering, composed of many units, added up to a complex sum.

Now, made wiser by experience, I wanted to find out what units created the suffering of the people on my list.

More accurately, I wanted to find out one of these units, for whose sake I had conceived my book.

No, this is not easy and not simple to do. It must be done very discreetly, with a full awareness of the environment of these people. These people were of various epochs, various characters, various directions. And consequently the forces which acted on them from outside were not the same. The things which caused their psychic conflict were not the same.

Not infrequently a psychic conflict arose which virtually bypassed the biological bases and acted on these people entirely from outside. Such, evidently, was the psychic conflict of Pushkin. The situation in Russia—this is what formed the basis of his conflict and what led the poet to disaster.

Only in such a complex calculation can one decide questions about the forces acting on man.

However, I will try to avoid such complex examples. I will choose only those people who were only too obviously affected by physiological forces.

I will choose examples of a clinical nature.

With the greatest caution I approach my brief investigation.

No, I cannot even call it an investigation. These

265

are materials for an investigation. These are rough drafts, sketches, outlines from which one can only partially reconstruct the true picture.

4

In the beginning of my book I recalled the name of Edgar Allan Poe, the name of a remarkable writer who exerted an enormous influence on the fate of world literature

His personal fate, on the other hand, was without a glimmer of joy, without a bright spot, horrible.

Edgar Allan Poe wrote:

"I am suffering under a depression of spirits which will ruin me should it be long continued... Nothing can now give me pleasure—or the slightest gratification... My feelings at this moment are pitiable indeed... Convince me that it is worth one's while—that it is at all necessary to live."109

He wrote these words when he was less than thirty years old. At forty he died. All of his conscious life was filled with misery, amazing despair, whose causes were incomprehensible to him.

I do not have sufficient materials on hand to investigate this man's life in detail. But even my scanty materials indicate an extremely sensitive psyche, a morbid consciousness, neuroses which cannot fail to be noticed.

I will note a few facts from his biographical materials. I will note those facts which strike me as characteristic, which had some significance or influence on the morbid psyche of Poe.

His parents lived in poverty. They died when the child was two years old. A foster father assumed the care of the boy.

When the foster father came to take the boy (writes a biographer), he was in a sort of stupor. The nurse had

266

calmed the boy by stuffing wine-soaked bread in his mouth.

At five years of age the boy came close to dying. He fell from a tree. Not only that, he fell into water, into a pond. They dragged him out of the water nearly dead—he had no pulse. They could hardly bring him back to life.

When he turned six he was taken to England. All his biographers note that the extended sea voyage made a very strong impression on him.

One of his biographers writes: "A voyage made twice over water predetermined much in the development of Poe's distinctive features."

Another biographer (Harrison) notes that "the two ocean voyages made a great impact on his impressionable character."

The same biographer notes that Poe could not learn to swim for a very long time, even though he persistently strived to learn. He tried to master this science with unusual tenacity. Yet he learned to swim only as an adult. And he even set a record once when he swam several miles.

Yet swimming frequently ended in misfortune. "Once (writes his biographer) he came out of the water covered all over with leeches" (!).

Frequently swimming ended in vomiting.

We see scenes of unusual clarity: the man undoubtedly overcame the tremendous internal obstacles which had been formed outside of his consciousness. We can boldly declare that water had an oppressive effect on Poe. The protective reflex accompanied every encounter with water. An unconscious fear appeared upon contact with the conditioned stimulus.

I do not propose to reconstruct the entire picture of Poe's psychoneurosis. But I can point out that the objects of fear and the conditioned connections attached to them are quite obvious. Edgar Allan Poe writes the woman he loves (Helen Whitman):

267

"I shunned your presence and even the city in which you lived..."[110]

It is interesting to note that Poe avoided this woman because he thought her to be married (without the least grounds for this thought). And only afterwards was he "abused" of his error.

His motive for shunning this woman was truly extraordinary. Artificial, contrived motives were required to justify his otherwise incomprehensible flight.

In another letter[111] Poe writes this woman:

"I *dared not* speak to you—much less see you. For years your name never passed my lips... The merest whisper that concerned you awoke in me a shuddering sixth sense, vaguely compounded of fear, ecstatic happiness, and a wild, inexplicable sentiment that resembled nothing so nearly as the consciousness of guilt."

With striking clarity Poe unfolds the picture of his misfortune. Without even suspecting it, he gives us a meticulous analysis of his psychic state. He finds these elements in his state: fear, joy and guilt.

There can be no doubt that here the school of Freud would see the so-called Oedipus complex. In other words, it would see here a secret and suppressed attraction to the mother. It would see here a moral prohibition and the fear of punishment, which is imposed on man by the conditions of civilized life.

Biographers note that Edgar Allan Poe loved the image of his mother. All his life he did not part with a medallion which contained her portrait.

Certainly the Freudian school would see in this small fact a true justification of its conclusions.

Nevertheless, these conclusions are not justified. We see here again something besides the Oedipus complex. And this is why:

The mother of Edgar Allan Poe died when the boy was two years old.

It is doubtful that a one-year-old boy could have

268

experienced moral anxiety or the fear of punishment for his infant feelings toward his mother.

And it is even more doubtful that the boy experienced these feelings and anxieties after two years of age. He could not have experienced them. He did not even see his mother—she had died.

Consequently, the boy could not have suppressed or prohibited his attraction to his mother, no matter what form it took. And consequently if a prohibition did arise, it arose from some other causes which do not justify Freud's views on the Oedipus complex.

In this case, what other causes could there have been? Only those which we have mentioned in our book.

Not moral motives and not the fear of punishment for his infant "drives," but a fear of a different sort—a fear of objects whose significance the infant misunderstood—this is what is important.

The protective reflex could have been established only on the basis of such "material" motives. Any other motives were dictated by the subject's later development. Without a doubt, these other motives could have exerted an influence on his behavior. But it is doubtful that they could have produced a pathological nature.

Thus, among Poe's morbid conceptions we find several very obvious elements: water—mother—woman. It may be assumed there were still other objects of fear.

Yet these objects alone quite clearly bespeak the pathological nature of Poe's attitude toward them.

Not understanding what was wrong with him and what the causes of his unhappiness were, Poe began to drink. In this way he wanted to rid himself of his numbness, the gloominess, the inhibition which arose in him upon contact with his objects of fear.

Poe died unexpectedly and under peculiar circumstances. He was traveling from Baltimore to Philadelphia. The train conductor found him on the floor in a peculiar stupor. They sent him to the hospital. And there he soon died. Witnesses to his death wrote that during the whole time at the hospital he was in some sort of convulsive condition.

The entire course of his life, his illness, despair and ruination shows traces of pathology. It shows, to my mind, traces of false conditioned connections which were established on his first brush with the surrounding world.

5

I shall make a more thorough investigation of Gogol's illness. For Gogol's psyche, distinguished by tremendous contradictions, is extremely complex. And it appears impossible to achieve an exhaustive analysis without certain materials of a type we do not find in the notes of Gogol's contemporaries.

I will note only that which strikes me as incontrovertible.

There can be no doubt that Gogol's illness derived from not only physical causes. Herzen, for example, believed that "Nikolai's regime drove Gogol into the madhouse." There is some justification in these words.

Gogol portrayed the Russia of Nikolai I with tremendous power. He found apt and merciless words to portray the life of the landowners, the rule of Nikolai I and the vulgar, false morality of society.

By taking these literary positions, Gogol was a revolutionary, a democrat, a true representative of the people.

Yet Gogol was frightened by the joyless pictures he drew and the revolutionary spirit he did not countenance.

There appeared a great split between the artist and the man, between real life and the desire to see Russia as something other than she was.

He wanted to tear himself out of the vise of this conflict. But he could not do it. He could not and did

270

not want to take the path of Belinsky, Chernyshevsky and the revolutionary democratic youth.

Gogol took a step toward a reconciliation with dismal reality, but this step landed him in the camp of his enemies.

This was Gogol's tragedy, the tragedy which reinforced his illness, hastened his ruin.

However, in addition to this tragedy, Gogol contained in himself another tragedy—a conflict of physiological order, which manifested itself so violently in his illness, in his psychoneurosis.

The features of this psychoneurosis are distinctly visible throughout Gogol's life.

These unhealthy features were noticed by those around him in his early childhood.

In 1815 (when Gogol was five or six) the "great lord and benefactor" Troshchinsky wrote Gogol's father:

"...I should inform you that I consulted with Natalinsky (a physician) about your Ñikosha's attacks of scrofula..."

These incomprehensible attacks of scrofula were to be repeated both in youth and in mature years.

On occasion these attacks became very severe. And then Gogol didn't know what to do with himself: "I couldn't lie down or sit down." In addition, his despair sometimes became so intense that he was once able to exclaim: "Hanging or drowning seemed to me like some sort of medicine or relief."

Yet the physicians did not find any serious organic illness in Gogol. They treated him for scrofula, for hypochondria, for "hemorrhoids," for gastric ailments.

The treatment had no success, and Gogol's physical condition steadily worsened.

Yet there were moments when Gogol's lifelong illness instantly vanished. And then he felt healthy again and as fresh as in youth. Gogol noticed this peculiarity of his illness more than once.

In 1840 Gogol wrote (to Pogodin):[112] "The road performed a miracle on me. I feel a freshness and hardiness as never before."

In a letter to Aleksandr Tolstoi[113] (2 January 1846) Gogol wrote:

"I am growing thin, sluggish and weak, and at the same time I feel that there is something in me which could cast all these maladies out of me with a single nod of the higher power."

It would seem that Gogol himself did not feel that this illness was something given once and for all, something organic. This unhealthy "something" could go away, simply vanish and not return to him. This circumstance alone permits us to suspect that Gogol's illness contains the illness described in our book.

Let us assume that our suspicion is correct. Let us assume that Gogol was traumatized by something in his infancy.

How can we investigate this trauma? How can we analyze the course of this illness?

It seems to me that this can be done by following the peculiarities and "oddities" which were characteristic of Gogol's behavior in his personal life.

What "oddities" do we observe in Gogol's behavior?

There are not a few of these oddities. But the main one may be considered his attitude toward women.

It is well known that Gogol never married. And he did not seek marriage. More than that, we do not know of even one significant infatuation in his life.

In 1829 Gogol wrote his mother of his feeling for an unknown girl whom he called "a divinity lightly arrayed in human passions."

The words he used to describe his feeling of love are unusual and extremely important for the investigator:

"An infernal despair with every possible torment raged in my breast. O, what a cruel condition!.. If hell was made for sinners, then it is not nearly so tormenting!

272

No, this was not love... In a fit of frenzy and the most horrible tortures, I thirsted, burned to drink in just one glance of her, I was athirst for just one glance... To glance at her one more time—that was my sole, my single desire... In horror I surveyed and examined my horrible condition. I saw that I would have to flee from myself if I wanted to preserve my life..."

Even if this is not a true love, but only a fantasy, an invention, still the analytic nature of this invention remains.

Fear, horror, torments, death—this is what goes hand in hand with women! This is what accompanies love.

And only flight can preserve life. And so we see this flight throughout Gogol's life.

He fled from women.[114] Although he understood that such a prolonged forbearance could not fail to tell on his health.

Gogol wrote about Konstantin Aksakov:

"If a man has not married by the time he reaches thirty, he will become ill..."

Undoubtedly Gogol addressed these words to himself. Nevertheless, he did not change his life. And he could not change it, since the obstacles were considerable and beyond his power.

What kind of obstacles were they?

Evidently: a fear which had not become conscious, which had arisen by virtue of the protective reflexes, that fear which Gogol so eloquently admitted in his letter about his feeling of love.

How did this fear arise? When? And what was its basis?

This fear could have arisen only in the infant stage. For only the period of infancy could have created a fear so completely devoid of logic.

But then this fear related to women. What was it that originally incited this fear?

Possibly it was incited by his mother—more pre-

273

cisely, by the objects of fear conditionally connected with his mother. For according to the law of conditioned reflexes, both the mother and the objects of fear connected with her frighten the baby, the only difference here being that this fear was complicated by contradictions and lived side by side with joy and longing.

In the future the image of any woman might evoke this contradictory fear.

But if the conditioned neural connections combined the image of woman with unhappiness, horror and even disaster, then these feelings should have appeared in relation to the mother as well.

Was this indeed the case with Gogol?

Yes, precisely the case. Gogol's attitude toward his mother was contradictory and odd in the highest degree.

His "respectful filial love" for his mother lived side by side with his reluctance to see her. He found various pretexts and motives for not traveling to her and for her not to travel to him.

He excused himself on account of business matters, poor health and the fact that he felt gloomy at home.

He wrote his mother (in December 1837):

"The last time I was at your place I think you yourself noticed that I did not know what to do with myself in my despair... I myself did not know where this despair came from..."

Another time, when traveling to his mother, he felt this despair in the carriage.

Gogol, who could bear any road wonderfully well and even believed that the road was his medicine, could not stand the road this time. His "nervous" condition rose to such proportions that he decided to return to Moscow.

And he actually turned back half-way in the trip, without reaching his family estate.

Gogol loved his mother at a distance and avoided meeting her in any way possible. He even went so far as sometimes to send letters from Moscow with the return address of a foreign city—Vienna, Trieste.

These circumstances have led many of Gogol's biographers into a blind alley. This deception seemed enigmatic, incomprehensible.

In point of fact it is very easily explained—by Gogol's reluctance to see his mother, by his flight from her. Let her think that he is abroad, otherwise she will insist on a meeting again.

But perhaps he did this to avoid taking long trips? Perhaps, being burdened by business matters and other concerns, he was simply not in the mood? No, his mother never insisted that he travel to her. She herself wanted to come to Moscow.

In this case, perhaps Gogol was ashamed of her, was embarrassed by her provincial appearance? No, judging by his letters, Gogol respected her, honored her, felt sincere feelings for her and tried to spare her any worry or bother.

Evidently something else kept him from meeting his mother.

This "something else" was unconscious, infantile. The conditioned connections obviously extended to the objects of fear: home, mother, woman.

These connections remained unsevered throughout Gogol's life and exerted a pernicious influence.

Once when he could not put off a meeting with his mother, Gogol used extremely cold and unpleasant words to report the anticipated meeting. He wrote Danilevsky[115] (December 1839):

"...Wishing to perform my filial duty, that is to give Mama a chance to see me, I am inviting her to Moscow for two weeks..."

Apparently the mother was an inadvertant perpetrator of an infant conflict.

Furthermore, in the infant's mind the mother is not only a mother, she is also nourishment, food and the joy of satisfying hunger. This means there should be oddities, "eccentricities" in regard to eating as well—

perhaps to an even greater degree than in regard to love, for here the conditioned connections are more firmly established, since "encounters" with this object are constant and there is no possibility of avoiding them.

We know how Gogol passed the last tragic days of his life. He refused to eat and mortified himself with hunger.

In his last days he stopped eating altogether, despite the advice and entreaties of those around him.

Then they began feeding him artificially, by force. He screamed and begged them not to touch him, not to "torment" him.

But Gogol's refusal to eat did not derive from any gastric illness or from a lack of appetite.

Doctor Tarasenkov writes:

"The pulse was weak, the tongue clear but dry, the skin possessed its natural warmth. By all considerations, it was obvious that he was not in a feverish condition, and one could not attribute his disuse of food to a lack of appetite..."

The same Tarasenkov writes:

"He did not want to eat anything that day and afterwards when he ate the sacramental wafer he called himself a glutton, a cursed soul, an intemperate person and was sorely penitent."

But was this not the "religious delirium" which many biographers see in his fasting?

No. The religious motive may have had some significance, but it was not fundamental and not even necessary.

We know that members of the clergy—a father confessor and a parish priest—exhorted Gogol to eat.

It is known that the parish priest practically forced Gogol "to take a spoonful of castor oil."

More than that, Tolstoi appealed to the Metropolitan Philaret[116] to bring his influence "to bear upon the deranged imagination of a repentent sinner"—to order Gogol to take food and to follow the dictates of his physicians.

The Metropolitan ordered that the command be communicated to Gogol that "the church itself directs that one submit to the will of physicians when indisposed."

Yet even this command from on high did not produce a change in the thoughts of the patient. For religious motives did not constitute the basis of his refusal to eat.

How did Gogol himself explain his refusal to eat? He found an extremely odd and at the same time revealing reason. Doctor Taransenkov writes:

"At dinner Gogol took only a few spoonsful of oat soup or cabbage brine. When offered something else to eat, he refused on account of illness, explaining that he felt something in his stomach, that his intestines were turning over, that this was the illness of his father who died at the same age and moreover because they had treated him"(!).

This infantile answer of Gogol's quite clearly explains the essence of his refusal to eat.

First, spasms and convulsions (symptoms of a protective reflex?) prevented him. Second, these words of Gogol's bespeak his reluctance to be treated, in other words—his reluctance to be healthy. Here lies the essence of his illness and ruin. It is better to die than to experience what he was experiencing.

It was in such a reckoning that the question of Gogol's fasting was decided.

But how can one reconcile his fasting with that passion for food which was so characteristic of Gogol? We read of this passion of Gogol's everywhere—in memoirs, in letters, in reminiscences.

From reminiscences we learn how Gogol on occasion conducted a "religious service" over dinner, how he ceremoniously sat down to eat and what significance he placed in good food.

In his letters (to Danilevsky) Gogol called a

restaurant a "temple" and even "a temple of gobbling"(!).

In the memoirs we read that Gogol on occasion prepared the food himself, cooked dinner. Moreover, he did this very ceremoniously and seriously.

Sergei Aksakov[117] writes:

"He took up this task wholeheartedly, as if it were his favorite trade. And I thought that if fate had not made Gogol a great poet, then he definitely would have been an expert chef."

Thus Gogol's attitude towards food was quite odd and even exaggeratedly ceremonious.

Moreover, this oddity was constantly in evidence and was noted by all the memoirists.

Mikhail Pogodin writes that the artist Bruni, in speaking of Gogol, exclaimed: "Sometimes we went for the express purpose of seeing Gogol at dinner, so as to stimulate our appetite—he eats enough for four."

Pavel Annenkov[118] writes:

"Upon receiving a bowl of rice to his taste, Gogol set to it with extraordinary voraciousness, leaning over it so that his long hair fell right down into the dish, and gulping spoon after spoon with passion and alacrity."

Sergei Aksakov writes:

"Gogol took upon himself the responsibility for our coffee, tea, breakfast and dinner..."

Mikhail Pogodin writes:

"Gogol's first concern was to arrange the morning tea. His stores of excellent tea were never exhausted. But his main task was to obtain various pastries to go with the tea. And where he ferreted out all those little cracknels, rolls, biscuits, only he, and he alone, knew... Then begins the pouring, the serving, the savoring, the regaling and the smacking of lips. It was never possible to finish with the tea in less than an hour..."

This amazing passion of Gogol's was noticed even by his comrades in grade school.

V. Lyubich reported:

"In his pants pockets he always had a considerable store of sweets—candies and cookies. And, taking a few out from time to time, he would chew up the whole lot without stopping, even in classes, during lessons..."

And another note on Gogol's school years:

"He constantly sucked on cookies, ate sweets and drank pear kvas. Gogol either prepared the kvas himself from pears soaked in water or bought it at the bazaar..."

Simultaneous with this extraordinary passion, Gogol sometimes complained of a lack of appetite, gastric indigestion, and every sort of indisposition. But on the whole his exaggerated and ceremonious attitude toward food remained intact.

Yet every time he sat down to eat (as witnesses to his dinners report) Gogol became "capricious," grew nervous, and sometimes even got angry.

Pavel Annenkov writes:

"Gogol shocked me, however, with his capricious, exacting attitude toward the attendant. Twice he sent back the dish of rice, finding it first to be overcooked, then undercooked."

F. I. Iordian writes:

"After requesting some dish or other, Gogol would hardly touch it before he called the waiter and demanded the meal be changed two or three times, so that the restaurant waiter nearly threw the dish at him and said: 'Signor Nikolo, it would be better if you did not come to us for dinner, no one can satisfy you.' "

It's as if some childish, infantile scenes were acted out before food. Some sort of extraordinary agitation is present before this ceremonious procedure.

We know how contradictory the feelings and desires of a man may be when they are based on his initial infant notions. Sometimes a fear which is connected with a desire does not extinguish it, but on the contrary reinforces it. A struggle, as it were, ensues for the object of fear, which might be taken away. And a temporary victory over this object increases the triumph of the victor. Yet the decisive victory remains on the side of the fear.

And sometimes the mechanism of this victory is founded on a weakening of control. It is well known to science that when the cortex of the brain weakens its control (due to fatigue, illness, old age) it permits the suppressed animal and infant forces to rise up again.[119]

Overfatigued, weakened by illness, Gogol's brain (more accurately, the cortex of his brain) ceased to maintain even that incomplete degree of control which was realized in the years of his youth. And so we see these tragic scenes of fasting, we see a fear which had not become conscious, which was constantly present in food. The infant notions and the animal forces, not being controlled by consciousness, gained the upper hand.

However, the conditioned neural connections combined not only food, woman, mother with danger. They combined a whole series of other objects: home, night, bed.

And as a result the "dangers" turned up at every step. And the struggle with these "dangers" was wearisome, beyond his strength. He could save himself only by flight. Only flight severed these connections, spared him the "dangers."

It is precisely flight which characterizes the behavior of Gogol. As soon as he got in the carriage he felt emancipation, rest, health.

How many times he wrote that the road healed him.

In the words of Smirnova (1840), "Botkin placed Gogol, who was half-dead, in the diligence..."

Gogol further reports about himself:

"Arriving in Trieste, I felt better. The road—my only medicine—did its work this time as well..."

And so it should have, for the road led him away from the dangers. The unconscious fear abandoned him.

280

This is what served as a cure...

But it was a temporary cure. The same road led him once more to women, to food, to treatment, after which came health, and after health—still greater "dangers," still greater possibilities for encountering objects which frightened him.

His situation was "inescapable," for even illness did not provide a release. Illness, you see, was connected with the bed, the berth. And the bed was conditionally "connected" with that wearisome drama which was once acted out in the period of infancy.

It is interesting to note that many biographers and memoirists noticed Gogol's odd attitude toward the bed. He almost never lay down on a bed, even when there was a bed in the room. And he did not always lie down even on a sofa. He preferred to doze in an armchair.

Pavel Annenkov was "distressed and alarmed" when he saw "such a whim" in Gogol.

Annenkov describes a night spent with Gogol as follows:

"Gogol rather frequently, and toward the end more and more frequently, came into my room and sat down on the narrow wicker settee, rested his head in his hands and dozed for a long time after I had already gone to bed and extinguished the candle. Then he went to his own place on tiptoes and sat down in the same way on his own straw settee and remained upright until daybreak..."

Gogol explained this oddity by the fact that some sort of "deadness" came over his body when he lay down on a bed and, besides this, he was "afraid of passing out."

Annenkov further reports:

"At daybreak Gogol pummeled and messed up his bed so that the maid who cleaned the rooms could not have the slightest suspicion of her lodger's caprice..."

Thus, not only did Gogol experience an infantile fear, but he also had to pretend that there was no fear and no flight.

What infantine scenes were acted out in his adult years! And with what tenacity they clung to Gogol!

Here is a striking example of a remarkable mind dominated by unconscious notions.

What wearisome sufferings the great poet experienced! What pain we feel for these sufferings of his! They would not have existed had control been established over the lower forces.

These sufferings which Gogol experienced do not diminish the image of a great artist, poet, writer. Do not darken our memory of him. Gogol was level with the knowledge of his time. But the level of knowledge was insufficiently high. In this area the science of that time was wandering in the dark. It could not help Gogol. Or even explain things to him as it now explains them to us.

6

Several more investigations lie before me on my desk. And their conclusions are equally compatible.

I will not encumber the reader with the details of these investigations. It seems to me that the two examples cited are sufficiently convincing.

Of what do they convince us? At the very least, of the necessity of controlling the lower forces with reason.

However I will cite a few more brief examples from the same category.

Nekrasov[120] attributed his gloomy state to his defective health, particularly a disease of the liver... Nekrasov writes:

"Doctor Zimmerman announced that I have a defective liver. And so I grow stupid from a defect of the liver..."

For many years Nekrasov was treated for this disease.

Yet after his death, his body was dissected, and his internal organs, including his liver, were found to be in good condition.

Doctor Belogolovy, who was present at the autopsy, writes:

"For 56 years of age, he was quite well-preserved. Aside from his specific constitutional disorder, he had no diseases."[121]

Melancholy accompanied Nekrasov throughout his life. Even as a seventeen-year-old boy, Nekrasov wrote:

And on a newfound path with gloom too far developed
I walked without a purpose then...

This "gloom too far developed" did not derive from any illnesses of the body. Its causes lay elsewhere. Even a superficial analysis is enough to convince us that unconscious notions were present and sometimes gained the upper hand.

It was assumed that Saltykov-Shchedrin[122] had a brain tumor. Since, as Doctor Belogolovy writes, he had "convulsive contractions in the muscles of his body which were so powerful that writing became not only difficult for him, but almost impossible."

"In 1881," writes Belogolovy, "these twitchings became extremely pronounced and took the form of St. Vitus dance."

Besides this, he developed "pains in the eyes not connected with any apparent affliction of the oracular apparatus."

These symptoms and the "tormenting fits of gloom peculiar to him" led the physicians to think that Shchedrin had "a tumor or a cyst in the brain."

Yet the autopsy revealed (as the same physician reports) neither tumor nor cyst, nor any changes whatsoever in the tissues of the brain.

The causes, undoubtedly, resided in functional disorders, in unconscious notions, in the sphere of mistaken feelings, mistaken responses to stimuli which did not correspond to the force and expediency of these responses.

Probably modern science would have made an analysis of the psyche before making hypotheses about a tumor in the brain.

Such an analysis, perhaps, might have saved the life of the great novelist Balzac.

The story of his love (for Ganskaya) is the story of his illness and ruin.

He corresponded with this woman for many years. He loved her as only a man of a great heart and a great mind is able.

At a distance (they lived in different countries) she was not "dangerous" to him. But when she wanted to leave her husband to come to Balzac, he wrote her: "Poor tethered lamb, don't abandon your stall."

Yet she "abandoned her stall." She arrived (in Switzerland) to visit with Balzac. Yet this was an unhappy meeting. Balzac practically avoided Ganskaya.

His behavior has led his biographers into a blind alley.

One of the biographers writes: "He was afraid to face the one he loved."

Another biographer writes: "He was frightened of too much happiness"(!).

A third biographer draws the conclusion: "He had a miserable room and was ashamed to invite her to visit him."

What nonsense! And what vulgar motives were found to explain his flight, protection, fear.

But then Ganskaya's husband died. All the moral reasons dropped out of the picture. There could be no further evasions.

Balzac was to travel to the Ukraine to marry Ganskaya.

One biographer writes that the decision to travel greatly agitated Balzac. "Once he sat in the carriage, Balzac very nearly remained there forever."

With each city that brought him closer to the goal

of his journey, Balzac felt more wretched and more horrible.

He became so short of breath that the rest of the journey seemed unnecessary.

Servants supported him by the arms as he entered Ganskaya's home.

He mumbled: "It seems I shall die before I give you my name."

Yet his condition did not protect him from the marriage, which had been set in advance.

During the last days before his marriage Balzac was nearly paralysed. They carried him into the church seated in a chair.

He died soon after. Died at fifty years of age. This was a man of tremendous physical strength, tremendous spirit. But this did not save him from defeat.[123]

From this example we see what strength the foe may sometimes acquire. And what protection is needed to conquer him, to conquer the false infantile notions which so terrify our unconscious world.

7

It would be possible to cite quite a few examples of defeat—examples of despair, illnesses and disaster. But I shall limit myself to the above.

I shall only remark that some people, without locating the cause of their own misfortunes, have regarded the mind as the chief perpetrator of these troubles. And here it was not difficult to be misled.

People saw before them, it would seem, such glaring examples: elevated minds had to bear sufferings more often than others. It seemed that these sufferings pertained to every elevated mind. It seemed that an elevated mind itself produces misery, woe, illness. Yet these sufferings by no means pertained to an elevated mind. They pertained to a mind which was primarily connected with art, with creativity—because of this mind's own special, specific qualities, its inclinations to fantasize, to seek highly sensitive perceptions. Precisely these special qualities of the mind (most often of an inherent nature) increased the possibility for the appearance of mistaken neural connections, which almost always are founded on the specious fantasies of an infant!

Yet this does not mean that all people in art, creators and fantasists, must of necessity bear illnesses and anxieties. These illnesses arise as a result of an unfortunate concurrence of circumstances. And the qualities of the mind represent only a fertile soil for their inception.[124]

Here is where the mistake lies. And here lie the sources of the blame placed on reason.

An elevated consciousness is not something dangerous. Even for a highly sensitive mind, inclined to fantasize, sufferings and psychoneuroses are by no means obligatory.

There are a multitude of examples which show that great talent and even genius were by no means accompanied by madness, neurosis, illness. On the contrary, we see in these examples absolute health and a normal disposition in all respects.

Absolute health by no means reduces the possibility of being a creator-artist. On the contrary, absolute health—this is the ideal for art. Only then may art achieve its full value. And become what it should be. True, an absolutely healthy person may on occasion prefer real life to fruitless fantasies. He will probably have no time to stuff his head with make-believe personages. He will prefer, perhaps, to think about living people, about genuine feelings. He will leave the fantasizing to those people who already stumble about among their fantasies, unable fully to realize their feelings because of their fears and inhibitions.

This is why we sometimes see art and illness in

dangerous proximity.

And this is why art may seem to be the exclusive property of unhealthy people.

But this is definitely not the case! It is precisely these people who surmised that reason causes misfortune. It is precisely these people who announced: "Woe to wit."

Perhaps they were not mistaken in regard to themselves. But they are mere iotas. They should not have ascribed their adversities to all people, who by no means share these miseries.

Here lies the common mistake of philosophers, writers, poets. Not infrequently they identify their feelings and conjectures with "all of humanity."

Lev Tolstoi deemed that "non-resistance to evil" would save people from myriad misfortunes. Perhaps it saved Tolstoi. But this idea was absolutely foreign to most people.

Goncharov saw Oblomovs among the Russian people. Perhaps Oblomovism was characteristic of the writer, but it by no means characterized the Russian people.

Balzac, in his novel *The Will Ass' Skin,* put forward the thought that life expires and accelerates with every aroused desire.

Fearing his own feelings and desires, Balzac proposed that all men fear them, intimidating the unruly with death.

This was a terrible mistake.

On the contrary, human life burns the brighter and the longer, the fewer unhealthy obstacles there are to this burning. The human organism is not a bucket with precious juices which might be spilled, be lost, be expended in its many encounters with life. This "bucket" fills up as it is used. But it empties if its contents are not used at all.

This mistake has confused many, many people.

Such mistakes have been made against society,

against physiology, against logic. In them we can perceive the logic of people who were not completely healthy, and sometimes definitely ill.

And in the light of these conspicuous mistakes we can understand the philosophical mistake of Dostoevsky, who said: "An excessively elevated consciousness and even any consciousness at all is an illness."

Dostoevsky was not a well man. His wife has left a note of her first impression of him:

"I saw before me a man terribly unhappy, beaten down, tormented. He had the appearance of a man who today or yesterday had lost someone close to his heart, a man striken by some kind of terrible misfortune."

One may assume that his unhealthy condition (epilepsy) doubtless worsened as a result of his immoderate mental work. And probably this permitted the writer to draw such an extreme conclusion.

But it seems to us that not work, but a complicated "response," a complex of "responses" to external stimuli, abetted his condition.

Perhaps in my book as well someone will perceive a mistake such as those I describe. But remember that I assert only that which refers personally to me and partially to people of art. As to that which refers to people of other professions and occupations, I make no assertions. I simply make the suggestion.

XI. REASON CONQUERS DEATH

Draws nigh the din of funeral horns,
Grows faint the breath of lips now cold... [125]

1

In one of Gogol's youthful letters there is a remarkable and sad passage:

"I figured out the science of a joyful and happy life, and I was surprised how people who thirst for happiness immediately flee from it once they encounter it..."

Thus Gogol saw not only his own "immediate flight from happiness," he also saw the flight of others.

Where did these people flee to? In what regions did they find salvation from the chimera they had created for themselves?

They fled to regions which most certainly did not save them. They fled to the regions of illness, the regions of madness, death.

They fled to these regions hoping that precisely such extreme measures would save them from horrors and fears, from miseries and anxieties which in fact they were not even conscious of.

Does this mean they fled to death? Could they really have seen relief in death?

After all, we know what madness it takes to instill the thought of death in a man. And, nevertheless, we see many examples of people striving for death, achieving it, viewing it as their salvation, escape, relief.

How can we "reconcile" two such extreme poles? No doubt we can reconcile them if we glance at what goes on beyond the threshold of consciousness.

A baby (or an animal) does not know what death is. It might view death simply as vanishing, going away, absence. But the meaning of death is still unclear to it. This conception comes with the growth of its mind. On the lower stories of the psyche death evidently is not considered the most terrible (or more exactly, the most "dangerous") act of the human condition.

In 1926, when catastrophe came too close to me, when contradictions and conflicts horrified me and I could find no escape, I had a strange dream.

I saw Esenin, who had recently died, had recently hanged himself, come into my room. He comes into the room rubbing his hands, happy, contented, merry, with rosy red cheeks. I had never seen him this way in life. Smiling, he sits down on the bed where I am lying. Leans toward me to tell me something.

I woke up shaking all over. I thought: "He has come for me. It's all over. I guess I'm going to die."

But the years passed. I forgot about this nocturnal episode. And only now, while recalling everything from the past, did I remember this dream. And all at once I understood what it meant for me at that time. And this

290

it what it meant: "Look how nice it is for me now, see how happy I am now, how healthy, how carefree. Dear friend, do as I did, and you will no longer be endangered by those horrible miseries which tormented us both."

This is the meaning of the dream which my lower story so conveniently supplied me, the lower story which evidently fears danger a great deal more than it fears death, for it does not understand what death is— more exactly, does not understand death the way we understand it through reason.

Does this not explain many ridiculous deaths—those deaths which result from nonsense, bunk, trivial illnesses? Do we not find here one of the reasons for those suicides which so resemble a hasty flight, the flight of an animal?

Such suicides are infantile in the extreme. Beneath this urge for death there appears only too obvious the "unconscious" childish fear of a dubious danger, a dubious conflict.

The pathological nature of this urge cannot be questioned. And once again we become convinced that the control of reason is necessary.

2

But perhaps the intervention of reason is super-fluous in certain cases, in those cases which may be called normal?

No, it seems to me that the control of reason is necessary in these cases as well.

Indeed. What feelings do we experience when we see death? What happens in our psyche, in our "upper story," when we look death "in the face?"

Most people experience fear, despair and even horror.

But isn't this right, if only from the viewpoint of the preservation of life? No, this is absolutely wrong, dangerous and even pernicious.

Here I am obliged to speak at greater length about

death—about that condition which is more unavoidable than any other condition in human life.

It seems to me that a discussion of this subject does not contradict the principles of socialist realism. With all its great optimism, socialist realism certainly does not close its eyes to everything that goes on in the world. And it does not hypocritically put off decisions to questions which need to be decided.

The attitude toward death: this is one of the greatest problems which a man must encounter in his life. Yet this problem not only has not been solved (in literature, in art, in philosophy), it has hardly even been thought about. The solution is left to every man by himself. But the human mind is weak, timid. It puts off this question until the last days, when it is already too late to decide it. And much too late to oppose it. It is too late to regret that thoughts of death have caught you unawares.

An anti-fascist German writer once told me of an amazing incident. A friend of this writer was put in a cell. There he was tortured. But he withstood the torture. Yet when he came up against the fact that he would die, his soul trembled. The thought of death came to him for the first time. It caught him unawares, when he was weak and tormented. This thought so terrified him that he renounced his idea in order to save his skin. He sent a penitent letter from jail frantically explaining what had happened to him.

Speaking of this incident, the writer told me:

"I used to think that we should leave questions of death to the writers of the old world. No, it is we who should write about death. We should think about this question no less than people think about love."

This is surely the case. And now you will see why.

3

Almost all the memoirists who speak of Gogol

have remarked on his fear of death.

Gogol was not a well man, of course, but he was still in satisfactory condition when once he became closely acquainted with death.The poet Yazykov's[126] sister, who was friendly with Gogol, died. At the first service Gogol felt horrible. He was shaken and stunned by this death. The very fact of death affected him so strongly that everyone around him noticed it.

Doctor Tarasenkov writes:

"Her death did not stun her husband and relatives so much as it stunned Gogol... Here, perhaps for the first time, he saw death face to face..."

This remark by a contemporary of Gogol was surely correct. Without a doubt, Gogol had seen death, but here, perhaps for the first time, he really began to think about it. And then, as he himself told his confessor, "the fear of death assailed him."

At the first service, peering into the face of the deceased, he said (according to Aleksei Khomyakov):[127] "It's all over for me..."

And truly,from that very day Gogol was constantly disturbed. And once, probably thinking of death and the life he had lived, he said: "It's all bosh, poppycock..."

He fell ill. According to P. A. Kulish[128] he fell ill "with the same illness which had killed his father—namely, he was seized by the fear of death..."

A few weeks later Gogol died.

We have described his end. It was a death without struggle, a death without complaint, an urge for death. The fear was present in his feelings. It hastened and promoted the end. It acted to that pernicious extreme noted by those around Gogol.

But then Gogol was not alone in experiencing such a fear. Many people experience it, the majority.

History, memoirs, letters—all tell us about this fear and even horror of the very fact of death.

Potyomkin[129] —the favorite of Catherine the Great—literally "howled with the fear of death." Contemporaries wrote about him: "A fainthearted fear and horror of death took possession of him, and he began to mope and despair."

Empress Elizaveta Petrovna[130] "was horrified of death" and even turned to drink to dispel her terrible thoughts about it.

Tsar Mikhail Fedorovich,[131] contemplating his end, "fell into immobility" and died "from much sitting, cold drinks and melancholy, viz.—heartache."

Death horrified people. And people of great talent were no less subject to this fear.

The sister of the composer Glinka writes:

"He was so afraid of death that he guarded himself against trifles to an extent that was laughable."

Despair harrowed Maupassant when he wrote:

"No matter what we have done, we shall nevertheless have to die. No matter what we believe in, no matter what we strove towards, we must all the same die. You feel crushed by the weight of consciousness..."

Lev Tolstoi wrote in horror:

"Forty years of work, torment and successes in order to understand that nothing exists and that from me there will remain only rotting and worms..."[132]

Tolstoi later changed his attitude toward death, and this remark of his becomes all the more interesting to us, if only for the comparison we will make below.

Frightened by death and no doubt wishing to see the finale as soon as possible, Blok wrote:

When comes the end? Persistent are the sounds.
They give no pause. No strength to hear remains.
It's all so terrible! So wild!
**   —My friend,**
Give me your hand, and we'll forget again...[133]

And so we see that an immoderate degree of fear is present when one comes into contact with death, even when one thinks about it.

At the same time we see that this fear disheartens people and makes them all the more acquiescent to death.

As it is said in Shakespeare:

Cowards die many times before their deaths;
The valiant never taste of death but once.
Of all the wonders that I yet have heard,
It seems to me most strange that men should fear;
Seeing that death, a necessary end,
Will come when it will come.[134]

These are precise and truthful words. Fear deprives one of the ability to struggle. It hastens one's downfall. It leads one more quickly, more precipitously to the end.

People who have been in a war know this very well. I remember (in that first war) how soldiers used to say with a snort: "The bullet will find a coward." And this is the way it really is. For a frightened person acts unreasonably, senselessly. He bumps about like a blind man, without sizing up the situation. Fear paralyses him, deprives him of flexibility, resistance. Such a person becomes physically weak, helpless, fidgety. And then the bullet finds him more easily.

And this applies in equal measure to the conditions of ordinary, peaceful life. Frightened, cowardly people perish sooner. Fear deprives them of the ability to manage themselves.

Thus, in these cases as well—in the "normal" state, so to say, reason should come to one's aid. It should eliminate fear.

4

Yes, but how can this be done? It is easy to say: there is no need to fear death. But try to persuade someone that death is not so terrible. He won't

295

believe you. You'll only make him laugh. And then he'll probably fear the end of his life even more.

What path can reason find to eliminate fear, to get rid of the fear of death? For reason can find it. We are convinced of this by numerous examples of absolute fearlessness, amazing courage, and by examples which inform us of a contemptuous attitude toward death, a disregard for it.

Here there is no need to recall the past. We see this in many examples taken from our own days.

We may recall, for instance, the Komsomolets Aleksandr Matrosov, who blocked the enemy's machine gun with his own body.[135] He did this consciously. He disregarded himself. The fear of death vanished with the desire to help his comrades, to save them, to attain victory.

An officer of the Red Army told me of a no less astonishing incident.

In a dugout, in a blind, there were twelve officers and two telephone operators. One of the officers accidentally dropped a hand grenade on the floor. The grenade started hissing. His terrible carelessness might destroy his comrades. The door of the dugout was closed. There was no chance of throwing the grenade out immediately.

How did this Soviet officer act? He had only a few seconds to think. He fell on the grenade. Covered it with his own stomach. And when it exploded it literally annihilated this officer. But not another man in the dugout was hurt. The officer absorbed the entire blast and all the fragments.

He saved his comrades. The fear of death was negligible in comparison to the feeling which this remarkable man bore in his heart.

Without a doubt, one may find not a few facts of this sort in the history of the past and in the history of our own days.

These facts tell us that reason, ideas and higher

feelings frequently conquer fear.

But surely, when speaking of the fear of death, we had in mind not exceptional cases, not those cases in which death was necessary for attaining a high goal. We had in mind not a heroic death, but the ordinary, so to speak, everyday death.

We wanted to see examples of fearlessness among the cases of this ordinary death. From these examples we wanted to learn how the reason of these people acted to eliminate fear.

Such examples of a fearless and courageous attitude toward death we find in great number.

Before his death Lomonosov[136] wrote:

"I do not bemoan my death: I lived, I suffered and I know that the children of the fatherland will feel sorry for me..."

To his friend at the Academy (Shtelin) he wrote:

"I see that I must die and look calmly and indifferently on death. I regret only that I cannot complete everything I have undertaken for the good of the fatherland, for the augmentation of the sciences and for the glory of the Academy."

Suvorov[137] died courageously and simply. On the deathbed he asked Derzhavin[138] with a smile what kind of epitaph the latter would write on his gravestone.

Talleyrand, the famous minister of Napoleon, and (as it seems to me) one of the wisest of men, wrote:

"I am slowly growing weaker and know how this may end. I am not grieved by this and do not fear this. My work is done. I planted trees, I built a home, and I did a lot of other stupid things. Isn't it time to stop?"

Lev Tolstoi (according to Gusev) said:

"I almost feel the possibility of dying joyfully."

A few months before his death Repin[139] wrote (to Kornei Chukovsky[140]):

"Please do not think that I am in a bad mood on account of my approaching death. On the contrary, I am gay... Above all, I have not given up art. All of my last thoughts are about it... For more than half a year I have been working on the picture 'The Hopak.' How vexing: I won't succeed in finishing it..."

Repin writes further:

"In my garden there are no reforms. Soon I will dig my grave. It's a pity I can't do it with my own hands, my puny strength would not suffice, and then again I don't know if they would permit it..."

It would be possible to cite quite a few similar examples of a calm and even businesslike attitude toward death.

Yet how did these people act to eliminate fear? What did they do for this? How did they attain fearlessness?

An incident which I once experienced suggested the answer to this question to me.

Many years ago, returning from a hunt, I stopped by a peasant hut. I stopped by to drink a cup of milk.

In the entryway I saw a cross. An ordinary birch cross, which is placed on graves. Evidently someone had died in this hut. And here was the cross prepared for the deceased.

I was about to leave, thinking that I had stopped by at the wrong time. But suddenly the door to the hut opened, and some old man, far from young, barefooted and dressed in rose-colored pants, invited me into the house.

After a cup of milk, I asked my host who had died here and where was the deceased.

My host, chuckling in his beard, said:

"No one has died. And there's no deceased. As regards the cross, well, I got it ready for myself."

My host's appearance gave not the slightest hint of death. His eyes shined merrily. His step was firm. And a rosy redness even played about his chubby cheeks.

With a laugh I asked him what his big hurry was.

Again chuckling, my host answered:

"Well. There was a touchy moment. But it passed."

As we parted I again went out into the entryway, and the host, slapping the cross with the palm of his hand, said:

"And do you know, dear friend, when I got this cross ready? Seventeen years ago."

"Were you sick then or something?"

"Why sick? I just got a bit scared of death. And I made myself a cross to remind me. And can you imagine—I've gotten used to it."

"And now you have no fear?"

"No fear. No death either. I'll get interested in dying another time—no, it's not coming, the damned thing. It must have gotten scared of my character..."

And so, recalling this little incident, I understood perfectly the secret of this man's struggle with fear. The secret lay in his habit. His habit of regarding death as something ordinary, natural, obligatory. The thought of death ceased to be accidental, unexpected. The habit of thinking this way eliminated fear.

We have mentioned that death horrified Gogol. Those around him saw his reaction. According to Vera Aksakova,[141] these people, wishing to alter the course of Gogol's thoughts, began to talk "about the possibility of training a child from his earliest years so that death would not be something unexpected for him."

The absence of "unexpectedness"—this is the main line of the struggle with fear.

Without a doubt, people who regard death so peacefully have thought about it well in advance. The thought of it did not come to them unexpectedly.

They saw death as a natural event, the conformity of constantly renewing life. They grew accustomed to thinking of it as an ordinary end. And therefore they died as man should die—without losing composure, without panicking, maintaining a businesslike calm. And this imparted some sort of majesty, even triumph to their lives.

Such a reasonable attitude toward death perhaps

even lengthened the life of these people, for the main foe was absent from their life—the animal, not always conscious fear.

5

The habit of thinking about death as something ordinary, natural, eliminates fear. Yet this habit may take extreme forms which are hardly needed in this matter.

We find examples of an excessively calm and even somewhat loving, tender attitude toward death. This strikes me as utterly worthless.

Instances of such an extreme attitude, however, are not devoid of their comic aspects, and they are tolerable in human life if only for this reason.

The famous librarian of the Hermitage (end of the 18th century) I. F. Luzhkov, according to his contemporaries, regarded all matters concerning funerals with love and zeal. Almost every day he was present at the burial service of someone completely unknown to him. He dug graves for the poor, free of charge. Had a passion for writing epitaphs. And sometimes he spent whole days at the cemetery.

Not content with this, he built himself a little house next to the Okhotinsky Cemetery. And the windows of his house looked out on the cemetery just as other people's windows would look out on a garden.

Luzhkov authored the following epitaph, engraved in the tombstone of one of his relatives:

"Pasha, where are you?"
"Right here."
"And you, Vanya?"
"Just a little further off."
"And you, Katya?"
"Still fussing about."

300

This regard for life as an unnecessary fussing about, which next to the majesty of death is superfluous, was glorified by yet another man. This was the retired vice-governor Shevelyov (the forties of the last century).

Shevelyov made a point of finding out from the undertakers where the recently deceased were located and, grabbing his pillow, paid them a visit. And when he found a spot he liked, he remained for two or three days with the permission of the caretakers. In addition, he took a most active part in the whole business of burials. He washed the deceased, equipped them for the final journey and read appropriate words over them at night.

Long before his death he personally ordered a coffin with some sort of special peephole. Of course, such a peephole would not have given the deceased any particular advantage. Through this peephole the deceased would have been able to see almost nothing. And he himself could not have been seen at all. But Shevelyov corrected the situation in time. He ordered them to enlarge the peephole to the size of his face.

In addition, he bought some sort of "thick porthole glass" which was adapted to the coffin. It turned out very nicely. One could admire the deceased through the glass without lifting the lid of the coffin.

Yet death did not hasten to come for this aficionado of burials. The coffin remained standing in his study for a number of years. And many guests "crawled into it out of curiosity" to see what kind of panorama would open up before them through the glass of the little window.

There were probably a few smiles when they buried this gentleman. It must have been amusing to look through the glass and see the serious, pensive face of the deceased, who had said the final word in the business of burying people, in the business of saving them from the fuss of the world.

This attitude toward life as some sort of vain fussing

about—this is that extreme measure which is characteristic of people who have become too accustomed to
thinking about death. It must be that a certain caution
and reasonable measure is required in this matter.

Then again, it is possible that the elevated style of
funeral orations requires the reminder that life is, so to
say, a vanity. It is possible that this is simply a manner
of speaking, of using pretty words and, so to speak, of
raising the spirit among the deceased.

This is evidently the case, judging by the epitaph
which until very recently adorned the Smolensky
Cemetery:[142]

> What's on the surface of the earth?
> Worldly vanity, adversities, a great blare.
> Beloved spouse, now heed my words:
> You find rest here, and not there.

What a scoundrel! He claims that rest is here, but
you couldn't have tempted him here from the surface
of the earth for love or money.

Evidently all this is simply a manner of writing,
dictated by tradition, by the heart's predilection for
elevated words.

One way or another, we can see in these extreme
measures a certain reasonableness in regard to death—
the habit of regarding it as a lawful natural end.

XII. REASON CONQUERS SUFFERING

The brighter and clearer the vault of heaven,
The more unsightly seem to us the clouds
Which fly across its blue expanse...

1

How many and how heavy are the sufferings which people may experience!

They experience these sufferings in nearly every circumstance of our wretched human life, at nearly every crossroads in their path.

These sufferings come from physical causes, from causes lying in the depths of the psyche, and from external causes, which may exert no small influence on that complex sum of actions and affairs which goes by the name of human life.

These sufferings are frequently accompanied by fear.

Fear adds the final touch to the picture of life.

Fear intensifies these sufferings, disarms these people and frequently, as we have seen, drags them to their death.

But reason conquers fear. Reason finds the way to happiness. Reason creates science—the science of a worthy and just human life.

People armed with this science have learned and continue to learn how to crush the obstacles in their path. They learn how to create different, better, worthier conditions for their existence.

And as they proceed down this difficult path, people step by step force back the fears which once relentlessly mastered them.

Thus, for example, in our socialist country people have rid themselves of the basic fear associated with the search for work and hence sustenance. And in this respect we have no people who might fear for their fate. (Of course, I do not consider the war years, when people experience unprecedented sufferings, including hunger in many cases.)

Reason has taught us the way to free people from many physical sufferings. Science struggles against these sufferings with an energy deserving amazement, joy and our hopes.

Science has studied many of these sufferings. It has studied the mechanisms of these sufferings. And the keys to many of these mechanisms have been found.

Yet the keys have not yet been completely assembled to those complex, intimate mechanisms which arise in the depths of our psyche and act upon us, as we have seen, with such inordinate power.

I have tried, not without misgiving, to assemble these keys. And if people may say that these keys do not fit their perhaps overly sensitive mechanisms, then I will reconcile myself to this. I will go off like a lock-smith who has forged a lock but not opened it due to his poor expertise or because he had too much to drink the previous night.

In short, I don't know about other doors, but the keys definitely fit mine.

Reason has spared me much suffering.

Whoever looks on nature with reason, said a certain philosopher, will find that nature looks on him reasonably.

2

Some people, without knowing the source of their sufferings, become resigned to them. And they become resigned by referring to God and to providence. And, perhaps because of their characters, they even try to take pride in this. We know how suffering has been elevated in art, in literature, in painting.

We remember what elevated words the literati have pronounced, saying that suffering enobles people, puri-fies them, raises them to the highest level of charity.

It's a sad and tragicomical spectacle—to see sufferers who urge people to flaunt their scabs instead of to struggle.

About two months before his death Aleksei Maksimovich Gorky sent me a remarkable letter:

I call this letter remarkable because it is an extra-ordinary, courageous letter about suffering. And Gorky wrote it when his own sufferings were great.

Here is what Gorky wrote:

"...Ah, Mikhail Mikhailovich, how good it would be if you produced a book in the same form[143] on the theme of suffering. At no time and with no one has man ever decided to ridicule suffering, which has been and remains the favorite profession of a great number of people. At no time and with no one has suffering ever awakened the feeling of disgust.

305

"Consecrated by the religion of 'the suffering God,' it has played the role of the 'first violin' in history, the leitmotif of life's dominant melody... But while the 'simple people' struggled against its supremacy, even when it meant making each other suffer, or running away from it into the deserts, into the monasteries, into 'foreign parts,' the literati—the prosaists and versifiers—deepened, broadened its 'universality,' despite the fact that even the suffering god himself found his sufferings repugnant, and he prayed: 'Father, let this cup pass me by.'

"Suffering is the shame of the earth, and we must hate it in order to eradicate it...

"...To ridicule the professional sufferers—that's a good idea, dear Mikhail Mikhailovich... To ridicule everyone who is disposed by the idiotic trifles and the inconveniences of his private life to look on the world with hostility.

"You can do this. You would do this work splendidly. It seems to me that you were born for this work. You are actually approaching it—but carefully, maybe too carefully!"[144]

And now, reading over this section of Gorky's letter, I am again struck by his words. And by the fact that Gorky, who was suffering himself, was able to find these words. And by the fact that he understood so precisely what was troubling me then. I was concerned then with precisely these questions as I collected materials for this book of mine, which first bore the title "The Keys to Happiness."

I wrote out a reply but did not send it, for I learned that Gorky had gotten worse. I did not want to bother him, a sick man.

In my reply I wrote that I intended to write just such a book. However (I wrote), I did not intend only to ridicule the "sufferers" in this book, but also to find at least a few causes of suffering in order to understand the source of these sufferings.

306

I promised to send Gorky the first copy of my book.

How painful and how sad it is that Gorky is no longer with us.

I dedicate my book to him in my thoughts.

3

Reason conquers suffering. But the "sufferers" do not want to surrender their positions at any cost.

It was precisely they who declared woe to reason[145] and began to flee it, having decided that all sufferings originate in it and in it alone.

In what way, however, did reason fail to please, in what way did it enrage and infuriate the sufferers?

We have found several causes which had cast reason and even its future into doubt.

We dethroned these doubts to the best of our meager abilities.

But perhaps we missed something? Perhaps we did not study something exceptional which would make us indisputably recognize reason as futile or guilty in the sufferings of humankind?

It would seem not. In my thoughts I survey everything that relates to people, everything that constitutes their life: distant journeys, meetings of friends, work, rendezvouses of lovers, speeches for the prosecution and the defense, performances in theaters, attempts to get something done in office buildings...

No, definitely not! Reason does not produce suffering. In any one of these matters reason does not prove to be superfluous. Quite the contrary. Quite the opposite. God in Heaven! What happy hopes would be ignited in our hearts if higher reason were present at every step, in every trifle, in every breath!

But perhaps there lurks the suspicion that love motives sound subdued in the presence of higher reason and therefore bring people melancholy and sorrow?

No. It would seem not. Everything is normal here.

What is left then? The loss of a, well, birdlike levity, the loss of a sheep's spontaneity? But surely this does not bring such suffering to people that they should deny reason.

Permit me to tell you a little story which will show you that in the final instance reason prevails in this area as well.

Once Flaubert underwent an operation. He had some sort of a boil on his cheek.

Apropos of this, Flaubert writes his beloved (Louise Colet) a melancholic missive about what unhappy creations people are: they are subject to an unceasing process of deterioration and decay.

Observe what incautious expressions Flaubert uses:

"As if all that rot and infection which precedes our birth and awaits us after death were not enough... Today you loose a tooth, tomorrow a hair, a wound opens up, a boil comes to a head... Add to this the corns on your feet, natural bad smells, secretions of every kind and taste—all this gives quite a charming picture of the human person. And just think—this thing is loved!.."

No, of course, you should never write this way. Especially to a woman you love. Here you should restrain your higher consciousness. Stop being so smart. Hold yourself back a little. At least excuse yourself for getting carried away by reason and saying something superfluous.

But then a lady of reason should not have become so angry as she did.

We do not know in precisely what words the beloved answered Flaubert, but judging by his letter, her words were really, and I mean really, unpleasant.

Here is what Flaubert wrote to exonerate himself, but without understanding his wrong:

"Formerly I seemed elevated to you—now I am

petty... What did I do, my God, what? You claim that I address you as a woman of the worst sort... I don't understand your insults and arguments..."

No, it all ended well. Flaubert made up with his beloved. Thus in this respect reason emerged triumphant, and higher consciousness showed the right way to behave.

The lady again brightened up and continued to consider Flaubert elevated. And the little love episode, in which wit had been present and spontaneity had been absent, was forgotten.[146]

No, I see absolutely no cause to fear higher reason. As you see: even in these matters everything turns out quite satisfactorily and without any real suffering.

4

Suffering is the shame of the earth, and we must hate it in order to eradicate it.

Thus spoke Gorky. And I share his opinion entirely. For the purpose of eradicating suffering there exists science. It has done quite a lot. But even more remains for it to do in the future. A great and shining path lies ahead.

Perhaps more and more keys will be found to open the secret mechanisms of suffering. Perhaps still other causes of suffering will be found, causes which we as yet know nothing about.

Perhaps something will be uncovered which now greatly occupies science—questions of radiation.

Science has so far taken only timid steps in this area. And without a doubt, reason lifts the veil from something which is more hidden from us than what was hidden in the secret mechanisms of the large hemispheres.

Perhaps in this area as well certain causes will be found of sufferings which one can be spared.

Everything living radiates. This is what modern

science has found, although without very great certainty. All living tissues are capable of radiating an energy whose properties are similar to electricity.

Various types of rays and various types of currents have been found.

Originally the opinion arose that these rays arise only as a result of the chemical reaction occurring in the blood. Thus, for example, it was found that a frog's blood emits ultraviolet rays.

A similar radiation was discovered in other animals and in man.

It was noted that the blood of sick people (those sick, for example, with sarcoma, cancer) does not radiate. Old age and decrepitude radiate to a lesser degree.

Later it was found that not only the blood radiates: the muscles, brain, skin, nerves all radiate.

It was found that the brain radiates electromagnetic waves. And these waves may actually be picked up by an antenna. And that these quite perceptible waves are created by the movement of electrons flying with the speed of light.

It emerged that the complex brain of man, which has a countless number of cells (more than 12 billion), is able to receive and retain an enormous number of electrons. In any event, it emerged that the brain is apparently the center of a complex electric network.

It was found that deranged brain activity manifests itself in a special form and special frequency of waves. In other words, the magnitude and intensity of the current changes with respect to the condition of the brain.

The brain of hysterics, neurotics, epileptics in certain cases create currents exceeding the norm by many times. This pertains in equal measure to certain kinds of psychic illnesses.

The rays arising in the tissues of living organisms have been named mitogenetic rays. This discovery has produced an extensive literature, yet the fate of this discovery is not completely known to me: I have heard that there is some doubt about these rays. The nature (and origin) of these extremely weak, low-intensity rays has not been demonstrated.

Yet the fate of this discovery does not change matters. The presence of currents and all sorts of radiations in our organism leaves no room for doubt. For a considerable time before this discovery it was known that certain animals, deep-sea ones in particular, possess the property of radiation. It is known, for example, that the sting ray stuns its prey with an extremely strong electrical shock (up to 80 volts).

It was known that people are also bearers of a certain electrical energy.

The famous artist Van Gogh writes of Gauguin in a letter:

"Oftentimes our discussions would become enlivened by an exceptionally strong electric fluid. Sometimes we would end our discussion with tired heads, like electrical batteries after discharging."

Evidently the discovery of biotics and of various radiations of the living organism is nothing new.

These radiations, these currents, are evidently something indisputable, inseparable from everything that lives.

This property of living tissues does not contradict the general principle which was found to pertain to all bodies. It was found that a complex electrical charge formed the basis for the structure of atoms.

And this pertains to the atoms of any substance.[147]

Consequently, a substance is the bearer of complex electrical charges.[148]

And consequently the electrical charge is in a sense the basic composition of matter, that is, evidently the primal material from which the world is formed.

Science does not fully know what electricity is and how many kinds of this energy there are.

Yet many correlations are known in this area.

One of the most elementary correlations is the fact that an electrical current of any sort produces magnetic forces around the wire through which it moves. And every change in the electrical field is accompanied by the emergence of magnetic fields.

And this principle pertains in equal measure to the currents of any property.

Consequently, every radiation is an electromagnetic radiation.

This pertains to light, and to warmth, and to radio, and evidently to biotics, for all the kinds of this energy arise with the aid of electrical waves.

These electromagnetic waves are transmitted in the form of rays, just as waves spread on the surface of water from a fallen stone.

If this is so, then electromagnetic waves should also exert an influence on the surrounding matter.

Consequently, the brain of man, which exists in a complex electrical network and in complex electrical relationships, doubtless experiences the most varied influences.

We may boldly state that the brain is not something detached, some sort of separate, isolated activity. It is not protected against all sorts of influences. It is not self-enclosed. This would contradict elementary principles.

We know that the activity of the large hemispheres is characterized by two basic processes: excitation and inhibition.

Consequently, if we are to speak of some influence from outside, then these influences in the first instance pertain to precisely these processes. And if the apparatus of our brain is truly not self-enclosed, then the influences from outside may affect one or another change of these processes. At the same time these changes evidently may correspond to internal impulses or contradict them.

In any event, if we admit that an influence from outside exists to at least the slightest degree, then the processes of excitation and inhibition do not proceed entirely from internal causes enclosed within the human body.

What is the strength of these influences and what is the origin of these influences—that is another question.

So far science has not been able to decide questions of this sort. And it has not proceeded any farther than hypotheses, sometimes very dubious.

However, it is not our task to decide this question. It is our task merely to suggest the presence of these influences and their possible effect on the large hemispheres of the brain.

It seems to me there can be no doubt: there is an influence from outside. The experiment conducted by G. Gurvich[149] is well known. The scientist demonstrated that when two onions are planted side by side, they influence each other. Short ultraviolet rays arising in one onion facilitate and promote increased cell division in the adjoining onion.

In any event, if these onions are separated from each other by a plastic shelf which cannot be penetrated by ultraviolet rays, then the growth of these onions slows down and the process of cell division becomes significantly weaker. And consequently such an influence from outside on living tissues is incontestable.

Evidently it is incontestable that all living creatures to a greater or lesser degree exert an influence on each other. Evidently not only the brain exists in a complex network of electrical relationships, evidently the whole organism of an animal is not something localized in its own activity.

We know a whole series of such external influences in the experience of our own lives. We know at least that an extreme degree of neurasthenia, of psychic depression, has an adverse effect on others. The others, in turn, begin in some measure to experience a similar depression. Sometimes even an unknown person who comes into the room has an adverse effect: the others begin to feel some sort of "uneasiness," constraint, they begin to feel that they are "not themselves."

Examples of this sort confirm that there are influences from outside. And that these influences first of all affect the processes of inhibition which take place in the brain.

If this be so, if these influences do exist, if the brain of man picks up radiations which originate outside, then how are these external fluctuations reflected on the human psyche? What significance does this external "background" have for the behavior of man?

It seems to us that we should not underestimate the significance of these influences. However slight it may be, they do play a role in the psychic life.

Let us assume that a man's brain begins to experience an extremely strong influence which expresses itself as an increased inhibition. Without knowing why this inhibition has arisen, the man will certainly try to motivate this depression of his by some sort of material or moral cause.

Such an accidental, sometimes spurious motivation is not particularly telling on the healthy psyche of a man. The inhibition goes away, and the motivation is forgotten. Yet for an unhealthy psyche (especially in the case of psychoneurosis) such an incorrect motivation is extremely telling, for the cause of depression will be sought among those "painful objects" which have been "encountered.' At the same time these "painful objects" will be even more decisively confirmed in the psyche as dangerous objects. In other words, the false proofs of danger will be confirmed.

Without a doubt, these questions are extremely difficult to analyse, and these hypotheses must be made circumspectly, yet the principle of correlations may already be seen.

All these questions are questions for the further investigations of science.

As regards the strength of the external influences

and their origin, these questions are even less accessible to calculation.

Scientists have repeatedly made hypotheses about cosmic influences, about the influence of the sun and stars on the organic life of the earth. These questions are of ancient origin. And the science of the past has repeatedly inclined to solutions which view the animal organism as a microcosm.

At any rate, modern science certainly does not reject the significance of those radiations and that energy which our planet receives from without.

So-called cosmic rays have been discovered. They represent a stream of enormous force and consist of electrical charges which bombard our earth. Falling on the rim of our atmosphere, they are able to deform themselves, able to transform themselves into other forces.[150]

The energy of these electrical charges is exceedingly great, yet as they fall on our earth, these charges greatly weaken.

At any rate, science is doing a tremendous amount of research into these radiations. In his time I. Usyskin, who perished in a stratospheric balloon accident, was concerned with this. He took measurements up to 22 kilometers. It was established that at a height of 5 kilometers the intensity of radiation exceeds the intensity at sea level by six times. At a height of 10 kilometers this intensity of rays is 40 times greater than at sea level.

Consequently, the energy of rays penetrating the atmosphere is greatly diminished. And evidently the magnitude of these rays is not so substantial as was once supposed by those who wish to belittle the significance of human life and human reason.

At any rate, the future science will decide the questions of the strength of this influence on man's psyche and behavior. And if it turns out that this influence has some significance and that people therefore experience certain sufferings of which they are unaware, then the reason of man will bring emancipation in this area as well.

XIII. REASON CONQUERS OLD AGE

But old age, may the devil take her, with her
pack and cane
Is knocking, may the devil take her, with her
bony hand.

1

Once I was walking down the street with my friend
and talking with him about old age.

My friend was inclined to believe that old age was
not so repulsive as many people think. He reminded me
of Tolstoi's words on old age: "I never thought that old
age could be so attractive."

I argued with my friend. At that time I looked
with terror on people who fade out, grow decrepit, turn

into miserable old wrecks.

I argued with my friend, claiming that old age was something horrible, more horrible even than death. It was a loss and weakening of feelings, desires, intentions. What could have been worse?

I had the wrong ideas about old age then.

As we conversed, we turned off Nevsky onto the Fontanka, and an unfortunate incident occurred. My friend made a misstep, and a passing truck clipped him. The injury was not too great. He was scratched on the cheek and neck. But his upper lip was pretty badly torn.

I called for an ambulance and took my moaning friend to the hospital. There they immediately put him on the table to sew up his torn lip.

I was present at the operation, squeezed the hand of my comrade tightly when he became terribly worried and moaned.

Before they began the operation, the surgeon (a young woman) addressed her questions to me, since the injured man's lip had swollen so much he could not answer. The woman-surgeon asked:

"How old is your acquaintance?"

I did not know. Shrugged. Said:

"What difference does it make? Get on with the operation. You see what condition he's in... He's probably about forty."

The woman-surgeon, also shrugging, said:

"It makes quite a difference. If he's no more than 40 to 50 years old, I'll give him plastic surgery. But if he's 50, I'll... well, sew him up... No, it'll be all right, just as it should be, but of course... it's not the same thing... as you get with plastic surgery."

Here the injured man, hearing her words, moaned and squirmed on the table. His torn lips did not permit him to enter into a dispute with the physician. Raising his hand, he thrust forward four fingers and shook them as if to say—only forty, only forty, damn it, give me

318

plastic surgery.

With a wry expression, the woman-physician began plastic surgery.

No, his lip was sewn up quite nicely, the scar was negligible, but the blow to my friend's morale had a lasting effect on him. He forgot that he had been hit by a truck, he was disturbed about something else: he could not forget the surgeon's words about fifty-year-old people whose lips could be stitched up the way they sometimes stitch up mattresses, quilting up the gash.

And so this spiritual pain remained with my aging friend for a long time. This pain also remained with me. And I began to think even worse of old age than ever before.

And I decided to struggle against it.

2

No, I never dreamed of living a long time, never wanted to live to see a hundred. I saw no charm or pleasure in this.

But I would like to live in a way that would keep me from growing especially old, that would keep me from knowing pitiful feebleness, decrepitude, despondency. I would like to remain relatively young to the end of my days. That is, a person who would not lose a certain freshness of feelings in his battles with life. This would reconcile me to old age. I would not begin to abhor the years before me. I would not await my old age with such resentment and repugnance as there was then in my heart.

"But how am I to do this?" I thought. "How am I to act so that I don't feel the embrace of old age too keenly? What can one do to make himself feel healthy, flourishing, if not young in old age?"

Could human reason really fail to avail us in this highly legitimate desire?

And then I began to pay greater attention to all

old men. From among them I chose those with bright cheeks, firm gait, smooth skin, strong hands and young, shining eyes.

I didn't find such old men so very often, but when I did find them I wouldn't let them out of my sight. I followed after them, looked into their lives, into their behavior, into their habits.

By observing them I hoped to draw some sort of rule for the preservation of youth.

I was unable to draw any such rule, for every one of these old men lived differently, in his own way, without adhering to any standard.

I began to interrogate many flourishing old men about their secrets. And they readily answered me.

But then every one of them answered me differently, every one had his own peculiarities and his own motivations which he thought accounted for the continued flourishing of his life.

One old man, who was 70 years old, answered me like this:

"I never smoked. Tobacco wears out the tissues. And that's probably the reason why I am young."

Another old man, who was no younger in years, said:

"Tobacco had no bad effect on me. But I was always active in sports, athletics. I slept under an open window. This is what probably had a favorable effect on me."

A third remarkable and even magnificent old man, hardy and fresh as a boy (I am speaking of Bernard Shaw), answered me at a supper given in his honor. With a chuckle the writer said:

"I haven't eaten meat for 35 years. Don't you find the reason for my youthfulness in this circumstance?"

No, I didn't find the reason for the youthfulness of this 75-year-old man in this circumstance.

I didn't find the reason mainly because right next to me there sat another 70-year-old man (I am speaking of F. Kon[151]), who said:

"I've eaten meat all my life. And all the same I'm hale and hardy. The reason is to be found elsewhere: I work, work engrosses me, I am as accurate and precise in my work as a clock. And that, perhaps, is the secret you are seeking."

Another old man (M., an outstanding figure in the arts) said:

"The reason for my youthfulness is work, inspiration. That's where I draw my relative freshness from. But when my work is finished, I deflate like a rubber toy pig punctured in the side."

Another remarkable old man (I am speaking of the people's artist Yu[152]) said:

"You see how things are: I eat a lot, work a lot, I do everything a lot, I don't limit myself in anything. I don't forbid myself anything I want. And I know: when I begin to limit myself, when I begin to fear, when the fear penetrates my heart—then I am dead. Then both life and youth will end simultaneously."

This answer greatly pleased me. But this rule was not for me: I am not accustomed to eating a lot and not accustomed to fulfilling all of my desires. And I did not intend to betray my habits. Yet the second part of the answer struck me as just.

Still another man, who was 70 years old and looked 40 (this was the Danish writer M. A. N.[153]), answered me with a glance at his young wife:

"I love."

Embarrassed, the wife of this man said:

"No, no, it's not only that. My husband loves his literary work. He works a great deal. And that's the reason you are seeking."

Another flourishing old man, who appeared to be 40, but was in fact 63 (this was the poet Ts.), told me with a heavy sigh:

"I am young because I eat tomatoes, cranberries and carrots. But what sense does this make?"

And then, with continued heavy sighs, the poet told me a little story that happened to him. A young girl—the university student N.—fell in love with him. She stayed with him once. And they were happy. In the morning when the poet went into the hallway, the girl, sitting before the mirror, accidentally saw his passport lying on the desk.

When the poet returned to the room he found the girl in tears.

Through her sobs she said:

"My God! I didn't know you were so old. I would never have come to you. My God, how low I have fallen."

I consoled the poet by saying that the girl was stupid. And that was why she had said that. Yet my heart contracted. But then I was consoled by the thought that I was not seeking youthfulness for any love encounters. And if there happened to be any, I could always hide my passport.

Another old man, who reeked of wine, told me:

"Wine alone keeps me strong. Wine alone has given me hardiness, youthfulness and, if you like, adolescence."

I looked closely at this old man. No, this was not youth or adolescence. A puffed-up face. Bleary red eyes and trembling hands told me something else. They told me of the epitaph which would serve to immortalize the approaching end of the old man:

> **Here rests a pitiful body**
> **Parted from a pitiful soul!**

In sum, I questioned a great many, a great many old men. And all of them answered differently. All of them found their own rules which might have suited them but not quite suited others.

Yet some of these rules were helpful to me, and I made good use of them. Nevertheless, my youth slipped away from me in my thirties.

And then I began to think about the rule required for my own needs, for my own life, for my own qualities.

And then it seemed to me that I had found this rule and that it suited me perfectly.

I have in mind the subject matter of this book.

I have in mind the control which I later established for myself in order to free my mind and my body from the lower forces, from their fears and horrors, from their actions expressed in a senseless, savage, mistaken defense against something which it was not necessary to be defended against.

And as a result of this my reason and my body were freed of a great number of obstacles and miseries. And freed of the sufferings which I had borne submissively, supposing that this was the way it should be.

And this gives me hope that old age will not affect me to such a horrible degree as we sometimes observe.

XIV. EPILOGUE

*Consciousness is a thing that
people acquire whether they want
it or not.* **154**

1

And now my book draws to a close.

What remains to be said? Quite a lot has been said
already. It remains only to add the fates of the heroes,
as is fitting in finales.

The main hero is partly myself, partly that suffering
person for whose sake my creation was undertaken.

Everything seems to have been said about me that
can be said.

The years of my boyhood were painted in black,

325

melancholy and despair held me firmly in their grip. The image of a beggar pursued me at every step. Tigers came up to my bed, even when I was not sleeping. The roaring of these tigers, strokes and shots added the final touch to the picture of my sad life.

And no matter where I turned my troubled gaze—everywhere I saw one and the same thing.

Disaster awaited me at every moment of my life.

I did not want to perish in such a lamentable way.

I decided to change my unhappy fate.

I took up the attack against the enemies which I discovered by means of a careful investigation.

One enemy among these—the unconscious fear—was routed along with his insidious defense weaponry.

My other enemies placed themselves at the mercy of the conqueror.

Some of them I destroyed. Others were put in irons and thrown back into their former dungeon.

I emerged the conqueror. I became another person after this battle. Not just another person: a new life awakened completely unlike what had been before.

At times the foe made attempts to regain his positions. But my reason controlled all of his activities, and these attempts broke off.

2

Can we be sure that reason conquered?

Does not this control, this constant vigilance, this watchful gaze in its turn occasion distress, misfortune, despair?

No. This control, this vigilance and watchfulness were needed only in time of combat. Later I managed to do without this and lived almost good-naturedly, as most people live.

But did my craft as an artist not suffer from these battles? Did conquering reason not drive out along with my enemies something precious to me—art?

326

No. On the contrary. My hand became more steady. And my voice more sonorous. And my songs merrier. I did not lose my art. As proof I offer this book of mine. It is written in many genres. And the genre of an artist, I dare to hope, is not the weakest among them.

Can we be sure that such control over the lower forces may be realized without any harm to oneself?

Yes. But such control should be established by people who are able to think professionally, who are able to analyse. Such control must be attained only with the help of a physician. I have warned the reader against dilettantish attempts by citing the example of my own initial defeats.

I know there is no small number of opponents who disparage and will continue to disparage this method of control, and even the idea of control itself.

What is the basis of this protest, and what conclusions do these opponents bring forward?

Some hold that such control cannot be realized. And if it is realized, then it is not really control at all, but something like self-hypnosis.

This, of course, is nonsense. Even if elements of self-hypnosis should arise on occasion, no harm comes from them.

Other opponents hold that such control and the entire process of analysis are accessible only to the very few. Presumably this is a science for the few, it presumably will not serve the masses as a method of treatment.

Well, so what? This illness connected with the psyche itself pertains to the very few. This illness likewise does not serve the masses. And therefore my opponent's argument is unfounded.

My opponents have yet another conclusion. Inhibition, they say, is in a sense a biological necessity. If an inhibition arises (even of a pathological nature), then it arises because it is demanded by this or that deficient organism, deficient since birth. Such an inhibition is in a sense the normal thing. One must become reconciled

327

to it. Just as one must become reconciled to despair and melancholy. For the happiness of mankind is found not in free will and not in free reason. Happiness is found in the vise which restrains people from their desires.

These arguments are usually forwarded by people who fear to look into themselves, people seized by fears, seized by the lower forces which do not permit them to raise their head and see the world illumined by the blinding sun.

It was precisely about these people that the poet said:

> O woe! To flee from the sunshine
> And to seek delights in a cell
> By the light of a lamp...

These people are content to spend their life by the light of the lamp, so long as their fears are not disturbed.

Every page of my book will make these people break out in a sweat.

I can already hear their whining voices.

Once a man who was not stupid, but who was extremely restrained, gripped by his unrecognized fear, nearly destroyed by it in his personal life, wrote to me:

"Don't think that I have cured myself of my neurasthenia, I have only devised a method... My neurasthenia consists of despair (for the most part). So I must assimilate despair into myself. That's the whole method. I convinced myself that this condition is unavoidable and that I must get used to it."

Do you understand what this man said? He said that you must get used to despair. Not drive it away, not destroy it, not investigate the causes of this despair, but get used to it, learn to love it.

What servile feelings! What servility in the face of fear! How patently obvious are the causes of protest!

328

Such examples of protesting "sufferers" convince me all the more that the control of reason is necessary.

In 1936 I received a horrible letter. A peasant (in the Voronezh district), seeking revenge, butchered the family of his neighbor with an axe. A feud had been raging between the two families for a long time, and finally this peasant, seized with a feeling of hatred, committed his bloody crime.

This man was, of course, given the most severe sentence. Locked in his cell, this poorly educated man read some books and among them came across my book *Youth Restored.*

I do not know what this man understood from my book, but one idea he did make out. He understood that a man can and must govern himself.

Struck by this simple thought, the criminal wrote me a letter which said that had he known about this— he would not have committed his crime. But he did not know that it was possible to govern your own feelings.

There can be no question of the lower forces getting the upper hand. Reason must conquer.

AFTERWORD

And so, the book is finished.

The last lines to this book are being put down in October 1943.

I am sitting at the desk in my room on the tenth floor of the "Moscow" hotel.

On the radio they have just reported the rout of the German troops on the Dnepr. Our valiant troops have made a forced crossing over the Dnepr. And now they are driving away the foe.

And so the black army, the army of fascism, the army of darkness and reaction falls back.

What happy and joyful words! But then it could not have been otherwise. It could not have happened that these men could conquer, these men who stood against everything dear to all peoples—against freedom,

331

against reason, for slavery, for the cry of the beast in place of human speech.

Our valiant Red Army is driving away and destroying the foe whose black thoughts have become still blacker.

Night. The pages of my manuscript lie before me.

I leaf through them and make the final corrections.

Dawn breaks through the curtained windows.

I open the door and step out onto the balcony.

A cold October morning. Silence. Moscow is still sleeping. The streets are desolate, empty of people.

But somewhere in the east the sky grows rosy. Morning approaches. Rasping its iron, the first streetcar goes by. The street fills with people.

It's cold.

I return to my room. Collect the scattered pages of my finished book. Mentally bid it farewell. For eight years this book has been on my mind. For eight years I have thought about it almost daily. Eight years—this is no small portion of a man's life.

Some farewell verses come to mind. Perhaps I will recite them sometime in the future when I bid farewell not to this book, and not to eight years of my life, but to my entire life.

They are the verses of a Greek poet:

Most beautiful of all I leave behind is the sunlight;
After that, the sparkling stars and the face of the moon;
Then apples, ripe cantaloupes and pears.[155]

To tell the truth, I am completely indifferent to the stars and the moon. The stars and the moon I will replace with something dearer to me. I will recite the verses this way:

Most beautiful of all I leave behind is the sunlight;

332

After that, art and reason...

And then in third place I can list some fruits—ripe pears, watermelons and cantaloupes...

NOTES

1. *Vozvrashchnonnaya molodost'*, published in 1933. (The author's notes will be identified; all other notes are by the translator.)

2. The Russian term for World War II.

3. Pavlov (1848-1936) led discussions from ten to noon every Wednesday in the Academy of Sciences.

4. Sophocles, "Oedipus at Colonus," included in *Three Theban Plays*, trans. by Theodore Howard Banks (New York: Oxford Un. Pr., 1956), 120.

5. Not long ago, while leafing again through Valery Bryusov's *Diary* I found the following lines: "Yaroshenko's good. A nice man. Foreign to life." *Author's note.*

6. Quoted from the last stanza of Bryon's *The Prisoner of Chillon* (l. 366-369). Zoshchenko cites the Russian translation by Vasily Zhukovsky.

7. Quoted from Poe's letter to Annie L. Richmond, 16 Nov. 1848. *The Letters of Edgar Allan Poe,* John Ostrom, ed. (Cambridge, 1948), II, 403.

8. Quoted from Poe's letter to John P. Kennedy, 11 Sept. 1835. *Ibid.,* I, 73.

9. These words are also found in Tolstoi's *Confession (Ispoved',* 1882), chap. 4.

10. A vacation resort on the eastern shore of the Black Sea, less than halfway between Yalta and Batum.

11. Also the title of Vasily Rozanov's series of reflections *(Oparshie listya,* part I-1913, part II-1915).

12. In the Russian system of grading, one equals "F," five equals "A."

13. The Russian secondary school, equivalent to our junior-high and high school.

14. "The Guardian," a minelayer in the Russo-Japanese war of 1904-1905. The monument was erected in 1911.

15. "Thunderbolt."

16. According to the religious custom, performed at midnight on Easter eve, Russians exclaim "Christ is risen!," respond "Truly he is risen!" and then exchange three kisses.

17. "New Village."

18. "Black River."

19. The final grade, equivalent to our twelfth grade of high school.

20. The heroine of the novel *A Nest of Gentlefolk (Dvoryanskoe gnezdo,* 1859).

21. An allusion to Tolstoi's play of the same name *(Vlast' t'my,* 1887).

22. Health resorts whose names mean, respectively, "Tart water" and "Mineral Waters."

23. "Tart waters" (a confusion of "Kislovodsk" and "Mineralnye Vody").

24. A covered cart.

25. Also the title of a famous story by Chekhov, usually translated as "Sleepy" *(Spat' khochetsya,* 1888).

26. The czarist army included a number of ranks with Germanic titles. This one is equivalent to sergeant major.

27. A cheap, coarse tobacco usually grown in the Ukraine.

28. A Russian unit of measure, equal to seven feet.

29. Low, wide sledges.

30. The litseya (=lyceum) was a special secondary school in prerevolutionary Russia for upper-class children.

31. State farm.

32. Flat bast sandals, laced up around the leg.

33. A title of respect, equivalent to "lord" or "sir," used by peasants in addressing landowners before the revolution.

34. A three-handed form of vint.

35. "Quiet Spell."

36. "Steep Streams."

37. A Russian unit of measurement, equivalent to 3500 feet.

38. Petrogradskaya Storona, the section of Petersburg (Leningrad) lying on the right bank of the Neva, across from the center of the city.

39. A refuge for writers, artists and musicians, founded in 1919 by Maksim Gorky. In 1923 it was converted into a complex of communal apartments.

40. Remizov (1877-1957), reteller of old legends and author of grotesqueries, created the facetious "Great and Free Chamber of Monkeys" and gave honorary titles to all his writer friends. He left Russia in 1921.

41. Zamyatin (1884-1937), author of *We,* worked for two years in England as a shipbuilder just before the Revolution.

42. Viktor Shklovsky (b. 1893) was one of the founders of Russian Formalism. Both he and Zamyatin read lectures to young writers in the House of Arts. Their pupils, who included Zoshchenko, formed the group called "the Serapion Brothers." (1921-1927).

43. Quoted from *Childe Harold's Pilgrimage,* Canto I, section LXXXIV. Bryon was actually twenty-one when he wrote these lines.

44. The Russian version which Zoshchenko cites uses the word "satiety" *(presyshchenie).*

45. M. Slonimsky, *Kniga vospominanii* (M. 1966), p. 153 says the cafe was named after the street number, not Blok's poem.

46. From "How my alarm arises toward night *"(Kak rastyot trevoga k nochi, 1913),* included in the collection *The Terrible World (Strashnyi mir, 1909-1916).*

47. Members of the Serapion Brothers. Maksim Gorky ("Maksim the Bitter," 1868-1936) invited the group to his apartment a couple of times before he left Russia in October 1921. He returned to Russia after several visits, in 1933.

48. Harun Al-Rashid (786-809)—Arab caliph of Abbasid Dynasty, known in legends (particularly *A Thousand and One Nights)* as a paragon of wisdom and justice.

49. Zoshchenko refers to one of his most popular stories, "The Bathhouse" *(Banya),* published in 1924.

50. Kuzmin (1875-1936)—a post-Symbolist novelist and poet, best known for the homosexual epic *The Trout Breaks the Ice* (1927).

51. The traditional monthly since the nineteenth century, which usually printed long novellas.

52. A "poema" is a longer verse form than a "poem" and usually tells a story. Esenin's poema "The Black Man" (*Chyorny chelovek,* 1925) begins as follows: "My friend, my friend, / I'm very, but very sick. / I myself don't know where this pain came from... / The black man, / Black, so black, / The black man / Sits down upon my bed, / The black man / Keeps me awake all night..." Esenin committed suicide in 1925.

53. "On This Day I Complete My Thirty-Sixth Year," second stanza. These lines are the closest equivalent found for

the Russian, which reads: "My genius faded like an autumn leaf, / My fantasy had lost its former wings. / And the brute force of harsh reality / Has turned my romanticism into spleen."

54. The title of a book of verses by Aleksandr Blok *(Strashnyi mir,* 1909-1916).

55. The word for slingshot is *rogatka,* the word for horns— *roga.*

56. Also the title of a famous play by Aleksandr Ostrovsky *(Groza,* 1859).

57. Both Katya and Katka are diminutives of Ekaterina, but the second expresses irritation.

58. Turnovers filled with meat or cabbage.

59. The poem is by the folk poet Ivan Nikitin (1824-1861): "Winter Night in the Village" *(Zimnyaya noch' v derevne,* 1853).

60. A Russian unit of weight, equal to 36 pounds.

61. An island in the Neva north of Petersburg (Leningrad), presently the location of the Kirov Recreation Park.

62. Also the title of a story by Aleksandr Pushkin *(Vystrel,* 1830).

63. Sung by the Miller after his daughter has drowned herself, in Aleksandr Dargomyzhsky's opera *The Mermaid (Rusalka,* 1856, based on Pushkin).

64. From Vasily Zhukovsky's translation of *The Prisoner of Chillon,* section IX. The original lines of Byron are: "And fixedness—without a place; / There were no stars, no earth, no time..." (l. 244-245).

65. Cf. Key to Translation, *strakh* and *strashnyi.*

66. From Vasily Zhukovsky's translation of *The Prisoner of Chillon,* section IX. These lines, which immediately precede those cited below, do not occur in the original (Zhukovsky adds four lines to section IX).

67. Zhukovsky's translation of *The Prisoner of Chillon,* section IX. Byron's lines read as follows: "For all was blank, and bleak, and gray, / It was not night—it was not day, / It was not even the dungeon-light / So hateful to my heavy sight, / But vacancy absorbing space, / And fixedness—without a place; / There were no stars, no earth, no time..." (l. 239-245).

68. The word *vrach* = physician, *vrachevanie* = healing.

69. Further events showed that one could find the cause of

a pathological inhibition by another means, not only through dreams. *Author's note.*

70. "Sands."

71. From the series "Dances of Death," in *The Terrible World (Staryi, staryi son... Iz mraka... 1914).*

72. An acronym for "Red Banner" Expedition for Underwater Operations in the Seas and Rivers of the USSR.

73. Zoshchenko's account *(Chyornyi prints,* 1936) of Epron's attempt to recover the British wreck of 1854.

74. A British submarine which sank in the Baltic Sea in 1919.

75. Shakespeare, *Macbeth,* Act III, scene 2, l. 13-14.

76. The episode entitled "Just Pretend." Cf. above, p. 154. Cf. also the episode "I Want Nothing," p. 73.

77. In Russian, a person is respectfully addressed by his given name and patronymic.

78. Chistyakov (1832-1919)—a historical painter and pedagogue, best remembered as a teacher of Serov, Surikov and Vrubel.

79. The largest island in the delta of the Neva, place of the university, The Academy of Sciences and other institutes of learning.

80. In Russian, the word "student" refers only to a university student or the equivalent.

81. A vacation spot on the Gulf of Finland.

82. Aleksandr Tinyakov (1886-1922)—a poet almost completely forgotten today, not included in any anthologies. Kornei Chukovsky writes of Zoshchenko's meeting with Tinyakov in his reminiscences of Zoshchenko: K. Chukovsky, *Sobranie sochinenii* (Moscow, 1965), II, 531-533.

83. One of the main prospects which cross Nevsky Prospect.

84. I.e., disrespectfully.

85. The last lines of "The Coming Huns" *(Gryadushchie gunny,* 1905).

86. The poem is by Konstantin Balmont (1867-1942): "The Vestments of the Fairy" *(Naryady fei,* 1905).

87. The poem is by Vladimir Solovyov (1853-1900): "My princess, she has a palace so high..." *(U tsaritsy moei est' vysokyi dvorets,* 1876).

88. Shakespeare, *Romeo and Juliet,* Act II, scene 2, line 1.

89. Let my condition serve to warn the reader against any

experiments of this kind. One should investigate the psyche and analyse dreams only under a physician's observation. My auto-therapy led me to dire consequences. And only my professional ability to think and analyse spared me from even greater distress. The reader should not follow my example. It is worse then dangerous. *Author's note.*

90. Cf. Key to Translation, *udar.*

91. Cf. above, p.

92. Cf. "The Student With a Stick," p.

93. Cf. "The Days Are Numbered," p.

94. Taken (slightly inaccurately) from Vasily Rozanov's *Solitaria (Uedinenie,* 1912).

95. Cf. above, p.

96. Zoshchenko means the episode entitled "In a Hotel." Cf. above, p.

97. Later, when everything was unraveled, I was able to determine the source of my cardial neurosis. This neurosis had had a well established past. It had existed with the blessings of physicians who had treated it with mixtures and hydrotherapy. I had borne this chronic illness submissively. Had even gotten used to it.

And so, when everything was unraveled, when the fears gradually began to abandon me, I once closely followed the course of a heart seizure. Without suppressing it, without taking recourse to medicine, I permitted it to begin and to continue to a degree which formerly had always frightened me. But now I controlled both the onset and the whole process, and to my surprise I discovered that the usual symptoms of the heart actually originated in gastral   and intestinal spasms. These spasms did not attain significant strength, but they pressed on the diaphragm, and the actions of the heart resulted from this pressure. Once again, fear must have lain beneath this attack. By dethroning this fear, I eliminated a serious chronic cardial neurosis with such ease that it seemed it had never even existed. *Author's note.*

98. Presently called Petrodvorets, a town founded on the shore of the Gulf of Finland by Peter the Great, site of his monstrous Grand Palace.

99. Also the title of *Les Liasons Dangereuses* (1782) by

Choderlos de Laclos, in its Russian translation *(Opasnye svyazi).*
Zoshchenko wrote a play with this Russian title in 1939.

100. Shakespeare, *Measure for Measure,* Act III, scene 1, 1.
16-17.

101. I have taken the term "painful objects" from Emil Du
Bois-Raymond. Painful objects are those which have made an
unhealthy impression on the infant, objects conditionally connected with some misery, pain, trauma. *Author's note.*

102. Evidently a loose paraphrase of something by Goethe.
Cf. "Analyse und Synthese," *Goethes Werke* (Christian Wegner
Verlag: Hamburg, 1958), XIII, 51-52.

103. Bryon, *The Prisoner of Chillon,* section XIII, 1. 356-
358.

104. This might be translated, "Is it satiety?" Cf. the citation
from Byron above, p.

105. *Gore umu,* the title given by Vsevolod Meyerhold to
his 1928 adaptation of the Russian classic *Woe from Wit (Gore
ot uma,* 1825) by Aleksandr Griboyedov. In Griboyedov's
play, the brilliant and "witty" hero Chatsky is undone by the
rumor that he is insane. Meyerhold's change in the title
suggests that woe does not come from wit, but is visited upon
it.

106. The rank of corporal.

107. I.e., a hospital assistant.

108. The last stanza of the poem "Euthanasia" (1812).

109. Quoted from the letter to John P. Kennedy, 11 Sept.
1835. *The Letters of Edgar Allan Poe,* John Ostrom, ed.
(Cambridge, 1948), I, 73.

110. Quoted from the original letter of 1 Oct. 1848. *Op. cit.,*
II, 384-385.

111. Actually the same letter.

112. Mikhail Pogodin (1800-1875)—publisher and editor of a
leading literary journal, *The Muscovite (Moskvityanin,* 1841-
1856).

113. Aleksandr Petrovich Tolstoi (1801-1873)—a government
bureaucrat and chief procurator of the synod, said to have had a
religious influence on Gogol.

114. The physician who treated Gogol, A. Tarasenko, left
the following note on him: "...No illnesses were detected in

him; he had not had any relations with women for a long time and himself admitted that he felt no need of this and never received any pleasure from this..." *Author's note.*

115. Aleksandr Danilevsky (1809-1888)—boyhood companion of Gogol and one of his closest friends.

116. Metropolitan of Moscow from 1826-1867.

117. Author of sketches and reminiscences, Sergei Aksakov (1791-1859) was also the father of Konstantin (1817-1860) and Ivan (1823-1868), two leading Slavophiles. In the Aksakov household Gogol was regarded as a genius and prophet.

118. Author of literary reminiscences and editor of Pushkin (1812-1887). He served for a while as Gogol's secretary.

119. This, for example, explains cases in which an old man "regresses into childhood." *Author's note.*

120. Nikolai Nekrasov (1821-1877)—the famous poet and editor.

121. Nekrasov did have a cancerous tumor of the rectum. This tumor was removed four months before his death. However, it may have appeared only shortly before the operation. *Author's note.*

122. Mikhail Saltykov-Shchedrin (1826-1889)—publicist and satirist, best known for the novel *The Golovlyovs (Golovlyovy,* 1876).

123. Before his marriage to Ganskaya, Balzac had had quite a few infatuations and affairs, but these relationships did not appear "dangerous": it was possible to sever them. Marriage prevented flight. The conflict become more complex, an "inescapable" situation was created. *Author's note.*

124. These qualities of an elevated mind may in fact facilitate a mistake in the sphere of conditioned connections. *Author's note.*

125. From Blok's poem "I have conquered her at last!" *(Ya eyo pobedil nakonets!,* 1909), included in *The Terrible World.*

126. Nikolai Yazykov (1803-1846)—one of the "Pushkin pleiade" and Gogol's favorite poet.

127. Khomyakov (1804-1860)—a leading Slavophile.

128. Penteleimon Kulish (1819-1897)—Ukrainian writer.

129. Prince Grigory Potyomkin (1739-1791)—dashing field marshal (he annexed the Crimea in 1783) and womanizer, best

remembered today for the battleship in his name.

130. She reigned from 1741-1761, encouraged the arts and sciences and increased the nation's debts.

131. The first Romanov, a weakling tsar who reigned from 1613-1645.

132. Apparently taken from chap. 4 of *Confession (Ispoved'*, 1882).

133. The conclusion to the poem "The years are flying. Worlds are flying. Empty..." *(Miry letyat. Goda. letyat. Pustaya...*, 1912), included in *The Terrible World*.

134. Shakespeare, *Julius Caesar*, Act II, scene 2. These lines are the closest equivalent found for the Russian, which reads: "...Fear brings on death, / But we are death's obedient slaves, / Giving ourselves over to death from fear without a struggle."

135. After this feat, Matrosov (1924-1943), a member of the Komsomol (Communist Youth League), was named a Hero of the Soviet Union and his artillery regiment was named after him.

136. Mikhail Lomonosov (1711-1765)—poet, grammarian, scientist, associated with the Academy of Sciences in Petersburg and the University in Moscow.

137. Count Aleksandr Suvorov (1730-1800)—great soldier (he captured northern Italy from the French in 1798).

138. Gavriil Derzhavin (1743-1816)—Russia's first great poet, he wrote "The Waterfall" *(Vodopad,* 1794) in honor of Potyomkin's death. (Potyomkin is said to have died simply, being left to lie in the steppe.)

139. Ilya Repin (1844-1930)—great realist painter; his portrait of Moussorgsky and "The Zaporozhye Cossacks Drafting a Reply to the Turkish Sultan" are probably his most famous works. Repin is buried in the garden of his estate outside Leningrad.

140. Kornei Chukovsky (1882-1969)—literary critic, expert on Whitman and Nekrasov, children's poet. Chukovsky was one of Zoshchenko's mentors in the House of Arts (1919-1921).

141. Vera Aksakova (1819-1864)—eldest daughter of Sergei Aksakov.

142. I.e., where Zoshchenko's parents were buried.

143. A reference to my *Skyblue Book (Golubaya kniga,* 1935) Author's note. The book consists of stories arranged under various headings, eg. "money," "love," "perfidy," etc. It is

dedicated to Gorky.

144. The letter dates from 25 March 1936. It is published in *Literaturnoe nasledstvo* (Moscow, 1963), vol. 70.

145. Cf. Key to Translation, *razum* and *um.*

146. Later Flaubert broke off relations with Colet because they interferred with his art.

147. Every substance consists of molecules, which constitute the smallest part of the substance. A molecule is the finest subdivision we can obtain without changing the chemical properties of the substance. For example, ice consists of water molecules. But if we divide a water molecule, it will no longer be water but atoms of oxygen and hydrogen. *Author's note.*

148. The atoms themselves are reserves of the greatest stores of energy. The breaking or splitting of the atom transforms matter into energy. *Author's note.*

149. Actually Aleksandr Gavrilovich Gurvich (1874-?)—Russian biologist who discovered mitogenetic rays in 1923.

150. A neutral atom (a positively charged nucleus with negatively charged electrons circling it) is capable of dividing into two charged particles. This process of division is called ionization. *Author's note.*

151. Probably Feliks Kon (1864-1941)—editor of party newspapers, museum director and publicist.

152. Probably Yury Yuryev (1872-1948)—actor named People's Artist in 1939; he played the roles of Chatsky, Romeo, Faust.

153. Probably Martin Andersen Nex (1869-1954)—socialist novelist, author of the five-volume *Ditte* (1917-1921).

154. Karl Marx, *Correspondence,* 1843.

155. The poem (untitled) is by Praxilla (c. 440 B.C.).

AFTER THE AFTERWORD

The Genesis, Art and Theory of *Before Sunrise*

> *We have scotch'd the snake, not kill'd it;*
> *She close, and be herself; whilst our poor malice*
> *Remains in danger of her former tooth.*

And so, the author has stepped out onto the balcony and seen the dawning of a new day, after so many years of needless despair. But does the reader not sense something sad in this scene? Does he not detect a shadow looming behind the back of the author? And is there a reader who does not find the last chapters of this, the author's masterpiece, in which reason takes on such fearsome opponents as death, suffering and old age, the least interesting and least convincing chapters of the entire book? Is there not something sad and even tragic about them?

1

Zoshchenko began writing about ennui, old age and the struggle against them quite early in his career. In 1923 he wrote a humoresque entitled "A Story About How A Certain Russian Citizen Went To Europe To Get Young" *(Rasskaz o tom, kak odin russkii grazhdanin poekhal v Evropu omolazhivat'sya)*. The protagonist, grown old and weary in Russia, goes to Germany, runs out of money and pays a quack his last funds for a youth injection, which kills him. The story falls in the tradition of spoofs, initiated by Nikolai Leskov, in which uncultured Russians misunderstand the customs, gadgets and thinking of "civilized" countries. Other stories in this vein by Zoshchenko are the better known "The Dictaphone," "The Trap," and "The Quality of Production." They represent merely a fraction of the hundreds of short satires which Zoshchenko penned in the twenties and which secured his popularity with Russian readers. But at the same time Zoshchenko began to compose a different type of story, a "sentimental novella," in which the humor was more mellow, bittersweet, and sadness began to show through the comical situations. The first step in this direction was "Wisdom"

(Mudrost'), also written in 1923. In this story, the hero (identified in the first version as the author's "grandfather") becomes a recluse after several years of drinking, skirt-chasing and brawling:

> But why he did this, what or whom his isolation served, no one knew. They only knew that the man was living his life, when suddenly everything in it appeared pitiful and pointless to him. All the best human qualities, as, for example, nobility, pride, love of fame, seemed like silly pastimes and jackstraws. And all the charm of his former existence, love, tenderness, wine, became silly and even demeaning.
>
> But whether this was basically physiological, from surfeit, so to speak, or whether it was related to spiritual vagaries, no one knew, and could not know, for with each year his distance from people grew greater.[1]

After 11 years of musty retirement, during which the flower of his youth has badly wilted, he suddenly has a change of heart. One morning he wakes up full of vim and vinegar. Surprised at himself, he spruces up, floods his dismal rooms with light, makes the rounds of his former friends and invites them to a party. In the process, he becomes younger, gay, a new man altogether. But just before the guests arrive, the revitalized and overexcited old guy has a stroke and dies. The ancient crone with whom he lives is left to explain away his demise to the famished guests. This ironic ending would seem to ridicule the hero's belated attempt to live a bright life, to preach the moral that "it's later than you think," but the point that a person's miseries may be self-induced and also self-treated has definitely been made. In this respect, the story recalls certain theories about the benefit of acting, current in the Russian theater early in the century. Nikolai Evreinov, in particular, proposed a "theater for one-self" in which one plays a role not simply to divert himself, but to improve and transform his life. If you have been sick a long time, and a cure does not seem forthcoming, advised Evreinov, it is time to "stage a recovery." Bring in a doctor friend, enlist a kindly neighbor as nurse, and run through the whole routine. The salubrious action of playing (which Evreinov found in all peoples, animals and children) will effect a cure. The inventions of art, put into practice, will become reality. (Evreinov also suggested "trying on deaths.")[2]

But Zoshchenko worked out his own theories. A melancholic since early manhood, he had already given up on the doctors and had begun to study the lives of great men, hoping to find there a remedy to his malaise. Perhaps at the same time he had begun to consider determination, willpower, the answer to his difficulties. Among the Serapion Brothers he was known as a diffident and sad person, easy to take offense on a matter of principle. The remark "Zoshchenko is offended!" became a standard joke within the group. Yet memoirists recall that he was becoming more open, more ready to laugh, less foreign and cold than in the first years. However this may be, his mental condition steadily worsened. Toward the end of 1926 Ilya Gruzdev, one of the Serapion Brothers, wrote Maksim Gorky:

> **Things are bad with Zoshchenko. This summer he suffered a strange illness—he was on the border line of insanity. He couldn't go out on the street alone. "I go," he says, "and suddenly the streetlamp grows incredibly large and hurls itself at me. A man comes and he grows large and—he's at me." Now Zoshchenko has recovered, he's merry, he says that by the force of his own willpower he mastered his hallucinations and even his heart seizures. But something else has appeared—great egocentricity. It seems he can neither talk nor think about anything but himself. And his opinion of himself—it's something Gogolian, horrendous. So let's keep this confidential. All the same, I love him a lot for his writing.[3]**

Evidently this report on Zoshchenko caught him at the first stage of his autotherapy, when he believed he had conquered his unseen foe and exulted in an easy triumph. The foe proved more durable. Zoshchenko, retaining his faith in willpower, continued his studies. In September 1927 he wrote Gorky (on the occasion of the latter's 35th anniversary as a writer):

> I very much wish you health and a long life, which, as it seems to me, depends mainly on a man's willpower.
> I read a remarkable phrase of Goethe's. When one of his friends died—a 70-year-old man, S.—Goethe said: "I am

347

surprised that people lack the courage to live longer."

Therefore, Goethe believed that for a long life one need only have the desire and evidently the notion, the assurance that one can live a long time and even as long as he likes.

And now every time I read about the long life of some great old man or other, I come to the thought that this is precisely the case, and that a man who has lived 60-70 years is either simply an animal or a very wise man who has made his life with his own hands, by directing and regulating his organism, just as, say, a workman regulates the machine on his bench.

I wanted to ask you, what do you think—is this true? Is it true that people, by themselves, with their own hands, make a long life for themselves. Is it true that people frequently create a philosophy for themselves (as, for example, Lev Tolstoi) which does not run counter to either their own strength or to their ability to live a long time.

Or am I deluded. And people live as they have to, consulting physicians from time to time about their indispositions and eating pills which support their life. It still seems to me that this is not the case.[4]

Gorky's response is not known, but, judging by the remaining nine years of correspondence between the two, we may assume that it was encouraging.[5] Still, Zoshchenko had not discovered the antidote to his anomie. Contemporaries recall him as painfully sullen and taciturn late in the twenties. Kornei Chukovsky tells the story of being invited to what promised to be a hilarious gathering of wits—Zoshchenko, Mikhail Koltsov, Ilf and Petrov. He arrived to spend four hours of awkwardness and gloom, brought on by Zoshchenko's dismal mood. "It's impossible even to smile in the presence of such a sufferer," remarked Ilf or Petrov.[6]

Zoshchenko persisted in his search for happiness through willpower. When he felt like being alone, he would force himself to visit good-natured people and mix among them. When he felt like quiet, he would seek out a noisy place.[7] After a few years, he again told friends that he had found the answer. This answer he gave to his readers in the novella *Youth Restored* (1933), his most important work on this subject prior to *Before Sunrise.*[8] It tells a story which, in a sense, combines both "Wisdom" and Zoshchenko's letter to Gorky. A 53-year-old professor, bored and ailing, decides "to breathe life into his broken body and to restore his youth." He first turns to physicians, who prescribe bromides and pills for him, give him shock treatments, hypnotise him and reduce him to a physical and emotional wreck. He decides to visit a neurologist, but here makes an important discovery. After shaving, changing his underwear, getting dressed and going out on the street, he notices to his amazement that these procedures have revived him. This caused him to ponder over his complaints and to devise his own plan to counteract them. He works out a program of moderate exercises, and his health improves. He traces his miseries back to his youth, and begins to change his habits. He links fresh feelings with romance and, abandoning his wife, begins to court the 19-year-old hussy next door, who has already run through "five husbands and seven or eight abortions." They marry, and the marriage works a miracle on the old boy until he finds his bride with a lover. He has a stroke, spends a month in the hospital, but does not die. Returning home, he resumes his exercises, reconciles himself with his politically-minded daughter and even listens to his wife for a long time, discovering that "she was not the ninny she had seemed to be for the last twenty years." His health and family life begin to flourish, but sometimes he casts a furtive glance next door and sighs over the lost hussy.

Even from this brief resume, it should be obvious that *Youth Restored* is hardly "an ordinary novella which writers write by the score," as Zoshchenko characterizes it in *Before Sunrise.* For one thing, it is ambiguous in a time of simplistic messages for the proletariat—both comic and sad, serious and ironic. For another thing, it is enclosed by seventeen introductions and seventeen postscripts, or "commentaries and articles to the novella." But above all, it is here (in the commentaries) that the author first develops his idea of autotherapy and touches upon the interrelationship of art and health. His rejection of an art which burns up its creator and his identification of intelligence with health is best illustrated by his commentary on Nietzsche:

Nietzsche wrote of his own mind as the highest

human aptitude. One chapter of his book *(Human, All Too Human,* I believe) is called "Why I Am So Wise."[9]

But was Nietzsche really so wise as he wrote of himself?

Examining his life, we see such a monstrous failure to understand himself and such a barbarian attitude toward his own body and brain, that in no way can we accept the mind of Nietzsche as "the highest manifestation of human aptitude."

Nietzsche forwarded the idea of the "superman," that is, a man who has the highest condition of physical and mental health, a man free in his views, convictions and actions.

This should have obliged Nietzsche even more to know something about himself.

But we see simply incredible things.

Approaching 35, having driven himself through inordinate work into a nervous, extremely irritated condition, having lost sleep, appetite and the ability to digest properly, he does not find it necessary to correct this situation by resting or planning a proper schedule. Without changing his schedule, he places all his hopes on a cure, only by means of pills and mixtures. Every day he gulps down a pile of medicines. For sluggish digestion he takes drops, for a headache—powders. For insomnia—the cruelest measure: veronal and chloral hydrate.

He takes these medicines every day.

For eleven years he almost never goes to bed without first taking a sleeping powder. When these powders don't work, he increases the dosage or replaces them with other measures which induce a brief, artificial, five-hour sleep.

Nietzsche's biographer cites the quantity of chloral hydrate ingested in the course of only one month: almost fifty grams.

Approaching 40, Nietzsche's health has become atrocious. Yet Nietzsche fails to see or to find the causes which put him in this condition. Worse than that, he finds these causes in the atmospheric pressure. He seeks relief from his sufferings in a change of place and a change of climate. He ascribes special curative properties to this or that place, but, once having arrived in the place, he quickly

350

becomes disenchanted.

He ascribes especially harmful properties to tobacco and tea. He absolutely refuses to take these things, which are actually innocent in comparison to veronal, narcotics.

At the age of 39 he writes in a letter:

"Terrible and almost uninterrupted sufferings force me to await the end avidly."

But he awaits the end for almost 20 more years. At the age of 46 he is afflicted by mental illness, and at the age of 57 he dies. He lives eleven years as a mental patient...

But was there no struggle for his health? Apparently, there was. In the last two years of his conscious life Nietzsche tries, as it were, to restore his strength. He tries to do this by psychic influence. He seems to talk himself into believing that he is essentially healthy. And at the very height of his illness he writes in his works that his health is quite sound.

Had this not happened, had there been no struggle for his health in his lifetime, then one could acknowledge only exceptional fanaticism, madness and the desire to know nothing but his work...

I do not judge the quality of a man by the length of his life. One person's short life may be more valuable than the century lived by another. But I believe that if an excellent short life is lengthened, that quality is not lessened.

Nietzsche could not do this and spent eleven years in madness.[10]

In the other sixteen commentaries, Zoshchenko offers suggestions for a reasonable attitude toward one's own "body and brain," drawing on the lives of great men, the advice of friends and his own experience as a neurasthenic. "These medical comments of mine are not copied down from books," he writes. "I was the dog on which all the experiments were made." Zoshchenko proposes that a person learn to rest as well as to work, for, as Lenin said: "Whoever does not know how to rest also does not know how to work." It is good to plan a schedule in which healthful actions become habitual, for "the organism is inclined to work like a machine," and when pernicious habits become fixed the organism regards them as normal and even necessary. Zoshchenko cites approvingly the regularity of Kant's life, which rid Kant of his early sickness and insured him his 81 years. True, Kant did over do it, he became a "maniac" of punctuality, and his innocence in regard to women was "tragic," but his experiment in controlling his own body was a "success."[11] It is also healthy to have a goal, a striving toward something, and the greater the goal—the greater the life-force. Zoshchenko recalls a rich, sated man who built a tower out of sheer boredom and then jumped off it once it was completed. Tolstoi wrote Fet, who was building a house: "Build a bit longer, dear Fet, or else a depression may come over you again."

Such, in a nutshell, are the positive pieces of advice which Zoshchenko gives the readers of *Youth Restored*. They are founded on the principles of attentiveness to one's body, moderation, reason. But they are insufficient by themselves, for many people are not in a position to follow them. Many people must first rid themselves of bad habits, physical malfunctions, nervous irritation, mental exhaustion, etc. before they can embark on a program of right living. Here Zoshchenko suggests methods founded not so much on reason as on a kind of self-hypnosis. The brain of a neurasthenic, he observes, dwells constantly on one theme, one problem, one memory, which gives it no rest, weakens the organism and prevents it from reacting directly and forcefully to its surroundings. Since it is impossible to remove this idée fixe with medicines, the only remedy is—to give it another interpretation. The sick person must tell himself that he is sick, unable to judge correctly, and then decide to rate his problem lower for a while, until he can cope with it as a healthy person. This will give him a breather and put him back on the road to health. In regard to psychosomatic complaints, the sufferer must simply refuse to pay attention:

> If a person has heart palpitations and he gets scared, the palpitations will be strengthened. If a person tells himself that he does not want these palpitations, that is, he suppresses them, they will not vanish. But if he tells himself that this is bunk, that this is an accident and will pass, and if this is said with full assurance and his attention is distracted from this to something else, then the heart palpitations will really pass, for they were born, if we may put it that way, in the psyche. (p. 150)

And finally, when one has minimized his problem, eliminated his complaint, found a goal and a program for life, he must forget that his neurasthenia ever existed:

> **"And if you do not forget, it will inevitably return. You must strike it out of your consciousness, at least in the first days. No traces of this illness should remain in your memory. Otherwise you will never part with the illness for good." (p. 145)**

These words are pronounced by a doctor who cured himself: as a vigorous young man he had been so afflicted by despair that both his legs were paralysed, but then, in this condition, he took up medical work and became happy. "What an unusual and cruel joke," remarks Zoshchenko, "to feel ill and unfortunate when you have no misfortunes, and to be healthy and joyful after losing so much." (p. 146)

In sum, Zoshchenko designs a double tactic against that ancient nemesis—mania, dementia, melancholia, neurasthenia, neurosis. First you must dismiss this nemesis as "bunk," and then you must live your life reasonably. This tactic, composed of so many wise maneuvers, seems in the final instance to skirt around the enemy—it leaves it unknown, untouched. Both the novella and the commentaries leave the reader with an uneasy feeling: yes, things have turned out for the best, but... The professor, directed down the slow road to health, glances wistfully at the fast road to hell. The author, having glorified reason and will-power, closes his work with their disappearance. He describes himself in Sestroretsk, sitting on the bed, looking out the window, at the sunshine, the clouds, dogs, children playing, a pretty woman pursued by an eager man, a little girl coming to visit his son, and he writes:

> **The well-being and unshakableness of these eternal scenes for some reason rejoice and console me.**
> **I don't want to think anymore. And with this I break off my novella. (p. 164)**

Other commentators on Zoshchenko find this conclusion uplifting. But this reader cannot escape the impression that the daily round of life has won, the eternal scenes will be repeated and will include all the miseries of man, whatever the mind thinks.

Youth Restored is an extremely unusual, engrossing work, but one that does not admit of an easy interpretation. The ironic story and the serious commentaries do not mix, or even mock each other. (The section of Nietzsche is given apropos of a dog which was said to be smart, but which stupidly chased cars.) To confuse even further the interplay of fiction and fact, the author appears in both the novella and the commentaries, wearing two masks, first as an acquaintance of the professor and then as an apologetic layman, the experimental "dog." One suspects the author feared to call his work a scientific study, yet the fictional "novella" occupies only a small portion of the work. Certainly Zoshchenko had a master plan, he was creating a new genre out of two dissimilar ones, but the effect is bewildering. To my mind, the work makes sense if we consider the novella the more "factual" part—this is what we might expect in life (accepting all of the fictional premises). The commentaries are the more "fictional" part—the theory, the beautiful ideal which we are not yet able to attain. But we must also remember that ambiguity may have been a protective device for Zoshchenko. In Stalin's time, it was sometimes healthier to say things indirectly. The acclaim won by *Youth Restored* (probably Zoshchenko's greatest success in his lifetime) and the opprobrium won by the more direct *Before Sunrise* proved the wisdom of this tactic.

Reviewing these several precursors of *Before Sunrise,* we find that Zoshchenko, in both his fictional and factual expressions, was mulling over the same themes—lost youth, exhaustion, tragic love, recuperation, control of the body by the mind. He did not yet have a definitive answer, a coherent theory—this is why he could espouse mental control, and yet advise flight from the enemy, methods how not to think about it. So far he had not determined the cause of despair, he could not account for imaginary aches and pains, and in any event he had not yet resolved to share his researches openly with the reader. In the story "Healing and Psychics" (1932), according to one scholar, he creates "an impression contrary to his own convictions," seeming to ridicule psychiatry, yet on closer inspection actually ridiculing the stupid remarks of the patients.[12] In *Youth Restored* he touches upon such subjects as inhibition, frustration, conflict, etc., but fails to discuss either Freud or Pavlov. Only by a minute analysis (sometimes of a kremlinological nature) can we determine what Zoshchenko knew and intended in these years. Nevertheless, we can make one simple generalization. In his evolution from humorist to the author of *Before Sunrise,* Zoshchenko moved constantly in the direction of self-control, reason, rationality.

Thus he aligned himself with two great figures in Russian literature: Tolstoi and Gorky. To be sure, he dismissed Tolstoi for his religion, but at the same time he admired the construction of a system which (so he supposed) answered Tolstoi's needs. More importantly, he created in *Before Sunrise* a modern parallel to Tolstoi's *Confession* (1882). The latter work begins by describing the author's youth, his quest for self-perfection and his inexplicable despair at the pinnacle of his fame. This states the problem of the book (more specifically, what is the meaning of life?), and in the remaining chapters the author deliberately, rationally, considers all the possible answers, examining the major philosophies, the world's religions, cataloguing four ways of dealing with death, etc. The same procedure is evident in *What Is Art?* (1898), where Tolstoi cooly reviews the esthetic theories of some sixty thinkers on the subject, before arguing his own. But beyond this, the paths diverge. In both books Tolstoi uses reason to extinguish itself and ignite faith, whereas Zoshchenko (to his own mind) remains steadfastly with reason.

In Gorky, Zoshchenko found a living paragon—a self-made man, a great humanist, a writer obsessed with the idea of ridding the world of suffering. In his self-imposed exile in Italy (1921-1932), Gorky seemed to stand above the literary polemics raging in Russia. With him Zoshchenko could share his thoughts and plans, and from him he could receive the support and encouragement often denied him at home. In Gorky's letters and writings Zoshchenko no doubt found ideas corresponding to his own. In particular, Gorky's article on Blok (1923) states the same concerns as *Before Sunrise.* The article begins with the words: "...Sometimes it seems to me that Russian thought is sick with the fear of its own self; by striving to remain outside of reason it disdains reason, fears it."[13] Gorky questions the suspicion of reason, the belief that great men are naturally depressed, the statements of writers (Tolstoi, Dostoevsky, Rozanov) that consciousness is an illness. Zoshchenko even uses some of the same quotations. Both regard Blok as the epitome of despair.

Perhaps it is not amiss to locate Zoshchenko's turn toward propaganda precisely in this rationalistic streak. It is logic and optimism, after all, which are the chief attractions of Marxism (to an intellectual). In the twenties Zoshchenko had signed the Serapion Brothers' statement against tendentious art ("An Answer to S. Gorodetsky"), he had joked that he would probably never be a Communist but was willing to "bolshevik around" ("About Myself, About Ideology, And Also About This and That"), and he had written satires strongly suggesting that human nature was incorrigible and revolutionary measures only complicated life. In 1930 he had defended his right to concentrate on the negative aspects of society: "my genre, that is, the genre of a humorist, is incompatible with the description of achievements."[14] But just as Maksim Gorky ("Maksim the Bitter") returned to Russia and earned the nickname Maksim Sladky ("Maksim the Sweet"), so Zoshchenko in the thirties tried to convert his art into a tool for the building of socialism. He simplified his syntax, his vocabulary, his thoughts; he wrote on assigned topics, accepted commissions, participated in writers' collectives; he gave speeches, worked on editorial boards, became an *aktivist*. The tenor of his optimistic works is exemplified by the conclusion to "A Story of One Life" (1933), the account of a rehabilitated thief. Readers of *Before Sunrise* will hear peculiar overtones in these words:

> And so, our entertaining story is finished.
>
> Now let us slice through the outer layers, so to speak, with the surgeon's scalpel.
>
> Three suppositions may occur to a sceptic who is used to doubting human feelings.
>
> Either R., having gone through fire, water and copper pipes, really reconstructed his psyche and became a man of labor.
>
> Or he pulled off a new "job."
>
> Or he weighed everything and decided that the criminal world would be busted and a thief had better requalify himself. And if this is the case, he did this not on moral grounds, but on the grounds of necessity.
>
> I place these three suppositions on the scales of my professional ability to analyse people. And I vote for the

first supposition.

So I would vouch for the new life of this man. But I make a reservation: I would vouch for him in our non-capitalistic conditions.

How glorious it will be to live in a country where the doors will not be locked shut and where people will forget those sad words of everyday life: thief, stealing, robbery and murder.[15]

How far Zoshchenko developed as a rationalist may be shown by one final comparison—with Evgeny Zamyatin. As a lecturer and writer, Zamyatin was criticised throughout the twenties for exerting and "ideological" influence over young writers, particularly the Serapion Brothers. His style matches Zoshchenko's at several points, but in terms of philosophy his works mark the end of the anti-rationalist line in Russian literature. Gogol-Dostoevsky-Belyi-Remizov-Zamyatin. (Current readers may wish to add Tertz.) It is interesting, therefore, that Zamyatin's novel *We* (1920) and Zoshchenko's novella *Before Sunrise* (1937, 1942-43) end with the same words. Yet when Zamyatin writes that "reason must conquer" *(razum dolzhen pobedit'),* the reader takes it as a mockery, for in the novel men have been converted into robots, soulless happy goons unable to feel or fantasize, all in the name of reason. But when Zoshchenko writes that "reason must conquer" *(dolzhen pobezhdat' razum)* it is meant as a triumph over the forces of darkness.

2

About a year after the abortive publication of *Before Sunrise* in 1943, Chukovsky met Zoshchenko in Moscow and gave his opinion of the work. The short episodes, he thought, were so simple, so natural, that it seemed the author did not even notice his own mastery. Zoshchenko needed only to pick them out of the surrounding text and publish them separately. With compressed lips and an offended tone, Zoshchenko replied: "What did you say? Pick... them... out? What do you mean, pick... them... out?" But Chukovsky, recalling this scene in 1965, maintained his opinion: "These short novellettes, as works of art, are much dearer to me than the entire book."[16]

Let us pursue this question. Assume that Zoshchenko's

357

conjectures on health, neurosis and conditioned reflexes are determined by science to be worthless, that nothing of use can be gleaned from his theory. What value would the book have then? In other words, what is the artistic merit of the work, apart from its message?

Our attention is drawn first to the short episodes, the recollections. In them it is possible to perceive the influence (or at least the methods) of Zoshchenko's two teachers in prose— Viktor Shklovsky and Evgeny Zamyatin. Once, in 1928, Zoshchenko paid tribute to Shklovsky for breaking up the old form of literary Russian: "He shortened the phrase. He let 'fresh air' into his articles. It became pleasant and easy to read... I did the same thing."[17] No further comment appears necessary: the recollections are compressed to the final degree. As Zamyatin, Zoshchenko offers a perspective which constantly expands or contracts, slowly or abruptly, as if the author were operating a zoom lens. Consider, for example, the first paragraph of Zamyatin's story "The Cave" *(Peshchera,* 1920). It is packed with nouns denoting things of various sizes. First, contraction: glaciers... wastelands... cliffs... caves... path... snowdust. Now expansion: mammoth... wind... roar... super-mammothish mammoth... winter. So too, Zoshchenko, less dramatically, more fleetingly, shifts our perspective. First, contraction: gates... officer... entry pass... student registration ("At the University," p. 30). Again: ballroom... windows... curtains... mirrors (between the windows)... piano... man in tuxedo... aster... buttonhole ("Feeling Sleepy," p. 37). Now expansion: operating table... white oilcloth... huge window... blue sky ("Torture," p. 29). Again: hand... knife... (pig's) belly... lard of immeasurable thickness ("Nerves," p. 39). Often there is a quick interchange of large and small. On occasion there is a comparison: the yellow ball on a stand... the yellow corpses laid out beneath it ("In the Garden," p. 45). The reader, once alerted to the feature, can pick out examples on almost every page of the first chapters. (The word order of the Russian is kept in the translation so as to retain this perspective, even though the English sentences must often be inverted.)

Another feature is one familiar to readers of Shklovsky, Zamyatin and the other Serapion Brothers: authorial distance. Zoshchenko describes many of the disturbing incidents in his life almost as if he were not present, or present as a non-participant. The most remarkable example of this device is the episode "Was It Worth the Hanging" (p.   ). In the original there is a subtle word-play which could not be retained in the translation. Where the translation reads "we decided... we gathered... we sang... we sang," in the original there are only the verbs, without subjects, which could also be translated: *"they* decided... *they* gathered... *they* sang... *they* sang" (the first and third person plural forms are identical in this instance). It's as if the persona of Zoshchenko were not really taking part in the outrageous celebration of the student's suicide. But then, in the last paragraph, the author specifically writes "we sang," and one understands that he also bears the guilt for this evening. A great distance is also felt in the similar episode "Five O'Clock Tea" (p. 55), where the author describes himself in an awkward position, but from the outside, without a word about his inner feelings. We see only his despairing expression and his gesture of helplessness at the end.

The similarity of these two episodes (there is senseless singing in both) points to the most curious feature of the recollections: the repetition of the same actions with different people. Leaving a woman, for example, becomes almost a ritual performance in these sketches. This impression is heightened by the repetition of the same words ("I leave," "I go away," etc.). Other repetitions: officers "standing beside saddled horses" ("Breakthrough" and "I Came For Nothing"), a "calm" death with "easy breathing" ("An Old Man Dies" and "January the Twelfth"), a melancholic looking away in a "near-dark" room ("The House of Arts" and "A Meeting"), a poet sitting down "ponderously" (" 'The Twelve' Cafe" and "At a Table"). One of the more suggestive repetitions is the phrase "just kidding" *(poshutil).* The persona wishes that a drowned boy would say: "Just pretend. I was just kidding." ("Someone Drowned"). A rough boy nearly drowns the persona, and says: "I pulled him by the leg, I was just kidding." The persona's grandfather gives him one drop of soup, and the grandmother says: "Grandfather was just kidding." Later Grandfather dies ("At Grandmother's"). And, finally, to show that these repetitions intertwine with others, the persona's mother holds him out to a beggar, and says: "It's just pretend." ("Just Pretend"). The association of "kidding" and "pretending" with fear and horror is most strange in the autobiography of a humorist. More importantly, we see that the author has linked together three "objects of fear": water-food-beggar. And when we note the interrelationship of titles ("On the Shore" and "At the Seashore"; "Cows Are Coming" and "Tigers Are Coming"; "It's My Own Fault" and "It's Not My Fault"), not to mention the use of quotations and classical titles, we see that these simple novelletes form a most complex pattern.

Does this mean that Chukovsky was right? Are the recollections self-sufficient? I think not. It is true that Zoshchenko invented a brilliant device for reviving the form of an autobiography. Each of these recollections is "illumined with a strange light"—the author's "emotional agitation." By selecting only such "snapshots" in his memory, Zoshchenko dispensed with the descriptions, interpretations and identifications which fill most autobiographies. But if each recollection is a little jewel, why did Zoshchenko not arrange them in chronological order, tell his lifestory and be done? The reason, I submit, is that a straight line of little jewels would be tedious, and it would fail to attract attention to its individual parts. It was necessary to piece together a mosaic, with each piece sparkling.

Zoshchenko therefore arranged the recollections into three blocks and set them in reverse chronological order. This was an artistic device. No one is fooled by the repeated claim that the author mistakenly limited himself, that he was forced each time to dig deeper into his past. The same author admits that he spent eight years on this book—he could easily have put everything in chronological order. But it was necessary to create interest, even suspense. For this purpose he made use of fictional devices. A mystery is stated at the outset: "I am wretched, and know not why." Recollections are then presented as clues toward solving the mystery. Each chapter brings the reader close to the solution. At the end of chapter five, all the clues are in, but the mystery remains. It is necessary to explain a system of decoding: the theory of Pavlov in chapter six. The theory is tested on dreams in chapter seven. The solution is achieved in chapter eight. Further confirmation is needed: examples of other people in chapter nine, and of great men in chapter ten. The triumphal conclusion, encompassing all of human life, comes in the next three chapters. The work ends with a frame structure: an epilogue and afterword to balance the prologue and foreword. The recollections therefore cannot stand alone: they are part of a pattern, an intrigue, well deserving the name of "novella."

One more word: if the theory is discounted by science, its merit as a unifying artistic principle is not destroyed. The associations of water-hand-beggar etc. unite the diverse materials of autobiography, biography and speculation. If science should reject this speculation, it will be welcomed by art.

3

But we must confront the theory. The final word, of course, will be said by the scientist, the experimental psychologist, the expert on Freud and Pavlov. As a layman, I can only offer a few observations made in the course of translation, and then close with a subjective appraisal.

Zoshchenko states his theory more directly in *Before Sunrise* than in *Youth Restored.* But he by no means loses sight of his time and place. He apologizes for the frankness of his recollections—they belong to the dead past, "this is the same thing as speaking of the dead." He plays down Freud and plays up Pavlov. He circumvents Freudian terminology: "complex combination *(slozhnaya kombinatsiya)* instead of "complex" *(kompleks),* "physician" instead of "psychiatrist," etc. He justifies his personal inquiry by linking it to the war effort, the national struggle against barbarianism, base instincts. He even associates Freud with Fascism, although Freud, no less than Zoshchenko, defended the "primacy of the intellect" against blind instinct, suffering and religion *(The Future of an Illusion,* 1927). He takes care to portray his positive attitude toward the revolution (the episodes "Five O'Clock Tea," "The Roads Lead To Paris," "We Play Cards"). He claims that a discussion of death is consistent with socialist realism, for socialist realism "does not hypocritically put off decisions to questions which need to be decided" (p. 292). (A statement which did not see the light for almost thirty years.) In short, Zoshchenko tries in every way to make his investigation acceptable to the higher powers. All these ruses need not distract us from the general theory.

Zoshchenko's ultimate defense is the assertion that the theory worked. He cured his own neurosis, "I don't know about other doors," he says, "but the keys definitely fit mine" (p. 305). We are therefore faced with two questions: is the theory defensible in its presentation, and did it really work in Zoshchenko's case? The answer in both cases is doubtful.

361

Zoshchenko combines Freud's theory of trauma with Pavlov's theory of conditioned reflexes. Despair is born in infancy. An infant is traumatized by an "unfortunate experience" which establishes a false conditioned connection between the objects in the experience. The trauma is reinforced by the repetition of the conditioned stimuli or by the overly sensitive psyche of the infant. Once established, the conditioned connection does not dissipate as the infant matures, but instead is confirmed, justified, even multiplied, by its imagination. The adult finds himself beset with fears, phobias, malfunctionings which have grown out of his illogical infantine mind. Despair evaporates when he reconstructs these infantine conceptions (by dream interpretation, by imagination) and explains them away with reason.

This draws a very strange picture of human life. Because he rejects the Freudian explanation of neurosis—a conflict between the inner world and the outer, between the primitive drives of the unconscious and the civilized standards of consciousness—Zoshchenko must ascribe special power to either the one or the other. A person can become neurotic by an unfortunate "concurrence of circumstances" which establishes false conditioned connections—in other words, by a run of bad luck, mere coincidence. Or, a person can become neurotic because, being more imaginative than a dog, he does not allow mistaken conditioned connections to die out, but fabricates justifications for them. Either you have bad luck, or you're too smart for your own good. Or both.

A more serious problem is whether the theory is internally consistent. Is the mystery "I am wretched, and know not why" solved by the clues and their decipherment? Is the despair of chapter two dispelled by the exposition of conditioned connections? That despair, the reader will recall, was a pervasive gloom, a "pessimistic view of life," a "certain repugnance for life." Zoshchenko quotes the words of great men who experienced such despair, some of whom he later analyses. He cites the words of Tolstoi: "It seems to me that my life has been a stupid farce." The despair at this point, in fact, is a Tolstoian despair—despair at the meaninglessness of life, despair in the face of death. But as Zoshchenko proceeds in his investigation, this despair becomes identified with phobias, idiosyncracies, psychosomatic afflictions—all legitimate sources of misery and all worthy of study, but not that all-encompassing despair with which he began. He has shrunk his despair into a theory, and something has escaped.

Even if we overlook this discrepancy, we must doubt the method of the cure. This is supposedly accomplished by shedding light on the remote corners of the psyche, discovering the hidden conditioned connections and severing them one by one. It is supposedly done by logic, the scientific method, but in fact all of the gaps are filled in by untested hypotheses ("it must be that," "without a doubt," etc.) and, one could say, by imagination, by art. You must "get down on all fours," think like an animal, an infant. Zoshchenko converts his art into therapy, but his art takes revenge. In *Youth Restored* he showed the professor, returned to his wife and his reason, darting a glance at the house of his lost lover. So too, the persona of *Before Sunrise,* dedicated to reason and overflowing with happiness, lingers over the memory of Nadya V., the woman he still loves, who rejected the revolution, who cast him out of her life. Reason conquers death, suffering and old age, but, evidently, not love.

In sum, Zoshchenko's theory fails to penetrate the chief cause of despair: the need to achieve one's identity, to become a significant human being, to give and receive love, to work out a relationship to eternity. By restricting his view to conditioned connections, his science to Freud and Pavlov, the author of *Before Sunrise* reduces himself to the level of a dog, without psychic needs and without destiny. Unconsciously, through the art of his autobiography, he attempts to create his own myth, to give his life a meaningful pattern, yet consciously he theorizes himself into a thing.

But did Zoshchenko himself, the historical person, snap out of his depression and find happiness? Chukovsky reports that he did. In 1937, during the horror of the purges, Zoshchenko courageously, forcefully, defended a fellow writer. In other meetings he gave the appearance of radiant health, listed the doctors who had confirmed his cure, worked enthusiastically on his new book *The Keys to Happiness* (the first draft of *Before Sunrise).* "It seemed," remarks Chukovsky, "that he really had succeeded in working a miracle—the conquest over himself, over his hypochondria." But also he had lost his sense of humor, he seemed like a man possessed.[18] His tragic fate is well known: the publication of the first half of *Before Sunrise,* his most optimistic book, brought the furies down upon him; he worked a few more years, and then Zhdanov chose to make an example of him. Zoshchenko was thrown out of Russian literature, forced to turn to translation. Ilya Ehrenburg recalls: "Once, at the beginning of the fifties, I met him (Zoshchenko) on Pushkin Boulevard; he was somber, looked ill. Mutual friends related that he was living through all this in extreme distress."[19] Chukovsky describes him in his last days: he wears a dull, fixed gaze, speaks with long pauses, forces himself to smile.[20]

Zoshchenko was right to rage against the night. No one can foresee a disaster. But he was wrong to think that the light of reason can shine all alone. Reason may conquer the physical world, but it is only one side of the mind. When it aims for absolute control, the dark side rebels. Chaos, irony, despair strike back at every victory. As Byron wrote:

> The serpent of the field, by art
> And spells, is won from harming;
> But that which coils around the heart,
> Oh! who hath power of charming?
> It will not list to wisdom's lore,
> Nor music's voice can lure it;
> But there it stings for evermore
> The soul that must endure it.

Of course, we must wrestle the snake. We must not grovel. But what do you think, reader, will the night ever slither away?

Gary Kern

University of Rochester
10 August 1973

NOTES TO AFTER THE AFTERWORD

1. Trans. by Priscilla Meyer in *The Serapion Brothers,* scheduled for publication by Ardis.

2. *The Theater in Life* by Nicolas Evreinoff, trans. by Alexander Nazaroff (NY: Brentano's, 1927), esp. 276-294.

3. *Perepiska Gor'kogo s Gruzdevym* (Moscow: "Nauka," 1966),88-89.

4. *Literaturnoe nasledstvo,* vol. 70, 157-158. (See Short Bibliography for full title.)

5. The preceding title prints a portion of Gorky's draft of a reply, which makes two initial objections: first, that longevity is "a biological question," and second, that Tolstoi's philosophy contradicted his talent—"his philosophy came from his mind, but his talent was lodged in the marrow of his bones." Three dots follow.

6. K. Chukovsky, "Zoshchenko," 541. (See Short Bibliography.)

7. *Ibid.,* 539-540.

8. An intervening short story, "Healing and Physics" (1932), relating to Stefan Zweig's *Healing Through the Mind (Die Heilung durch den Geist),* is discussed by Vera von Wiren-Garczynski, "Zoshchenko's Psychological Interests," 6-7. (See Short Bibliography.) Both Zoshchenko's and Zweig's works have the same Russian title: *Vrachevanie i psikhika.*

9. The chapter is actually the first of *Ecce Homo.*

10. M. Zoshchenko, "Vozrashchyonnaya molodost', *"Izbrannye proizvedeniya v dvukh tomakh* (Leningrad, 1968),   130-133. Following excerpts come from this edition.

11. It is odd that Zoshchenko never cited the life of Pavlov as a model. Pavlov believed that science could cure all ills, he lived according to a rigid schedule and he worked right up until his death—in fact, he studied the process of his own dying. And he lived 87 years.

12. Vera von Wiren-Garczynski, *op. cit.,* 7.

13. M. Gorky, "A. A. Blok," *Sobranie sochinenii v tridtsati tomakh* (Moscow: "Goslitizdat," 1951), 327.

14. Quoted by Rebecca A. Domar, "The Tragedy of a Soviet Satirist, or The Case of Zoshchenko," 215. (See Short Bibliography.)

15. *Izbrannye proizvedeniya* (1968), 468. Some revision was done on the work in 1935.

16. K. Chukovsky, *op cit.,* 549-550. Chukovsky had read the "entire book" in manuscript.

17. "O sebe, o kritikakh i o svoei rabote," *Mikhail Zoshchenko: Stat'i i materialy* (Leningrad, 1928), 11.

18. K. Chukovsky, *op cit.,* 546-548.

19. I. Ehrenburg, *Sobranie sochinenii v devyati tomakh* (Moscow: "Goslitizdat," 1967), vol. 9, 492.

20. K. Chukovsky, *op cit.,* 551.

APPENDICES

1. Dates in Zoshchenko's Life

1895   Born August 10 in Poltava. Father Mikhail is Ukrainian nobleman, an artist of the Peredvezhniki movement. Mother Elena is Russian, an actress in her youth.

1904   Family moves to Petersburg.

1913   Completes 8th Gimnasiya of Petersburg (with poor performance in Russian composition). Enters law school of Petersburg University.

1914   Spring. Works as a train conductor on the Kislovodsk-Mineralnye Vody line. Gives private lessons. Fall. Expelled from the university for failure to pay tuition. Takes accelerated military course, goes to WWI front as an ensign.

1915-17   Serves in Mingrelsky Regiment of the Caucasian Division, commands a battalion, is wounded, gassed, promoted to 2nd Captain.

1917   February Revolution. Returns to Petrograd (formerly Petersburg), works as postmaster, then as adjutant of Arkhangelsk militia. October Revolution. Returns to Petrograd, works as cobbler on Vasilevsky Island, poultry breeder in Mankovo, border patrolman in Strelna and Kronstadt.

1918   September. Volunteers for Red Army, serves in First Model Regiment of the Village Poor.

1919   Demobilized due to heart trouble, works as detective in Ligovo-Oranienbaum.

1920   Works as office manager in Petrograd military port. Visits newly opened House of Arts, attends seminars of Zamyatin, Shklovsky, Chukovsky.

1921   NEP. Becomes member of the Serapion Brothers, shares their desire to remain apolitical and their belief in the freedom of the individual writer.

August 10. Marries Vera Kerbits.

1922   Publishes a story "Griskha Zhigan" in *The Petersburg Anthology (Peterburgskii sbornik)*. Publishes first book, *The Stories of Nazar Ilich Mister Bluebelly (Rasskazy Nazara Il'icha gospodina Sinebryukhova)*. The book is a tremendous success.

1922-26   Publishes over 20 different collections of humorous stories, sales go into the millions, Zoshchenko becomes the most popular Russian writer of the decade. His neurosis reaches the stage of extreme hypochondria and hallucinations.

1928   First five-year plan. Dominance of RAPP (proletarian writers) in literature. Numerous critical articles identify Zoshchenko with his negative characters.

1932   Abolition of RAPP, formation of Union of Soviet Writers, preparations for doctrine of socialist realism.

1933   August. Sent as a member of a collective of writers to glorify the forced-labor construction of the White Sea Canal. Contributes "A Story of One Life" *(Istoriya odnoi zhizni),* the account of a rehabilitated convict. Publishes *Youth Restored (Vozvrashchyonnaya molodost')* after 4 years of reflection and 3 months of writing. Favorable reception. At this point Zoshchenko calculates that he has written 480 stories, several novellas and three comedies.

1934   First Conference of the Union of Soviet Writers.

Andrei Zhdanov expounds the principles of socialist realism.

1935   Zoshchenko publishes *A Skyblue Book (Golubaya kniga),* a cycle of stories arranged as a parody of history.

1936   Critics dislike *A Skyblue Book.* Pravda (May 9) joins in the attack.

1937   Zoshchenko writes historical works: *Kerensky* and *The Black Prince (Chyornyi prints).* Begins *The Keys to Happiness (Klyuchi schat'ya,* the first version of *Before Sunrise)*

1939   Awarded the medal of the Banner of Red Labor.

1940   Writes *Stories About Lenin (Rasskazy o Lenine).*

1941   WWII. June to October. Works for Leningrad radio, newspapers and the satirical journal *Krokodil.* October. Evacuated to Alma-Ata, works for Mosfilm, writes scenario *A Soldier's Happiness (Soldatskoe schast'e).*

1942   August. Begins to rework *Before Sunrise (Pered voskhodom solntsa).*

1943   March. Returns to Moscow, works on the editorial board of *Krokodil.* Summer. First two installments of *Before Sunrise* appear in journal *Oktyabr'.* Work is finished in October. Publication suspended as critical campaign mounts against Zoshchenko.

1944-46   Concentrates on plays. *The Canvas Portfolio (Parusinovyi portfel')* is given 200 performances.

1946   April. Zoshchenko is awarded medal for heroic work during the war. August. Andrei Zhdanov, secretary of the Central Committee, begins a purge of the arts. Zoshchenko is recalled as a

Serapion Brother, the author of *Before Sunrise,* and is branded as a "brainless scribbler." Zoshchenko is expelled from the Union of Soviet Writers. The film *Crime and Punishment,* with Zoshchenko's scenario, is withheld.

1947-53   Turns to translations, particularly works by the Finnish novelist M. Lassila. Lives in poverty, as an outcast.

1953   June. Reinstated in the Union of Soviet Writers 3 months after Stalin's death. Works for *Krokodil* and *Ogonyok.* Publishes bland stories.

1958   July 22. Dies and is buried in Sestroretsk. Kornei Chukovsky records his last meeting with Zoshchenko (April 1958):

> I attempted to talk with him about his works...
> He simply waved his hand.
> "My works?" he said with his even and measured voice. "What do you mean, my works? No one knows them by now. I myself have forgotten about my works by now..."
> And he changed the subject.
> I introduced him to a young literary man.
> He looked sadly at the youth and said, quoting himself:
> "Literature is a dangerous production, just as harmful as the preparation of white lead."

Sobranie sochinenii, vol. 2, 552.

2. Key to the Translation

As Kornei Chukovsky has shown in his book on translation, *The High Art (Vysokoe iskusstvo,* 1964), the meaning of a word matches its standard foreign equivalent only in certain contexts, but not in others, so that a constant one-to-one relationship in a translation may disfigure the sense of the original. On the other hand, when one Russian word is translated by two or three English words, the reader misses certain associations made in the original. The following key is intended for those who wish to trace associations. It contains groups of related Russian words, other words of particular importance in the text, and scientific vocabulary. The first English listing is the most frequent translation, the others are occasional.

assotsiatsiya n : association
assotsiirovat' vb : to associate

beda n : misery, misfortune, trouble
bednyi adj : poor
bedstvie n : poverty

begat' vb : to run
　—*ot* : to flee from
begstvo n : flight, evasion
　izbegat' vb : to avoid, to flee;—*vstrechi* : to avoid contact

bespokoistvo n : unrest

boleznennyi adj : unhealthy, morbid (re: Poe)
　—*konflikt* : painful conflict
bolezn' n : illness, sickness, affliction, disease (re: Nekrasov)
bol' n : pain
bol'noi n : patient, sick person; adj : ill, sick
　—*predmet* : painful object
　—*reaktsiya* : painful reaction

borot'sya vb : to struggle
bor'ba n : struggle

boi n : battle

burnyi adj
  —*more* : stormy sea
  —*otvet* : violent reaction

dokazatel'stvo n : proof
  lozhnoe— : false proof
  podlinnoe— : genuine proof

gibel' n : ruin, disaster, downfall, ruination; wreck (of a ship)

gore n : woe, grief

khandra n : gloominess, gloom, depression (in quotations)

melankholiya n : melancholy

neschastnyi adj : unhappy, unfortunate, wretched
neschast'e n : unhappiness, misfortune

nishchenkii adj : beggarly
nishcheta n : penury, indigence
nishchii n : beggar
  prositel' n : pauper

obraz n : image
  —*nishchego* : image of a beggar, beggar-image
  —*tigra* : image of a tiger, tiger-image
simvolicheskii— : symbolic image

ochag n : nidus
  —*vozbuzhdeniya* : nidus of excitation

opasat'sya vb : to save oneself
opasnost' n : danger
opasnyi adj : dangerous

pishcha n : food
pitanie n : nourishment
  eda n : food

pobeda n : conquest, victory
pobeditel' n : conqueror, victor
pobezhdat' vb : to conquer

razdrazhenie n : irritation, stimulation
razdrazhitel' n : stimulus

razum n : reason
  um n : wit, mind

reagirovat' vb : to react
reaktsiya n : reaction

refleks n : reflex
  oboronnyi— : protective reflex

sluchainost' n : coincidence
sluchainyi adj : accidental, coincidental

snovidenie n : dreaming, dream
son n : dream, dreaming; sleep

sovest' n : conscience

soznanie n : consciousness; *vysokoe—* : higher consciousness
  osoznat' vb : to be aware of
  neosoznannyi strakh : unconscious fear, fear which has not
                          become conscious
  podsoznatel'nost' n : the unconscious

stradanie n : suffering
  nervnoe— : nervous disorder

strakh n : fear, terror
strashnyi adj : terrible, frightening
  ustrashat' vb : to frighten; *—sya* : to fear, to be frightened
  ob"ekt ustrasheniya : object of fear
  predmet ustrasheniya : object of fear

stremlenie n : drive, urge, longing
  impul's n : impulse

vlechenie n : drive

svyas' n : connection
  nervnaya— : neural connection
  uslovnaya— : conditioned connection
  lozhnaya uslovnaya— : false conditioned connection
  nepravil'naya uslovnaya— : incorrect conditioned connection
  nevernaya uslovnaya— : untruthful conditioned connection
  oshibochnaya uslovnaya— : mistaken conditioned connection

toska n : despair

trevoga n : alarm, apprehension, anxiety

udar n : blow, stroke
  —groma : clap of thunder
  —molnii : clap of thunder
  —serdtsa : (heart) stroke
  elektricheskii— : electrical shock

ugnetyonnost' n : oppression, depression

um n : wit, mind

uzhas n : horror
uzhasnyi adj : horrible; violent (re: opponent of Freud)

volnenie n : agitation, anxiety, excitement
  dushevnoe— : emotional agitation
volnovat'sya vb : to be agitated
vozdykhaniya n pl : anxieties

vrach n : physician
vrachevanie n : healing
  doktor n : doctor

zashchita n : defense

zatormozhenie n : inhibition
  tormozhenie n : inhibition

3. Short Bibliography

I. Works by Mikhail Zoshchenko
    A. In Russian:

Sobranie sochinenii v shesti tomakh. Leningrad:"Priboi," 1930-31.

Povesti i rasskazy. New York: "Chekhov," 1952.

Izbrannye proizvedeniya v dvukh tomakh. Leningrad: "Goslitizdat," 1968.

Pered voskhodom solntsa. Povest'. Munich-New York: "Inter-
Language Literary Associates," 1967. (The Foreword and
first 6 chapters of *Before Sunrise.)*

Pered voskhodom solntsa. Povest'. New York: "Chekhov," 1973.
(The complete text of *Before Sunrise.)*

Literaturnoe nasledstvo, vol. 70. Moscow: "Akademiya Nauk,"
1963, 157-168. (Correspondence with Gorky.)

    B. In English:

Russia Laughs, trans. by Helena Clayton. Foreword by Whit
Burnett. Toronto: Longmans, 1935.

The Woman Who Could Not Read, and Other Tales, trans. by
Elizaveta Fen. London: Methuen, 1940.

The Wonderful Dog, and Other Tales, trans. by Elizaveta Fen.
London: Methuen, 1942.

*Scenes from the Bathhouse, and Other Stories of Communist
Russia,* trans. with an introduction by Sidney Monas. Ann
Arbor: Univ. of Michigan Pr., 1961. (Contains excerpts from
the first 6 chapters of *Before Sunrise.)*

Nervous People, and Other Satires, trans. by Maria Gordon and
Hugh McLean, with an introduction by the latter. London:
Victor Gollancz, 1963 (Contains large sections of the first
6 chapters of *Before Sunrise.)*

Anthology pieces:

B. G. Guerney (ed.), *An Anthology of Russian Literature
in the Soviet Period.* New York: Vintage, 1960. (Contains
2 short stories.)

F. D. Reeve (ed.), *Great Soviet Short Stories.* New York:
Dell, 1962. (Contains 6 stories.)

Mirra Ginsburg (ed.), *The Fatal Eggs, and Other Soviet Satire.* New York: Grove, 1964. (Contains 4 stories.)

II. Works About Mikhail Zoshchenko
A. In Russian

Mikhail Zoshchenko: Stat'i i materialy. Leningrad: "Academia." 1928. (Contains articles by M. Zoshchenko, V. Shklovsky, A. Barmin, V. Vinogradov.) Reprinted by "Ardis," 1972.

Konstantin Fedin, "Mikhail Zoshchenko," *Sobranie sochinenii v devyati tomakh.* Moscow: "Goslitizdat," 1962, vol. 9, 388-399. (One of the earliest sympathetic accounts of Zoshchenko, dated 1943.)

Kornei Chukovsky, "Zoshchenko," *Sobranie sochinenii v shesti tomakh.* Moscow: "Goslitizdat," 1965, vol. 2, 484-552 (A wise survey of Zoshchenko's entire career.)

Veniamin Kaverin, "Za rabochim stolom," *Novyi mir* No. 9, 1965, 154-156. (A timely appreciation.)

Mikhail Slonimsky, "Mikhail Zoshchenko," *Kniga vospominanii.* Moscow: "Sovetskii pisatel'," 1966, 145-171. (Further confirmation of Zoshchenko's melancholy and striving for long, serious stories.)

B. In English

Rebecca A. Domar, "The Tragedy of a Soviet Satirist, or The Case of Zoshchenko," *Through the Glass of Soviet Literature,* ed. by Ernest J. Simmons. New York: Columbia Univ. Pr., 1953, 201-243.

Hugh McLean, "Zoshchenko's Unfinished Novel," *Survey: A Journal of Soviet and East European Studies* No. 36 (April-June), 1961, 99-105. (An analysis of the first half of *Before Sunrise.*)

Vera Alexandrova, *A History of Soviet Literature 1917-1962.* New York: Doubleday, 1963. Contains a full chapter on Zoshchenko, 97-109.

Marc Slonim, "Mikhail Zoshchenko: The Condemned Humorist," *Soviet Russian Literature. Writers and Problems 1917-1967.* New York: Oxford Univ. Pr., 1967, 90-96.

Vera von Wiren-Garczynski, "Zoshchenko's Psychological Interests," *The Slavic and East European Journal,* Vol. XI, No. 1 (1967), 3-22. (The author has written a complete monograph on Zoshchenko, scheduled for publication by Twayne Pr.)